Proletarian Philosophers

No education is of any use to the workers which does not aim at the emancipation of the workers. But your masters will do their best, here as elsewhere, to put you off with SHODDY GOODS

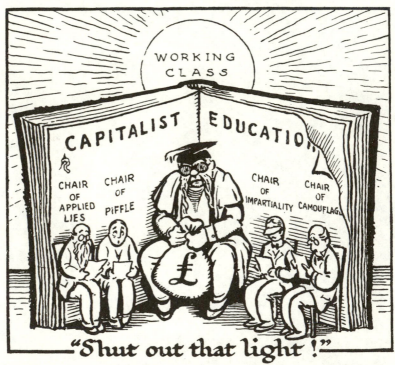

From the pamphlet 'What is Independent Working-Class Education?' published by the Plebs League in 1920. Reproduced by courtesy of the Fabian Society.

PROLETARIAN PHILOSOPHERS

Problems in Socialist Culture in Britain, 1900–1940

Jonathan Rée

Clarendon Press · Oxford
1984

Oxford University Press, Walton Street, Oxford OX2 6DP

London Glasgow New York Toronto
Delhi Bombay Calcutta Madras Karachi
Kuala Lumpur Singapore Hong Kong Tokyo
Nairobi Dar es Salaam Cape Town
Melbourne Auckland
and associated companies in
Beirut Berlin Ibadan Mexico City Nicosia

Oxford is a trade mark of Oxford University Press

Published in the united States
by Oxford University Press, New York

© Jonathan Rée 1984

British Library Cataloguing in Publication Data
Rée, Jonathan
Proletarian philosophers: problems in socialist
culture in Britain, 1900–1940.
1. Communism and philosophy
I. Title
335.4'11'0941   HX533
ISBN 0-19-827261-8

Library of Congress Cataloging in Publication Data
Rée, Jonathan, 1948–
Proletarian philosophers.
Includes bibliographical references and index.
1. Socialism — Great Britain — History — 20th
century.   2. Socialism and education — Great Britain
— History — 20th century.   3. Labour Party
(Great Britain) — History — 20th century.   I. Title.
HX243.R385 1984   335'.1   83-17348
ISBN 0-19-827261-8

Typeset by Hope Services, Abingdon,
and Printed at the University Press, Oxford.

Preface

This essay on several years in the life of the British Labour Movement is simultaneously a history of education, a history of philosophy, and a history of politics. It has not been easy for me — a vagrant philosopher, not a historian — to stop the three lines of enquiry from diverging, so I am particularly thankful to friends and others who have kept me to it. The first draft was written in 1980, but originated three years earlier, as part of an enquiry about philosophy and socialism undertaken with Tim Putnam and Anne Phillips. I am extraordinarily indebted to them both. I also acknowledge generous gifts of information from D. Bartkiw, Andrew Davies, Eric Homberger, Sidney Hook, Yvonne Kapp, David McLellan, Raphael Samuel, James Young, and especially Helena Sheehan. I have had valuable comments on my draft from Mollie Adams, Roy Edgley, Jean McCrindle, Lesley Morton, Denise Riley, and David Selbourne. I am thankful for assistance from librarians at Ruskin College, and Bodleian Library, Middlesex Polytechnic, the National Library of Scotland, and the Marx Memorial Library, and have benefited in various ways from the help, encouragements, and criticisms of Chris Arthur, David Attwooll, Rosalyn Baxandall, Roy Bhaskhar, Wendy Carlin, John Clayden, Hans Fink, Andrew Glyn, Ranajit Guha, Harry Hendrick, Bridget Hill, Christopher Hill, James Hinton, Allen Hunter, Dick Leith, Melanie McFadyean, Stuart Macintyre, Margo McRobbie, John Mepham, Mark Nash, Henry Pachter, Elisabeth Peretz, Dieter Pevsner, Jonathan Powers, Harry Rée, Betty Reid, Margaret Rose, Kate Shuckburgh, Nick Stanley, and Tom Steele.

My approach owes much to conversations with British socialists who were active in the 1920s, thirties, and forties, including Harry Clayden, Lawrence Daly, Dudley Edwards, Lesley Morton, Vivien Morton, and Jock Shanley. I am aware that some of these informants disagree with my interpretation of situations which they lived through. 'You have killed the past', one of them has told me, unhappy at what he must have considered an abuse of his hospitality and trust. Another has insisted, for similar reasons, on not being named.

These disagreements grieve me, but I cannot see how to avoid them. Part of the problem is that the documents I have used sometimes prove the existence of serious implicit differences in politics or philosophy, and of truculent open hostilities, between individuals who are nevertheless remembered, across the years, as the best of comrades. The other difficulty is that some of the most acclaimed and influential work in Marxist philosophy is, by any reasonable standards of comparison, lamentably unintelligent. There was enthusiasm for some very bad books, and excitement and zeal about works that had not been read properly, and about debates that had not been comprehended. So the story I have to tell is, at some points, one of ignorance, haste, and useless clash: but — I hope it is evident — all for the sake of the causes I care for most.

Jonathan Rée
Wolvercote
April 1983

Contents

Contents

Introduction: Marxism and Philosophy

Everyone knows, it seems, that Marxism contains a philosophy, perhaps called 'dialectical materialism'. But what on earth is it? Nearly all Marx's writings contain vestiges and hints of various philosophical ideas; but the same applies to the works of most great authors, and it does not make them all works of philosophy. Marx actually never mentioned the philosophical system which he is supposed to have created. Indeed he wrote very little about philosophy, and published far less; and anyway, this was all early work, mostly done in his effusive and unstable twenties. Besides, in these writings, rather than promising to found a new philosophy, Marx apparently came to the conclusion that the whole enterprise of philosophy was ineradicably wrong-headed, and should be abandoned in favour of scientific criticism.[1]

It was Engels who, thirty years later, began to compose what were to become the canonical texts of Marxist philosophy. There is his ponderous and cantankerous *Anti-Dühring,* which came out in German in 1878 (in full in English in 1935),[2] the lucid review-essay on 'Ludwig Feuerbach and the Outcome of Classical German Philosophy' which appeared in 1886 and was translated in 1903,[3] and the astonishingly ambitious *Dialectics of Nature* which was unfinished when Engels died and was not published at all till 1925 (translated 1934).[4]

The idea behind these works by Engels was to underpin Marx's theory of history with a foundation of 'Marxist philosophy'. For this purpose, Engels adopted an orthodox academic conception of philosophy, seeing it as a lattice of intersecting debates on a small number of fundamental questions — eternal questions on which 'philosophers' had allegedly divided into 'warring schools' ever since Socrates if not before.[5] The two 'battles' which Engels believed to be essential to philosophy were between idealists and materialists, and between dialecticians and metaphysicians. The idealists, according to this scheme, defended the mysterious ultimate reality of God, the soul, or some other spiritual entity, while the materialists, on the contrary, believed that science would ultimately expel mystery from the world by explaining everything in terms of matter and motion. Plato, Aquinas, Descartes, and Berkeley could probably be discerned in the ranks of the idealists, and Aristotle, Democritus, Diderot, and Hume were conspicuous amongst the opposing forces. However, the two groups of philosophers — so the story goes — shared a tendency to see things in rigid, immutable, hard-edged, unhistorical, and black-and-white terms, and were to this extent allies of 'metaphysics'. It was left to Hegel, at the beginning of the nineteenth century, to lead an insurrection on behalf of 'dialectics'. In spite of the remarkable success of Hegel's coup, however, his régime was — so the story continues — fissiparous and unstable, and this was because it relied on support from the idealist camp. So, after a materialist revival led by Feuerbach, a new philosophical treaty was concluded, and an unbeatable alliance was formed. Materialist metaphysicians and idealist metaphysicians had been at each other's throats for centuries; then the idealist dialecticians led by Hegel had achieved a splendid but brief ascendancy. Clearly, within this conceptual range there was only one option left — materialistic dialectics. Here, evidently, was the philosophical foundation which Marxism needed.

This Engelsian philosophical tapestry has since been embroidered by various revolutionary leaders, activists, and intellectuals — Plekhanov (who, incidentally, launched the phrase 'dialectical materialism' in 1891),[6] Bukharin, Deborin, Lenin, Stalin, and Mao, to mention only a few. So one might have expected the philosophical foundations of Marxism to be, by now, well and truly laid.[7]

It turns out, however, that the champions of Marxist philosophy present a remarkably disunited front, and that they have been able to disagree spectacularly about the pedigree, legitimacy, and validity of their supposedly fundamental philosophy. Amongst philosopher-Marxists in recent years, for instance, you will find that while Timpanaro discovers that dialectical materialism really goes back to a wholesome eighteenth-century tradition of militantly anti-clerical atheist materialism,[8] Colletti is able to exhibit it — just as persuasively — as an offshoot of the conceptually bankrupt authority of late nineteenth-century idealism — a soft-minded, religiose spiritualism.[9] Meanwhile, Peter Ruben commends it as the most adequate philosophy of modern physics, and considers it to be rooted in Marx's esoteric and incomplete early writings on natural science,[10] and Dominique Lecourt condems it as an anti-scientific imposture originating in Stalin's writings of the 1930s.[11] Others have joined the pursuit of Marxist philosophy as though dialectical materialism had never existed.[12]

The common belief that there must be a special, if elusive, Marxist brand of philosophy is, though, a long way from being self-evident. One likely and influential alternative to it begins by rejecting the idea that philosophy is essentially a matter of siding with materialism, idealism, or any other 'school'. For philosophy may, instead, be defined simply as the aspiration to map the horizons of all one's knowledge and values, the attempt to understand life, virtue, beauty, truth, and justice properly, or at least to traduce them less. Even if it fails, perhaps inevitably, to yield definite knowledge, it may still foster a lucid, sagacious, and poised uncertainty, which could be preferable to confident and possibly erratic partisanship. And so Marxists may then claim that commitment to working-class socialism is not based on adherence to a special 'school' of philosophy, or a particular manual of doctrines, but on a conviction that proletarians are destined to fulfil the hopes of philosophy in general, translating its bookbound transcendental ideals into the actual happiness, wisdom, freedom, and equality of real human beings. This position was, indeed, affirmed by Marx himself when, an exiled and unemployed twenty-five-year-old Doctor of Philosophy, he became enchanted by the working-class socialists of Paris. 'Philosophy finds its *material* weapons in the Proletariat,' he wrote, 'just as the Proletariat finds its *spiritual* weapons in Philosophy.'[13] A fight for socialism, in this perspective, is just a continuation of philosophy by other means.

Both these interpretations of the 'philosophical basis' of Marxism can, however, spill over into a very different, and apparently opposed attitude — namely that Marxism is basically *against* philosophy. For if Marxism rests upon 'dialectics' rather than 'metaphysics', and if philosophy was metaphysical until Hegel's precarious revolution, then Marxism must be in deep disagreement with nearly everything that has ever actually been achieved in philosophy. And in any case, philosophy in the style of Hegel, as indeed of his predecessors Hume and Kant, obeys a curious and poignant paradox, since it involves the idea that philosophical discussion is inherently self-defeating, its only possible outcome, apart from illusion, being insight into the impossibility of attaining the goals it sets itself. In this sense, philosophers loyal to their tradition must be committed to ending philosophy, and it is less surprising than it might seem that Marx, whilst reverencing philosophy as 'the head of emancipation', also called for its 'abolition' and 'negation'.[14]

The intention of 'abolishing' philosophy may then be eagerly taken up in a raucous refrain: what need has Marxism, or socialism, of philosophy anyway? Is it not, of all theoretical pursuits, the one most distantly removed from 'practice', that grand inquisitor of Marxist thought? What if a weakness for philosophical speculation should be, in fact, one of the besetting vices of Marxism? May it not be that Marxists ought to shun philosophy as they do religion, and that friendship towards the proletariat entails enmity toward philosophy? Perhaps philosophy and Marxism are incompatible, the philosophicalness and the proletarianness always inversely proportional? In this case the idea of Marxist philosophy must be a folly or a hoax from beginning to end.

The conflict between these three attitudes — that Marxism is based on a special kind of philosophy, that it is a continuation of philosophy in general, and that it can dispense with philosophy altogether — is further complicated by the fact that each of them will, to some minds, count against Marxism rather than in its favour. Who, it might be asked, could trust a social theory which is affiliated to the recondite, sectarian, and implausible dogmas of dialectical materialism? . . . or which is taken in by the grandiose conceits of traditional philosophy? . . . or which has turned its back on the philosophical heritage?

It is impossible to provide a direct analytical resolution of this debate, because, in the first place, the different parties start not just from different opinions but from different definitions of the basic terms. But secondly — as the episodes dealt with in the following pages testify — none of the attitudes involved can be measured against a purely philosophical scale: they cannot be appraised apart from the ambivalences about education and culture in the midst of which they have been adopted.

For uncertainty about education and culture has troubled socialist labour movements since their beginnings. From one point of view, it has been evident to socialists that education is a mechanism of enslavement to capitalism and the bourgeois class. From another, though, it is equally clear that education is the way in to a cultural treasure-house, and that working people are justly incensed at a social system which excludes them and their children from it. Again and again, the difference between these points of view has led to awkward misunderstandings between working-class socialists, looking forward and upward to a better and perhaps more cultured life, and their educated allies, often deprecating their own cultural advantages, and unaware of the overbearing, embarrassing, or dispiriting effects of what I shall call their 'universitarian' manners, values, and opinions.[15]

Philosophy has had a special salience in this tricky terrain. In the early days of working-class socialism, it was the sovereign discipline of University culture. Towards the end of this period, a special longing for philosophical education developed in certain self-educated proletarians — including, in Britain, the formidable T. A. Jackson, who will be the main character in the narrative which follows. Before long, though, the University intellectuals forsook their high opinion of philosophy, and questions about its status and value also became matter for fiery debate amongst socialists. In the ensuing contention, the hopes — intelligent, vigorous, and stubborn hopes — of the proletarian philosophers became perplexed, derided, and stifled; and finally, so far as I can see, utterly defeated.

Chapter 1

Socialists and Autodidacts 1880–1910

1 Autodidacts and the University

An important figure in the history of socialism, is that of the working-class autodidact — the man (it was unlikely to be a woman) who, with only the most rudimentary education, but possessed by a searing desire for knowledge, acquired massive, even ponderous, learning by boring through book after book, borrowed from clergyman or schoolteacher, or from Trade Union or Chartist or Public Library, or even purchased with hard-earned money and gloated over with miserly pride: little boys reading by candle-light when they should have been in bed asleep,[1] or learning to write with improvised materials in snatched moments down the pit;[2] tradesmen with a book always open beside them on the bench;[3] devotees of evening institutes and working men's clubs and colleges or participants in educational self-help groups like Leatherland's 'Mutual Instruction Society', Thomas Cooper's 'Mutual Improvement Society', Joseph Gutteridge's 'Coventry Mutual Improvement Class', and Tom Mann's 'Shakespeare Mutual Improvement Society'.[4]

Sometimes, this desire for knowledge might raise a working man up and up to a great institutional eminence. Joseph Wright is a case in point: he was born just outside Bradford, in 1855, and started work at the mill at the age of six. He benefited hardly at all from his 'half-time schooling', and cared little for it. But when he was fourteen, he overheard some of his fellow wool-sorters discussing newspaper reports about the Franco-Prussian war. Emulously, he decided to master the art of reading for himself. This he did by attending evening classes and Sunday schools, and going without sleep; and then he went on to French and German. He topped up his mill wages by conducting evening classes of his own, and became a full-time schoolteacher, eventually saving enough money to travel to Germany for higher education. When he was thirty, he took a doctorate *cum laude* in comparative philology at Heidelberg, and then moved to Oxford in search of teaching work. He became a pioneer of women's education at the University, and was appointed Professor of Comparative Philology there in 1901, becoming a driving force behind the recognition of English and Modern Languages as legitimate subjects for academic study, and compiler of the monumental *English Dialect Dictionary*.[5]

The working-class autodidacts do not always seem pleasant to modern eyes: it is easy to suspect them of University fetishism or bibliomania, rather than genuine intellectual curiosity, or of treacherous social ambition masquerading as devotion to truth. For instance, take George Tansley, an early student at the Working Men's College in London, who loved it so much that it became his 'second home'. He was, we are told, intellectually dim, but 'captivated by the atmosphere of the older universities; . . . it was his dream that the Working Men's College should one day become a university'. It is hard to avoid a condescending smirk at such infatuation; it is tempting to relax with such an amusing companion as Sir Charles Prestwood Lucas, CB, KCMG, KCB, distinguished civil servant and barrister, alumnus of Winchester and Balliol, and eventually Fellow of All Souls, a patron of the Working Men's College, who found Tansley remarkable mainly for his ignorant 'reverence for learning, for seats of learning, and for the degrees which ought to but do not always indicate that their possessors have learning'.[6]

Poor Tansley!

2 Books and Socialism

On occasion, then, working men with a love of book-learning and University culture could expect to find some career, or fantasy of one, open to their talents. But more often than not, they ran into cruel obstacles. There must be many, sunk without documentary trace, whose aspirations led only to heart-break — patterns for Thomas Hardy's fictional character Jude Fawley, languishing in Oxford, excluded from its

University, and dying, appropriately enough, with a waltz from a lavish college gaudy nagging at his ears.

Others, however, reacted to educational frustration with militancy, vindictiveness, and proud defiance. John Burns, one of the greatest working-class socialist agitators of the time, remembered: 'I have deprived myself, as many of my class have done, of hundreds of meals on purpose to buy books and papers.' And Tom Mann, in his agitation for the 'Eight Hours League', characterized the typical socialist as 'a workman who through youth and early manhood has been battling against long hours in order that he might attend the institute, listen to lectures, and read the works of able men, and who by these means has succeeded in having a mind worth owning'.[7] Partly it was that their success in acquiring some literary culture against the odds filled them with a somewhat acrid feeling of proletarian righteousness — a bullish pride that they could achieve, in the spare moments of a hard life, as much culture as their so-called superiors with all their leisure, prosperity, tutors, schools, and Universities. Nothing, for instance, could rival the relish with which Harry Pollitt recalled his victory in a debate about 'Liberalism versus Socialism' in Bootle before the First World War, which proved, as he said, 'that Penny Pamphlets enabled a worker without formal education to wipe the floor with a supposedly educated schoolmaster'.[8]

But it was not just the exhilaration of having filched something which their oppressors wanted to keep for themselves that fuelled the subversiveness of these autodidacts; there was also something disruptive about the theoretical content of what they learnt. The world of knowledge into which they had forced their way was, to many of them, a world of radicalism, if not of socialism: it contained some substance which seemed to corrode the ideological compound which, they felt, their bosses used to keep them down. They read Darwin, Huxley, and Haeckel, or studied botany and phrenology, and the unction of natural theology curdled.[9] They read Buckle or studied history, and existing social arrangements began to seem contingent and provisional. They read the poetry of Shakespeare and Burns (but not Morris — his works were too expensive[10]), and perhaps glimpsed the possibility of escaping from the narrow, puritanical circle of a joyless, sexless deontology of work. And beyond that, their athletic enthusiasm for self-improvement through intellectual exercise provided them with a model of social progress: they had a sense that they themselves were shifting, by their own efforts, from a crabbed, superstitious, and fearful parochialism to a bold and oceanic inclusiveness of vision, in which the infinite universe could be grasped as a whole. Surely, this individual betterment could be repeated on a social scale, and then the divisions between classes, nations, or groups would be accorded their true (that is to say, their vanishingly small) significance. Politics, for the autodidacts, became part of world history, and world history a chapter of cosmology. Tom Maguire, active in the Leeds Socialist League, was sardonic in his recollection of the debates of the 1880s:

Some [he reported] thought that we might advantageously limit the scope of our ideal to the five continents, while directing our operations more immediately to our own locality. Others were strongly of the opinion that our ideal was too narrow, and they proposed as the object of the society the internationalisation of the known and undiscovered world, with a view to the eventual inter-solarisation of the planets.[11]

Cosmic socialism (to coin a phrase) grew in the minds of hundreds of the proletarian autodidacts of the 1880s and 1890s: it was the red blood of the energetic creature which is now pickled in a bottle labelled reformist, Second International, evolutionary socialism. The movement grew mostly from books about science, philosophy, or history: books about socialism, in fact, were few and far between. There were some works by Hyndman, the first and most notable being *England for All*; several novels, such as Shaw's *An Unsocial Socialist*, Morris's *News from Nowhere*, and Bellamy's *Looking Backward*; and a few tracts ranging from Blatchford's *Merrie England* and J. L. Joynes's *The Socialist Catechism* to *Fabian Essays*. From these, it would be possible to glean something about the difference between feudal and capitalist forms of exploitation, about class struggle, and about the supposedly Marxist 'Iron Law of Wages'.[12] Of Marxism, however, there was almost nothing. In 1885, J. L. Joynes brought out a translation of *Wage-Labour and Capital*; then Engels edited the English translation of Volume One of *Capital* which came out of 1887; and only a tiny selection of other works (extracts from Engels's *Anti-Dühring* and the

Condition of the Working Class and some of his articles on *Revolution and Counter-Revolution or Germany in 1848,* together with Marx's own *Value Price and Profit* and — by a curious fluke[13] — *The Poverty of Philosophy*) could be added to the English socialist's book-shelf by the end of the century. Even the *Communist Manifesto* was hard to get. Until the English edition of 1888, which shortly became unavailable, readers had to seek out stray copies of the translation which had appeared in Harney's *Red Republican* in 1850.[14] Socialists were bookish, but their books were not socialist.[15]

3 The Education of Tommy Jackson

In 1879, a talented son was born into the family of a skilled compositor, a Radical named Thomas Blackwell Jackson, in Clerkenwell in the East End of London. At the age of seven, he began to attend the local School Board school in Upper Holloway. Here he learnt not only the standard elementary subjects, but also Darwinism and general science. He left school at the age of thirteen, becoming a printer's reader and then an apprentice. But his heart was elsewhere: in a 'passion for book collecting and devouring' which, he recalled later, 'was so inordinate that I used to embezzle my dinner money to buy books'. He decided to acquire and read the entire series of cheap editions of the classics known as 'Sir John Lubbock's Hundred Books', and one Christmas Eve he discovered a copy of G. H. Lewes's *Biographical History of Philosophy* in a second-hand furniture shop. He beat the price down to sixpence. Reading Lewes over Christmas 'changed my mental orientation for life', he wrote, and 'opened before me an entirely new world of adventure. . . . Thereafter', said Jackson, 'I wallowed in philosophy.'[16]

During the years of his apprenticeship, T. A. Jackson worked his way through Plato, Aristotle, Bacon, Hobbes, Locke, Spinoza, Kant, and Hegel; and when he reached his majority in 1900, he was a shy, gangling, short-sighted bookworm, a Radical like his father but with a head full of philosophical jargon, and his young feelings hurtling vertiginously from joy to despair as he contemplated the appalling eminence

of the Great Men in the philosophical pantheon. Years later,
he criticized these attitudes:

The trouble was that all these books — masterpieces though they might
be — belonged to the Past, both in their origin and in their mode of
expression. Insensibly, preoccupation with these 'classics' treated as a
single category — the Best — caused a student to slip into regarding
Culture as a fixed Mind-world in which one either ascended with the
geniuses to supreme heights or sank with the dullards and the dunces
to the uncultured slime.[17]

But Tommy Jackson's view of his fellow workers as 'uncultured slime' was soon to change. In 1900, he attended a
Radical rally against the Boer War at Highbury Corner. The
event was disrupted by a counter-demonstration, but the
vulnerable and bespectacled Tommy Jackson was rescued
from Tory fists by members of the Highbury Branch of what
was then England's main Marxist organization — the Social
Democratic Federation. He went off to a pub with them,
and listened eagerly to their talk about Marx, Engels, and
Socialism. It was disquieting. He went back home and looked
out an old copy of *Merrie England*, which he had cast aside
in disgust some years earlier.

I reacted instantly — and realised that I had become an Atheist and a
Socialist overnight. The shock was stunning. . . . In 1900 we got converted
to Socialism . . . almost literally in the same way that . . . men became
converted from sin to 'Salvation'. . . . The adoption of Socialism meant
for us a cruel wrench, a breaking of all personal ties, an alienation of
friends and relations. . . . I actually did succeed in concealing my
change of opinion from my parents until a full two years later.[18]

But his conversion was also, in a way, a logical continuation of
his extraordinary philosophical self-education.

Jackson set off 'hot foot in search of every line of Marx
and Engels I could discover'. He was disappointed: as he soon
learned, 'there was surprisingly little'.[19] One day however, he
'happened upon a second hand copy of that masterpiece of
popularisation, Engels's *Socialism, Utopian and Scientific*'.
This in turn told him, in a footnote, of 'the immortal *Communist Manifesto* by Marx and Engels'.[20] The literature
secretary of Jackson's SDF branch had not heard of the
Manifesto but he soon acquired a copy for the keen new
recruit. Its effect on Jackson was extraordinary. 'Never in
my life', he wrote,

have I been so instantaneously exalted, or to such transcendent heights, as by my first reading of the Communist Manifesto. . . . In the years of my adolescence I had stuffed myself omnivorously with all the books within reach. I had accumulated an incredible amount of miscellaneous information which I had incorporated as well as I could into the general pattern of the world-outlook given me by my 'pastors' and 'masters'. Under a succession of blows this world-outlook had been shattered into a million fragments leaving me nothing to cling to but my newly-found Socialist hope. Here in the Communist Manifesto I found a vital core around which I could reorganise my learning as a completely integrated whole. It gave me as in a flash of blazing revelation, a completely inter-related Universe, in which mankind and human society and their history were details in an endlessly developing whole — the triumphant Revolution and realised Socialism emerging as sub-details in the magnificent sweep of its irresistibly compelling whole. How did I get all that from the *Communist Manifesto*?

How indeed! Well,

One gets from a book in proportion to what one brings to its compre-hension. The *Manifesto* came to me when — with the aid of Hegel's *Philosophy of History* and Buckle's *History of Civilisation* superadded to Huxley, Tyndall, Darwin and Haeckel — I was groping for a concept of the 'becoming-process' of human society. Here before me was the vital clue I had searched for. All the myriad fragments of my miscel-laneous learning slipped easily into place and I had — something far better than a hope — a faith, a rational certainty by which to live and guide my steps.[21]

In 1900, then, Jackson read the *Manifesto* as a brilliant epitome to Lewes's *History of Philosophy*. Recalling his adolescent encounter with philosophy, Jackson was to write, much later: 'I was, in fact, unknown to myself, acquiring a grasp of the Universe, objective and subjective, as a unity in multiplicity in perpetual process of self-transformation. I was, though I would not have known what you meant if you had told me so, preparing myself for — *Marx*!'[22]

The Marxist socialism which now grew in Tommy Jackson's philosophically cultivated mind soon began to diverge from that of the leadership of the Social Democratic Federation. With James Connolly, Tom Bell, and George Yates, Jackson was prominent in opposing the elder statesmen of the SDF, by advocating the policy of inciting and organizing a revo-lutionary enthusiasm for socialism amongst the working class, which might then rally to a party of its own, untainted by bourgeois parliamentarianism or electoral compromise.[23]

Jackson and the other 'impossibilists' (they adopted the Hyndmanites' sneering designation with pride[24]) drew their inspiration from America — especially the Socialist Labor Party and the theoretical work of its leader, the mercurial Daniel de Leon[25] — and from the socialist books published by Charles Kerr in Chicago and by the New York Labor Publishing Co.[26] The British Socialist Labour Party was founded in 1903, and a small breakaway group, the Socialist Party of Great Britain, a year later. Tommy Jackson became General Secretary of the SPGB in 1906 but resigned after three years.[27] (He appears to have been quite feckless about party membership at this time, and eventually found himself enrolled in the SLP without knowing it![28])

It was these American-inspired 'impossibilist' organizations that introduced into Britain what was to become by far the most significant debate within twentieth-century socialist politics — the conflict between revolution and reform, centred on the hypothesis that a purely parliamentary road — however thickly paved with Marxist intentions — might never lead to socialism. The impossibilist alternative would stand on its own two feet — industrial (as opposed to political) power, and education.

The impossibilists' concern with education arose from the idea that, as de Leon put it in 1904, 'a ruling class dominates, not only the bodies, but the mind also of the class that it rules'.[29] The inference to be drawn by socialists was that working-class ideas are full of 'errors', and that these must be eliminated by education:

By echoing the errors of the masses of the working class we may ingratiate ourselves with them TODAY. But what of the MORROW, when bitter experience will have taught them that we were no wiser than they? . . . Not the echoing of our fellow wage slaves' errors is our task. Such a task is easy. Ours is the task of uprooting their errors....[30]

So the impossibilists looked to education to open the workers' eyes to the tricks played by the conjurors of bourgeoisdom, who produced compelling illusions of freedom, plenty, and justice out of the realities of poverty, exploitation, and arbitrary power. Education, if it was sound, would reveal to the workers the boundless opportunities for human happiness following the overthrow of capitalism. Thus, when it came to report on its achievements amongst the 'awakened' working class during the first year of its existence, the Socialist Labour Party of Great Britain claimed that it had been 'generally successful in changing their crude and untutored discontent into intelligent and educated revolutionary thought and action.'[31] So it appeared that the workers' desire for education could be used to steer their energies in the direction of socialist revolution. Meantime, however, and far beyond the reach of the impossibilists, the relations of education and social class were being remodelled from within the traditional educational institutions themselves.

Chapter 2

Dilemmas of Working-Class Education 1880–1920

1 The Extension Movement

So, each generation of working people in nineteenth-century Britain contained a scattering of enthusiastic autodidacts seeking knowledge not for any reckonable material advantage it might bring, but because they considered it to be an ultimate value, to be pursued for its own sake. They might linger affectionately on the particulars of grammar, spiritualism, botany, geology, phrenology, or some other detailed science, but their mind would always be fixed on a target beyond — on the hope of acquiring an inclusive grasp, or vision, of human and natural history as a whole: in short, a philosophy.

From the beginning, autodidacticism had had affiliations with non-conformity, radicalism, and secularism; and by the end of the century connections were also being made with socialism — 'cosmic socialism' — and even with a certain rather majestic kind of Marxism. But the socialist autodidacts were heading towards a dilemma, not to say a contradiction: the learning which they revered was embodied in persons and institutions which they resented. The colleges of Oxford and Cambridge, with their rituals, their libraries, and their scholars, were not only unrivalled bastions of knowledge, but also nurseries of an arrogant ruling élite; the Universities, in effect, provided the ruling class with hostages which the socialist autodidacts, however militant, would shrink from placing at risk.[1]

The autodidacts were approaching the Universities, caps or bombs in hand; but at the same time, and in rather different ways, the Universities were trying to open themselves up to working people. From the middle of the nineteenth century, young men in Oxford and Cambridge had been stirred by sincere enthusiasm for the social gospel, their consciences tortured by the plight of the poor, their imaginations haunted by a fear that the working people, understandably angered by undeniable injustices, would smash the social system — destroying, in their fury, not only unfairness and exploitation, but also civilization itself. Hence a succession of remarkable initiatives from University men: the Working Men's College (1854); the University Extension Classes, with Cambridge and Oxford dispatching lecturers round the country to give evening lecture courses to working people (1873, 1876); and — in a deliberate diversion of missionary zeal from the colonies to the metropolis — Toynbee Hall in the East End of London (1884) and the Settlement Movement which developed from it.[2]

If the proletarian autodidacts were aspiring, ultimately, towards a philosophy, a view of the world as a whole, the educational missionaries from the University were moving in the opposite direction, consciously setting out from an explicit philosophy — an anti-individualistic, anti-utilitarian social and educational idealism which had received its clearest expression in the writings of the ʻ'Oxford Hegelian' T. H. Green. For Green and his followers, society was more than the sum of its parts. Drawing on Plato, Rousseau, and Hegel, they developed a notion of community, of a body of people united not by interlocking material interests, but by common participation in an inherited conglomerate of values, institutions, laws, and works of art. On this view, the state was much more than an instrument either of mere rational administration or of simple physical coercion. It was the supreme guardian of the communal national culture, and the composer of social harmony: its dignity even seemed to demand, for many of its theorists, not only that it be obeyed implicitly, but also that its name be spelt with a capital 'S'. The State, as Green put it, was 'that complex of institutions without which I literally could not have a life to call my own'.[3]

Plainly, the State, so conceived, had an obligation to initiate children into the traditions of the community by means of a compulsory comprehensive system of education; and the Universities, especially their philosophical faculties, would have the executive responsibility, as it were, for ensuring cultural reproduction and should therefore extend their influence into the lives of all the members of the community. To be excluded from the University was to be debarred from full citizenship, for, as Mark Pattison put it as early as 1852, 'the ideal of a national University is that it should be coextensive with the nation'.[4]

The extensionists did not conceal the political motives behind their schemes of educational reform. They were alive to the possibility of class warfare, and aware of the enthusiasm with which, by the end of the century, many socialists viewed the prospect of a working-class offensive. They were even, many of them, committed to socialism in some form, at least if they could construe it as essentially the opposite of philistine, materialistic bourgeois individualism. But they considered the class divisions which fissured society to be lamentable, and deplored the prospect of their being enlarged by misguided militancy in the name of socialism. In this context, the purpose of their educational work was clear: they would carry to the workers the larger, more philosophical view of individual, community, and State which had been elaborated by Green and other University philosophers: the workers would then come to see all citizens as, implicitly, participants in a single spiritual community, and would realize that there was no value which deserved to be exalted above that of citizenship within an overarching corporate State.[5]

In one way, the Extension Movement succeeded quite spectacularly: it led to the control of schools by Universities through the agency of University-administered school examinations and teacher-education institutions, to the creation of a comprehensive state education system, and to the foundation, after 1870, of dozens of new Universities. But the achievements of the Extension Movement were not quite what its original apostles had planned. In the first place, the students did not, on the whole, receive a liberal education in idealistic social philosophy; instead, they were educated in the new, optional, non-classical, specialized disciplines, dealing with such subjects as English, modern history, or modern languages or — worse still — with such technical, utilitarian sciences as chemistry or biology. This was not the kind of curriculum which, in the extensionists' dreams, was going to integrate the working class into the spiritual life of the community. Secondly, University Extension did not contribute to Green's scheme for a 'socially united people'. In fact it reinforced the separation, deplored by Green, between 'the educated few and the uneducated many'.[6] The educational 'ladders' which Green had envisaged conveyed a few select individuals across the chasms which separated classes; they did not close them up and produce a consciously unified community. And thirdly, the ladders of opportunity did not seem to reach the right people. Edward Carpenter, an extension lecturer in astronomy from 1874 to 1881, recalled his disappointment:

> It had come on me with great force that I would go and throw in my lot with the mass-people and the manual workers. I took up the University Extension work perhaps chiefly because it seemed to promise this result. As a matter of fact, it merely brought me into the life of the commercial classes; and for seven years I served — instead of the Rachel of my heart's desire — a Leah to whom I was not greatly attached.

University Extension, in short, was taken over by a new class — the suburban 'lower middle' class, and mostly, as Carpenter wearily noted, 'the "young lady" class';[7] it did not serve the urban proletarians for whom it had been wishfully designed.

2 University Extension and the Working Class

In spite of the efforts of the Extension movement, it was evident by the turn of the century that working people were not getting the education they needed or desired. In 1899, American money and initiative were applied to the problem, and Ruskin Hall was founded in Oxford. The purpose of this institution was to provide both postal instruction and six-month residential courses for working men and (in theory at least) women too. Correspondents told Thomas Hardy that 'when Ruskin College was . . . founded it should have been called the College of Jude the Obscure'.[8] But it is not clear that Jude would have been pleased. In the first place, the founders planned to offer instruction in 'science, history, and modern languages, and generally in the duties of a citizen, and in practical industrial work', but proscribed the traditional apotheosis of University education, classics and philosophy ('metaphysics'), not to mention theology. Second, although they intended to enable their students to 'lead a life worthy of a citizen and a man', they made it clear that they did not wish to give them access to the University or to political power: 'it is not intended', they wrote, 'that a man should rise out of his class to swell the already-crowded professional classes'. This attempt to keep workers on a separate educational track, segregated from the Universities and the professional classes, would hardly have appealed to Jude Fawley.

Who then, would it have pleased? Not, for a start, the members of the Shoreditch branch of the SDF, who, in 1900, opposed the Ruskin plan on the ground 'that Oxford and Cambridge, and other endowed seats of learning, were the rightful inheritance of the people, and that to attach themselves to any other educational institution would be to give their acquiescence to this deprivation of their rights'. A speaker at the Oxford Union agreed that Ruskin would divert proletarians from the University, but welcomed the prospect and took pleasure in the thought that Ruskin would then enable workers to take up culture 'in much the same way that a professional man might take up gardening'.[9]

As it turned out, however, another policy for Ruskin was to prevail. In 1903, Albert Mansbridge, himself a lower-middle-class autodidact, and always tormented by the consciousness that he had never had the opportunity of a University education, rallied certain elements of the now dispirited University Extension movement, by allying it with Trade Unions and Co-operation, thus forming what was to become the Workers' Educational Association. The aim of the WEA was to direct the aspirations of proletarian autodidacts towards a Green-tinged corporate state, pleading 'after Emerson, that the co-operative wagon be hitched to the university star' and entreating the University to 'call down upon democracy that uniting wisdom which is the necessary antecedent of high moral power'.[10]

Ruskin College (as it was now called) came to see things in the same light. Rather than providing an education away from the University, it would become a preparatory school for it. In this way, it would enable leaders of labour to approach other politicians as educational equals, and, no doubt, to sympathize with their idealistic social philosophy. The economist Alfred Marshall was worried about the 'rapid growth in inclination of the working class to use political and semi-political machinery for the regulation of industry', and argued that

This new power may be a great good if well guided, but it may work grave injury to the working class and to the nation if guided by unscrupulous and ambitious men, or even by unselfish enthusiasts with a narrow range of vision. Such persons have the field too much to themselves. There is need for a large number of sympathetic students who have studied working class problems in a scientific spirit, and who in later years, when their knowledge of life is deeper and their sense of proportion is more disciplined, will be qualified to go to the root of the urgent social issues of their day and to lay bare the ultimate as well as the immediate results of the plausible proposals for social reform. If this is once granted to be sound reasoning, then the establishment of Ruskin College can need no apology.[11]

In the same spirit, the influential 1908 report on 'Oxford and Working-Class Education', produced jointly by the University, Ruskin College, and the WEA, proclaimed that 'The Trade Union secretary and the "Labour Member" need an Oxford education as much as the civil servant or the barrister.'[12] And so the idea of a separate working-class educational system began to fade, and many Labour leaders were glad to be rid of it.

3 Independent Working-Class Education

But Ruskin College's increasing subordination to the University provoked a hostile reaction amongst its students. Thanks to the educational work of the SDF, the SLP, and other socialist organizations, many of them arrived at the college with a good grasp of the Marxist theory of capitalist economics. Then they were confronted with tutors who knew nothing of Marx or of Socialism, and who offered them Marshall and Marginalism instead.[13] These 'University Men' would refer to their students, with insufficient irony, as 'the manual workers, "the mutable rank-scented many"', and describe the college, in baffling Latin, as 'an idealist experiment *in faece Romuli*'.[14]

In 1908, a group of Ruskin students, indignant and offended at such treatment, formed a national organization to campaign for the cause of independent socialist education and to prevent the affiliation of 'Ruskin to the University with the consequent permeation of University ideas in the minds of the young blood of labour', which threatened to dissipate 'the main source of the future strength of the labour movement . . . into channels useless to the workers'.[15] They called themselves 'the Plebs League' and launched a monthly journal of Marxist education, *The Plebs Magazine,* in the following year.[16] In adopting the name 'Plebs' they were identifying themselves as revolutionary, 'impossibilist' socialists by taking up a historical analogy proposed in one of Daniel de Leon's denunciations of reformist 'Labor Leaders'.[17]

In March 1909, incensed by an attempt to sack the only socialist at the college, its principal Dennis Hird, nearly all the Ruskin students went on strike, and after a fortnight, seceded from the college. With support from the South Wales Miners' Federation and the Amalgamated Society of Railway Servants and miscellaneous militants like Tommy Jackson,[18] they set up a Central Labour College, first in Oxford, and then, after 1911, in the Earls Court district of London. The new college was committed to 'Independent Working-Class Education' by residential and correspondence courses,[19] and also encouraged lectures and evening classes for part-time students all round the country on a basis of non-residential local 'Labour Colleges', some (for instance the Leeds and Bradford Colleges, run by Tommy Jackson during and after the War)[20] with a full-time Organizer.

The early 1920s were the great days of the IW-CE movement, as the Plebs League called it.[21] Numerically, its strength grew till it had 30,000 part-time enrolments,[22] its greatest failure being that men outnumbered women in a ratio of twenty to one.[23] And spirits rose because of events abroad, especially in Russia. In an infectiously affirmative book published in 1921, Eden and Cedar Paul — a marvellously industrious husband-and-wife team of writers devoted to the Labour College Movement — referred to the All-Russia Proletcult Congress of Autumn 1918, which had advocated an independent proletarian line in culture. They spoke with admiration of the work of Bogdanov, Kollontai, and (with reservations) Lunacharsky, and connected it with the legacy of Ferrer in Spain, with French syndicalism, with Ferrer schools and workers' colleges in America, and with the educational enterprise of the communists in Germany. Proletcult, they claimed, had been inaugurated in Britain by the Ruskin strike, and it was 'practically synonymous with what is generally known in this country by the cumbrous name of Independent Working-Class Education'.[24]

This internationalistic optimism was to fade during the 1920s, and morale was also depleted by events at home, especially the General Strike. Still, the 'IW-CE' movement did not close down until 1964,[25] and throughout the twenties and thirties its members put up a vigorous defence of the idea of socialist education free of ruling-class influence, and engaged in constant warfare on educational questions with the WEA, Ruskin, and the Universities, not to mention with socialist political parties. And the 'Plebs' (many of them at least) regarded philosophy — 'proletarian philosophy' — as an indispensable part of a revolutionary socialist education.

Chapter 3

Joseph Dietzgen and Proletarian Philosophy

1 Joseph Dietzgen's Philosophy

In the winter of 1927-8, a young University-trained philosophy teacher was taking University Extension classes amongst groups of miners in South Wales. She was bewildered by her students' idea of philosophy: 'Almost invariably when Philosophy was suggested as the subject for the class, the immediate reply was, "That's Ditchkin, isn't it?"' At first Dorothy Emmett did not know what they were saying, but she soon realized that she had stumbled upon what she quite accurately called 'a kind of underworld of philosophy of which the universities hear singularly little and perhaps care less'. This 'underworld' was a direct product of the work of the Plebs movement. It was conscious of itself as possessing a 'Proletarian philosophy', and Dorothy Emmett went on to report that it 'exercises such an influence over the minds of our fellow countrymen that they look upon the man who gave it some sort of formulation as literally the greatest philosopher who ever lived'.[1]

The 'greatest philosopher', unknown in the Universities, was Joseph Dietzgen, a tanner by trade, who had been born near Cologne in 1828, and divided his life between America, Russia, and his home village of Siegburg. He was a genial, complacent, self-employed family man, hard-working but not poor. He was an enthusiastic autodidact, who always had a book open beside him as he worked; and the consuming passion of his life was philosophy. He was widely read in the history of philosophy, and spent his spare time composing books and articles on philosophical questions. He loved to receive recognition from University men, inspiring in one of them the reverent comment that 'no professor could rise from his desk more spiritualised than did this tanner from his manual labour'.[2] In addition, Dietzgen was a revolutionary Social-Democrat, and one of the first people to identify themselves as 'Marxists'. As early as 1866, he was propagating Marxist theory amongst German-speaking workers in St. Petersburg,[3] work which he continued in New York and Chicago for the next twenty years. Dietzgen considered his own philosophical studies as having a kind of supportive, subordinate relation to Marxist economics, and claimed that this attitude was authorized by Marx himself:

'Once my work on Economics finished,' wrote Marx to me privately, 'I shall write a Dialectics. The laws of Dialectics have been formulated by Hegel, though in mystical form. What we have to do is to strip it of that form.' Being afraid it might be long before Marx could undertake such a work, and having since my youth thought a good deal on that subject, I shall try to throw some light on dialectical philosophy. It is in my opinion the central sun from whom light goes forth to illuminate not only Political Economy, but the whole course of human development and it will finally, I expect, penetrate to the 'final cause' of all science.[4]

In this spirit, Dietzgen produced an enthusiastic outpouring of writings designed to expound a philosophy for Marxists — what he called a 'proletarian logic' or a 'Social-Democratic Philosophy'.

Dietzgen's starting point was respect for science. The virtue of Marxism, he argued, was that it represented 'scientific' or 'inductive socialism'. 'Scientific socialists', he asserted, 'apply the inductive method. They stick to facts.'[5] 'Social-Democracy', he wrote elsewhere, 'is scientific and science is social-democratic.'[6] One of the chief attributes of the scientific temper, according to Dietzgen, was its abhorrence of all dualisms. Wherever common sense might dichotomize, the scientist would find a way of interpreting the apparent dichotomy as a difference within a wider unity. But, according to Dietzgen, this scientific procedure had been neglected in the field where it mattered most, namely in the welter of distinctions associated with human nature: soul and body, mind and matter, thought and object, value and fact, the human and the natural. The brusqueness of Dietzgen's attack on these problems is well conveyed by the title of his first major work, translated as 'The Nature of Human Brainwork, by a manual worker'. This essay, which dates from

1869, begins by praising 'inductive science' at the expense of metaphysical speculation, and then claims that although past philosophers wasted most of their time in idle verbiage, their labours had nevertheless resulted in one positive achievement: the recognition that thinking consists in the activity of the human mind in developing general categories out of concrete experience. The present task of philosophy, then, was to explain that this principle applied even to such concepts as 'soul' and 'thought'. To common sense and metaphysical philosophy, these categories indicated the unique and privileged ontological status of 'man'; but to scientific philosophy they were no more than the artefacts of the self-infatuated human brain. 'Man' was part of the material world, like everything else, and 'thinking is a function of the brain just as walking is a function of the legs.'[7]

After many pages on the techniques of 'brainwork', Dietzgen turned to 'Practical Reason', dismissing all attempts to tie morality down to any particular set of supposedly 'eternal' values, and proposing instead that it be seen as an evolving institution, part of society and ultimately of nature, and functioning indirectly to satisfy human social needs.[8] Dietzgen summarized this view of morality in the phrase 'the end justifies the means', which was destined to have an eventful career in Marxism. In this statement, according to Dietzgen, 'the developed theory of morality finds its practical expression'.[9]

But what did all this have to do with the proletariat? Dietzgen connected his monistic philosophy with the revolutionary doctrines of proletarian Social-Democracy by the following kind of reasoning: the enemies of socialism were committed to a divided society, so they saw divisions as inherent in the natural order of the cosmos. They also wished to conceal the mutability and malleability of social arrangements, and consequently were attracted to ideas of 'eternal values' and 'the eternal soul'. However, these intellectual subterfuges ran counter to the proper, natural uses of the organ of thought, and the proletariat, which had everything to gain from the abolition of social divisions, had an interest in exposing them. Hence the mission of the Proletariat was identical with that of Science, or of Scientific Philosophy:

the oppressed fourth estate, the working class, is the true exponent of this organ [the faculty of thought] , the ruling classes being prevented by their special class interests from recognising the demands of general reason. . . . So long as conditions are not equalised for men in general, but vitiated by class interests, our view of things is limited by these class limitations. . . . Not until historical development has proceeded to the point of striving at dissolution of the last society based on a ruling and a serving class, can prejudices be overcome to the extent of enabling the faculty of understanding to grasp the nature of human brain activity in the abstract. It is only a historical movement aiming at the direct and general liberty of the masses, the new era of the fourth estate . . . which can dispense with the spirit cult sufficiently to be enabled to expose the real author of every spook, the 'pure' mind. The man of the fourth estate represents at last the 'pure' man. His interests are no longer mere class interests, but mass interests, interests of humanity. . . .[10]

Dietzgen elaborated the ideas of 'The Nature of Human Brainwork' for the remaining two decades of his life, attempting in particular to relate his 'materialistic' and 'proletarian' outlook to traditional philosophical thought. In 'Social-Democratic Philosophy' (1876) he wrote that 'the critical attitude taken up by the old man towards his past is just the attitude of social-democracy towards philosophy'.[11] Our 'anti-philosophic philosophy' would enable us Social-Democrats to be 'proud of our philosophic descent'. It would turn us into 'materialists', which, Dietzgen explained, is 'the appellation of those who strive for the liberation of the human mind from all metaphysical magics'.[12]

These themes were taken up again in Dietzgen's next major work, the 'Letters on Logic, especially Democratic-Proletarian Logic', of 1880–3. Even by Dietzgen's own rather disappointing standards, this is an extremely repetitious book. It is based on the idea that 'untrained prejudice' and the 'uncultivated brain' are incapable of understanding 'the organic unity of all things', their 'universal connection'. Dietzgen alleges that 'formal logic' has colluded with common sense in this respect, and that the task of proletarian logic, therefore, is to attack them both. It would do this by demonstrating that 'all distinctions which are ever made constitute but a nibbling at the universal unit', and that 'error, pretense, lies, death, are only phenomena, formalities, passing trifles compared with the one thing, that thing of all things which is being, truth, life'. 'The universe', Dietzgen declared, 'is the absolute which includes everything, while the world and the thought of it, each by itself, are but classifications or relative things.' Swaying precariously on his stilted rhetoric, Dietzgen now used this inclusive notion of 'the Universe' as a way of mollifying much of his former enmity towards religion:

If he is an atheist who denies that perfection can be found in any individual, then I am an atheist. If he is a believer in God who has the faith in the 'most perfect being' . . . then I am one of the true children of God. . . .

If you would give the name of pantheism to this world philosophy, you should remember that it is not a sentimental and exhausted, but a common sense pantheism, a deification which has the taste of the godless.

But Dietzgen never ceased to insist on the revolutionary proletarian affiliation of his increasingly anodyne philosophy. This resided in its complete hostility to the narrowness of the bourgeois frame of mind:

The horizon of the everyday capitalist minds does not reach farther than they can see from the steeple of their church. . . . The old man who plants a tree the fruits of which he will perhaps never see is not such a capitalist mind, otherwise he would sow seeds that would ripen during this year's summer.

The working class, on the other hand, possessed 'the science of truth' which furnished it with 'the logical justification to renounce all clerical and mystic control':

The thought on which the proletarian demands are based, the idea of the equality of all human beings, this ultimate proletarian idea, if I may say so, is fully backed up by the deeper insight into the tortuous problem of logic. . . . My logic deserves its proletarian qualification for the reason that it requires for its understanding the overcoming of all prejudices by which the capitalist world is held together.[13]

Dietzgen completed his final work, 'The Positive Outcome of Philosophy', in 1887. It was intended to replace the 'Letters on Logic' with which Dietzgen was understandably dissatisfied. It is comparatively terse and business-like, and faces up to a contradiction that always lurked unrecognized amongst Dietzgen's earlier formulations — namely that if he wanted to march under the banner of 'materialism', he could not consistently present the categories of 'matter' and 'mind' as equally arbitrary human artefacts, imposed on a universe which embraced and confounded them both together. In his later work, Dietzgen got out of this difficulty by adopting a trenchant realism, claiming that thought in general involves mental representations of an objective material reality entirely independent of it. Already in the 'Letters on Logic' Dietzgen had compared the mind to a camera;[14] in the 'Positive Outcome', he developed this metaphor into a theory of the pictorial or reflective nature of thought:

Compared to the wealth of the cosmos, the intellect is only a poor fellow. However, this does not prevent it from being the most perfect instrument for clearly and plainly reflecting the finite phenomena of the infinite universe.

Its function, Dietzgen went on, was that of 'tracing a human picture of cosmic processes': 'conceived things are pictures, real pictures, pictures of reality.'[15] And it was this picture-theory of thinking, according to Dietzgen, which constituted the 'positive outcome' of centuries of philosophical thought, the end of philosophy and the beginning of socialism:

We maintain that philosophy so far has acquired something positive, has left us a legacy, and that this consists in a clear revelation of the method of using our intellect in order to produce excellent pictures of nature and its phenomena.[16]

The proletarians therefore required an education in logic, in order to perfect the 'picturing' activity of their brains, and to avoid being misled into dualism by it; in short, to master the rules of the Science of Understanding:

Thus our science of understanding finally culminates in the rule: Thou shalt sharply divide and subdivide and further subdivide to the utmost the universal concept, the concept of the universe, but thou shalt be backed up by the consciousness that this mental classification is a formality by which man seeks for the sake of his information to register and to place his experience; thou shalt furthermore remain aware of this liberty to progressively improve the experience acquired by thyself in the course of time, by modifying the classification.[17]

Dietzgen died in Chicago in 1888, a year after completing the 'Positive Outcome'; and by that time, he had amassed impressive credentials as the sovereign philosopher of Marxism.[18]

2 Dietzgenism and Marxism

In the late 1860s Dietzgen became acquainted with Marx, who is said to have referred to him affectionately as 'das Dietzchen';[19] and in 1868 Dietzgen wrote a review of the first volume of *Capital,* which was duly acknowledged by Marx in the Preface to the second edition. Dietzgen was naturally delighted when Marx presented him to the Hague Congress of the First International in 1872 as 'our philosopher'.[20] And in 1886, Engels gave Dietzgen an accolade for the 'independent discovery' of the 'materialist dialectic'.[21]

By 1907, most of Dietzgen's writings had been translated into Russian,[22] and they attracted considerable interest from Russian socialists. In 1908, Lenin insisted with emotion on the essential unanimity of Marx, Engels, and Dietzgen on the central questions of philosophy. The most urgent of these, in Lenin's opinion, was the debate between 'materialism' and 'empirio-criticism'. The 'empirio-criticists' — chiefly Mach, Avenarius, and Karl Pearson — were contemporary philosophers of science who were pushing a seemingly hard-headed, materialistic scientific empiricism to some surprisingly soft-minded conclusions. Science (they argued hard-headedly) had to be based not on metaphysical speculation but on actual sensory experience; and it followed (they concluded soft-mindedly) that science was an expression of consensus amongst scientists about their subjective sensory worlds, rather than an attempt to describe a 'real world' of matter independent of their minds. 'Materialism' thus became, in their view, a 'metaphysical' postulate, unnecessary for science. Lenin was appalled by the popularity of this line of reasoning amongst Russian Social-Democrats — Bazarov, Bogdanov, Lunacharsky, and others — and had no difficulty in pinning the label 'idealist' on it. (His hostility was presumably based on the fact that empirio-criticism implied that a revolutionary party could never be competent to challenge a majority opinion in the name of Marxist 'science'.) Lenin gratefully made use of Dietzgen's 'pictorial' theory of thinking — the 'reflection' theory, he called it — to rebut this attack on 'materialism', and angrily repudiated those who had (not quite groundlessly) classified Dietzgen with the 'empirio-criticists'. Lenin admitted that Dietzgen was sometimes tempted into an eclectic, soft-minded, pseudo-religiosity — evangelical, millenarian, and a priori; but he also argued, quite correctly, that there was more to Dietzgen than this. Alongside Dietzgen 'the muddleheaded', said Lenin, was Dietzgen 'the materialist' — open, empirical, atheistic, and strictly realist about science.[23]

Dietzgen's works were well known in America too, where he had left a number of devoted disciples.[24] His son Eugene had stayed in Chicago after his father's death, and in 1906 he supervised the publication of English translations of his father's works, in two volumes — *Some of the Philosophical Essays* and *The Positive Outcome of Philosophy*. Together, these books offered a quite comprehensive sample of Dietzgen's writings — they even included the rather dubious 'Letters on Logic'; and they instigated an extremely reverent attitude towards his authority in the years to come.

The volume entitled *The Positive Outcome of Philosophy* contained an introduction by the Dutch Marxist Anton Pannekoek, which stated that 'it is the merit of Dietzgen to have raised philosophy to the level of a natural science, the same as Marx did with history.' Pannekoek went on to claim:

Marx has disclosed the nature of the social process of production, and its fundamental significance as a lever of social development. But he has not fully explained, by what means the nature of the human mind is involved in this material process. Owing to the great traditional influence exerted by bourgeois thought, this weak spot in Marxism is one of the main reasons for the incomplete and erroneous understanding of Marxian theories. This shortcoming of Marxism is cured by Dietzgen. . . . Dietzgen's work demonstrates that the proletariat has a mighty weapon not only in proletarian economics, but also in proletarian philosophy. Let us learn to wield these weapons. . . .[25]

In the second volume of English translations, the *Philosophical Essays*, the same high note was trumpeted even more stridently. In an introductory essay, Eugene Dietzgen presented his father's philosophy as a mystical cosmic socialism, and explained excitedly how it

develops the dialectics of Marx and Engels, which is a theory of development through antagonisms to a higher stage, by perfecting it and pointing out that the universe is the last and highest organic unit, which combines monistically all other syntheses. By means of this understanding, the dialectics became a theory of the cosmic and organic interrelation and interpenetration of all phenomena. . . . Dialectics in its restricted sense found its culminating point in the cosmic interpretation.

This 'cosmic interpretation' in turn led to socialism, in other words 'the dialectically organised society', whose desirability and necessity were bafflingly explained as follows: 'A society of equals is evidently more powerful than any individual member, and the cosmos, finally, is more powerful than human society.' Moreover, socialism was ensured by 'the determinism of cosmic interrelations':

Dialectically organised society secures the freest expression to science and art by abolishing the cares for the daily bread. The proletariat is the bearer of this greatest of all social movements ever recorded. The individual who consciously takes part in it, avows to himself: I entrust my affairs to the understanding of the laws of society and of the universe, to which I owe the knowledge that I must develop my personality, not in a struggle against, but in alliance with those social and cosmic interrelations, whose proudly modest member I am.[26]

It was therefore a bland and semi-religious thinker — 'Dietzgen the muddlehead', in Lenin's terms, rather than 'Dietzgen the materialist' — who became known to English-reading socialists at the beginning of the century.

3 Dietzgenism and the Labour Colleges

The impossibilist revolt in Britain was sustained, intellectually, by books imported from America, and particularly from the Charles Kerr Co-Operative in Chicago, publishers of the English translations of Dietzgen. So it was that the Ruskin strikers, the de Leonite impossibilists, and the Plebs Leaguers eventually encountered 'Proletarian Philosophy'. With their desire for an education which would be liberal and elevating but also anti-bourgeois and anti-universitarian, they were powerfully attracted by Dietzgen's idea of the proletariat as the true inheritor of that most prestigious of intellectual traditions — philosophy. Dietzgenism appealed in this way, for instance, to W. W. Craik, a railway worker from South Wales, effectively the first editor of *Plebs Magazine,* one of the original students at the Central Labour College, and subsequently a member of the staff there from 1910 to 1925. Half a century later, he recalled how, in his view, Dietzgen had 'helped to fill the gap left by Marx' by constructing a proletarian view of philosophy. Craik saw Dietzgen wreathed in the folksy laurels of dignified manual labour — 'when he was not tanning hides in his tannery in the little Rhineland town of Siegburg, he was,' Craik wrote, 'in his leisure hours tanning the hides of the decadent philosophers.' The doctrines of this amiable worker-philosopher, Craik believed, would enable workers to see through the subterfuges of capitalism, Ruskin College, and the WEA, guiding them in 'consciously employing the faculty of thought in accordance with its actual nature, methodically and objectively . . . [rather than] ignorantly taking the faculty and function of cognition as a matter of course, like that of, say, the stomach.'[27]

Under Craik's influence, the early Labour College Movement was deeply suffused with Dietzgenism. Alongside Economics, Industrial History, Literature, Grammar, and Evolution, the local Labour Colleges provided lecture courses on 'Philosophical Logic',[28] based on outlines written by Craik, these in turn being derived from the translations in *The Positive Outcome of Philosophy*.[29]

Craik seems to have emphasized the practical or logical as opposed to the philosophical or systematic side of Dietzgenism. His starting-point was the (designedly provocative) thesis that thinking is only a physical activity of the brain, and his aim was to make his students aware of the otherwise automatic and unconsidered activities involved in their own 'brainwork'. To Craik, it seemed obvious that all knowledge comes from the senses, and that any thinking which could not be traced back to them must be invalid. A dexterous brainworker was one who was adroit and knowledgeable about the brain-activities of abstracting and generalizing; and it was for such skill in thinking that the honorific title of 'dialectical' was reserved. A historical survey of Western philosophy from the pre-Socratics to the present was given as a kind of backdrop, and the Dietzgenite technology of brainwork was put forward as the ultimate achievement, the 'positive outcome', of the history of philosophy.[30]

In the pages of *Plebs Magazine,* Craik campaigned for recognition of the need for philosophy and for 'dialectic method' in economics, urging students and tutors to follow 'the road opened up by Marx, Engels, and Dietzgen';[31] and the case seems to have been generally accepted, the only resistance coming from those who felt that Dietzgenite 'philosophical logic' should be offered as an option for 'advanced students', rather than as an essential preliminary course.[32]

When the Labour College movement started to pull itself together after the War, however, a conflict began to develop within it. On one side stood the Central Labour College, essentially a national institution administering a range of correspondence courses and running a full-time course based in London for residential students sponsored by nationally affiliated Trade Unions (principally the South Wales Miners and the Railwaymen). On the other side, there was a variegated array of local Labour Colleges, promoting lectures in the evenings or on Sunday afternoons for local working people — free to members of locally affiliated unions, and otherwise at a small charge.[33]

Craik had become acting Warden of the Central Labour College in 1917, and in 1919 he had entrenched his Dietzgenite 'Science of Understanding' course in the correspondence department.[34] Following his appointment as Principal in 1920, he was able to ensure that 'the theory of brainwork or knowledge . . . became a priority in the order of the studies' of full-time students.[35]

Meantime, the Plebs League, which mainly represented the part-time students in the local colleges, held a conference in Manchester in January 1920 with the aim of launching a series of 'Plebs Textbooks' — which would, of course, bypass the CLC. The conference agreed that Dietzgenism or 'The Science of Understanding' should be one of the four pillars of Independent Working-Class Education, along with Economics, Industrial History, and Economic Geography.[36] Soon, plans were laid for collectively written textbooks on each of these subjects, to be discussed as widely as possible at every stage of their composition. The proposals for the philosophy textbook, however, got off to an idiosyncratic start, with Alice Pratt, an experienced teacher of 'philosophical logic', drawing attention, in a courageously autobiographical essay, to the despair and self-doubt that might result from too sudden an exposure to Dietzgenism. She recalled her own first encounter with the subject:

I retired from that lecture feeling as though my brain had been stirred with a porridge spoon. . . . Joseph 'took it out' of me, very considerably. All the same, I felt sure something valuable lurked behind this maze of unfamiliar words, for the lecturer was obviously so infatuated with his subject. . . . I went to sleep feeling that this is a hard world for a working woman seeking a reliable brand of truth.

Intrigued by her tutor's incomprehensible enthusiasm, Alice Pratt tried to study the *Positive Outcome of Philosophy,* but without great success. There was an avalanche of philosophical jargon, 'hurtling through the mental atmosphere, now and then giving one a nasty blow in the self-esteem, and necessitating a desperate offensive and defensive alliance with the dictionary'.[37] Alice Pratt's conclusion was that there was an urgent need for a textbook putting Dietzgenism into plain English, and her proposal was ratified by a special 'Textbook Conference' held in Bradford in April 1920, Craik being asked to produce the first draft. But a few months later, he was reported to be behind with the work, and it was announced that Eden and Cedar Paul would, in the meantime, produce an 'Outline of Psychology'. The textbook committee expressed its confidence that the book would interest 'every student of Dietzgen and of the Science of Understanding', although in fact the Pauls ignored Dietzgenism entirely. The projected Plebs textbook on philosophy never appeared.[38]

Meantime, the power of the full-time Central Labour College, along with that of its Dietzgenite principal Craik, was being eclipsed by the part-time local Labour Colleges, which had, in 1921, strengthened their position by organizing themselves into the National Council of Labour Colleges. One effect of this shift was that the attempt by the CLC to impose a central curriculum — particularly one which emphasized a subject which students found difficult — became pointless. Part-time students in local colleges would study what they liked, and in spite of Craik's blandishments, this was more likely to be Economics, History, or Geography than Philosophy or 'The Science of Understanding'.[39] And in 1923, the NCLC began its own Postal Courses Department, based in Edinburgh, which promoted Economics, Social History, and English language, at the expense of Philosophy, and which soon took the wind out of the sails of the CLC correspondence department.[40] The decline of the CLC, and with it of the championship of Dietzgen in the Labour College movement, was accelerated in 1923 when the College Secretary George Sims, a close and long-standing associate of Craik, absconded, taking the account books with him. And in 1925, Craik himself fled the country, accused of embezzling CLC and Railwaymen's Union funds, allegedly to pay off drinking and gambling debts. Henceforth, it was impolite to mention Craik or his ideas in Labour College circles.[41] The CLC closed, in an atmosphere of considerable bitterness, in 1929.[42]

Still, although Dietzgenism had lost its principal power base, it was kept alive by individual Labour College tutors in certain regions, and especially in Lancashire, thanks to the tireless efforts of an eccentric crippled watch-maker from Bury. His name was Fred Casey and he had been born into a Roman Catholic family in 1876. Like many other working people of his generation, he had moved from a thirst for book-learning to a passion for socialism. He recalled that 'A combination of physics, astronomy, biology and philosophy, including the rationalist literature, spoiled my Roman Catholicism, though it did not settle the "great" questions — it took the "Positive Outcome" which I met later to do that.'[43] Casey first encountered Dietzgen's work in 1912, when he was thirty-six. This was a result of attending local Labour College lectures given by Craik. His family commitments prevented him from accepting a CLC scholarship that same year, so he devoted himself to studying the *Positive Outcome* on his own. During the war, he conducted Dietzgen classes in Labour Colleges in the Manchester area, eventually converting his lectures into a brief textbook, published — but not by the NCLC or the Plebs League — in 1922.[44] The book was in two parts: a history of philosophy from Thales to Marx and Dietzgen, supplemented by two large wall-charts, and a section on 'Logic, or the Science of Understanding'. This continued Craik's development of Dietzgenism as a technology of brainwork, a 'method of thinking'. It was based on the idea that the brain operates by dividing the data of experience into various units, and then reshuffling them to create complex ideas. An explicit study of brain processes, Casey thought, would enable students to appreciate how their brain-begotten categories could mould their experience, and to recognize that they did not necessarily correspond to divisions in the nature of things themselves.

In 1925, Casey sent a copy of his book to Eugene Dietzgen, a genial business man, proud of his father Joseph, and fond of congratulating himself on his dialecticalness in combining socialistic views (of a very mild variety — he deplored all talk of 'class warfare') with his comfortable existence as a well-to-do bourgeois now living in Zurich. Eugene was vastly impressed by Casey's book, sent him money, and financed a second edition published by Charles Kerr in Chicago. This edition was even more fervent in its claims for Dietzgenism than the first: 'the mental reflex involved in Marxism,' it said, 'that is the dialectics of the thought process, was never fully worked out by them [Marx and Engels] but was ultimately explained by Joseph Dietzgen who, by this means, completed the great work of Marx and Engels so that "Marxism" is really Marx-Engels-Dietzgenism.'[45] Casey devoted himself to the promotion of Marx-Engels-Dietzgenism in the Manchester area with redoubled vigour, holding series of twelve three-hour training classes with groups of about half a dozen students at a time, dictating his lectures and getting students to repeat their lessons the following week. He was delighted when, in spite of indifference from the NCLC, the Manchester Council of Labour College Tutors resolved that in their district 'no teacher of whatever subject must henceforth go out unless he has taken training in Scientific (Dialectic) thinking', that is to say, Casey's philosophy course.[46]

In 1928, Casey linked up with Eugene Dietzgen in Zurich, and the disgraced Craik, now working on the State Lottery in Hamburg, to try to co-ordinate international recognition of Dietzgen's centenary in December. Casey produced a brief celebratory article for *The Plebs*, as well as publishing privately a substantial pamphlet written specially for the occasion. The *Sunday Worker* ran a feature-article on Dietzgen and celebrations were held in six centres in the United States, as well as in Manchester and London.[47] All in all, however, the centenary was rather a disappointment to all concerned, demonstrating the cranky disarray of Dietzgenism by this time, rather than its strength.

In spite of such discouragements, Casey produced another

book in 1933, under the title *Method in Thinking*. It was advertised as an 'application' of Marxism to 'human brain-work', and it pressed home the thesis that 'thinking is a physical process' in which the brain collects its 'sense-perceptions' and then 'puts them together in different ways'. It also offered step-by-step instructions in clear thinking and exceedingly mystifying examples designed to show how the 'method' would enable traditional philosophical problems to be solved.[48] This book did not contain any trace of the rapid survey of the history of philosophy which had been the more popular part of Casey's earlier book, *Thinking*. The NCLC refused to be associated with *Method in Thinking*, so a number of voluntary tutors in the South East Lancashire Labour College clubbed together to publish it privately.[49] This curious and deeply flawed book was not successful, and although Casey continued to hope against hope for a revival of Dietzgenism, he eventually concluded, despairingly, that the attitude of the NCLC had 'killed it'.[50]

4 The Attack on Dietzgenism in the Plebs League

The leading teachers of Dietzgenism within the Labour College movement — Craik and Casey — tended to reduce Dietzgen's philosophy to a technology of 'brainwork', for whose benign political and intellectual effects they made large but unargued claims. Their courses on 'brainwork' were really a rather degenerate offspring of Dietzgen's robust philosophical work, but many of their students seem to have skirted the obstacles created by their teachers, and discovered some of the original motives of Dietzgen's thought for themselves. Maurice Dobb recalled that in the 1920s, 'if one stayed overnight . . . in a South Wales miner's household, there were his [Dietzgen's] works . . . in a prominent place and treated with reverence as a sacred text'.[51] And Dorothy Emmett, quoting essays by her Dietzgenite students, claimed that Dietzgen's reflections on morality, rather than brainwork, were 'the part which is chiefly fastened upon by his followers'. Students were preoccupied with the idea that, as one of them put it in an essay written for her, 'there is no more an absolute morality than there is an absolutely green pea. . . . At present morals are relative to the needs of the dominant class, and . . . under a different mode of production we will have a new code of morals.' Dorothy Emmett commented, too, on the 'extraordinary fervour and pertinacity' with which these Dietzgenite doctrines were adopted and expounded.[52]

The experience of Jock Shanley illustrates the verve and depth of Dietzgen's influence. Shanley was an upholsterer by trade, with little formal education. But as a young man, he obtained a scholarship to the Central Labour College, which he then attended from 1924 to 1926. In a recent interview, he recalled how, at that time, he read various Marxist classics,[53] but above all, *The Positive Outcome of Philosophy*. 'This is the one that was central', he said. For Shanley, as for numerous working people before him, contact with philosophy, and especially with the notion of dialectic, produced a revelation:

The first thing — complete mental consternation and confusion. . . . It was completely contrary to any principles I'd been taught . . . God had disappeared, heaven had disappeared. Slowly, it began to be something I came to be always looking for . . . the dialectic leap was working in my mind constantly . . . so everything I read, everything I did, had a different context: it was as real as that.

The notion of dialectic was 'real' to Shanley because it combated an attitude of mind in which he had been brought up — where something's mere existence was taken as an argument for its permanent necessity. Dietzgenism taught him never to underestimate the changefulness of nature and society; in a word, the idea of 'evolution'. ('That may not mean a lot to you. But coming as we were without any tradition of being taught concepts of evolution in the ordinary school, this to us was mind-opening.') Nor was it only a theoretical enlightenment. It provided Shanley with a beacon to guide his activities as a leader of the Amalgamated Union of Upholsterers and the National Union of Furniture Trades, where he consistently criticized reactionary craft unionism, lecturing his members on the inevitable eclipse of their special skills, and the consequent need to make common cause with young and unskilled workers.[54] However, Shanley's vivid practical appreciation of 'dialectics', though learned at the Central Labour College, was actually to set him at odds with the doctrines of leading NCLC tutors, especially Casey.[55]

Dietzgenite philosophizing might have sunk under its own weight, or conceivably it might have been overthrown by students insisting that there was more to Dietzgen than the techniques of 'brainwork'. But as it happened, Dietzgenism was deliberately sabotaged from within the Labour College Movement — by a group of young, University-trained intellectuals who committed themselves to the movement in the period after the First World War. They were, above all, moved by the Russian Revolution. As Arthur Ransome wrote: 'There was the feeling, from which we could never escape, of the creative effect of the Revolution . . . the living, vivifying expression of something hitherto hidden in the consciousness of humanity.'[56] These enthusiastic new recruits were, in one way or another, scientific rationalists, in politics and everything else: they felt that the Revolution had transformed socialism from an inconsequential philosophical Utopia into a palpable scientific fact, which they, as trained intellectuals, had a duty to study, publicize, and promote. They believed in Independent Working-Class Education, but they did not think it should oppose the intellectual values of the University — only, perhaps, prize them more highly than did the bourgeois professors. So to the minds of these young universitarians, Dietzgenite proletarianism was pointless, unintelligent, and in rather poor taste.

The first expression of this line of thought was an article in *Plebs Magazine* in May 1919. Lancelot Hogben, a twenty-three-year-old medical graduate from Cambridge University (and a graduate, too, of Wormwood Scrubs, where he had been imprisoned for resisting conscription) advocated there a view of historical progress as consisting in the gradual triumph of science over religion, philosophy (especially Hegelianism — the 'dying gasp' of anti-scientific obscurantism), and other intellectual vanities. Hogben proclaimed that 'the method of the scientist started not with human "reason", but with facts.' And Marx and Engels, to Hogben, were scientists in this sense. Their 'materialist conception of history' had been a generalisation which to ourselves is as fundamental for a coherent comprehension of the data as the theory of organic evolution in the world of living organisms. It meant that philosophy must abandon many of its problems to science and admit that others were . . . meaningless. . . .

Ingeniously, Hogben claimed that Dietzgen himself would have shared this hostility to philosophy. It was, he said, what 'Dietzgen styles the Positive Outcome of Philosophy. . . . Thus in much the same relation as Marx stands to the social study of his time does Dietzgen to contemporary philosophy.' Hogben entitled his scientistic attack on philosophy, 'The Wisdom of Joseph Dietzgen: An Appreciation'.[57] But in parading his scientific rationalism under the flag of Dietzgen Hogben was really being quite disingenuous. It is true that his attitudes paralleled some of those to be found in Dietzgen's writings, but they were a total negation of those by which British Dietzgenism was inspired. Hogben's position implied that philosophy, far from being an all-important element of working-class education, ought really to be left to a few experts, like Hogben's fellow Trinity man, Bertrand Russell, or to Radical Empiricists and Pragmatists at Harvard.

The attacks on Dietzgenism built up over the following year. A correspondent with the *nom de guerre* of 'P.L.E.B.S.' (possibly Hogben), writing of the need for scientific education in the Labour College Movement, argued that 'mere repetition of Dietzgen's phrases will not bring us any nearer to the goal which Dietzgen foreshadowed'.[58] Philosophy was not mentioned in the Plebs League's 1920 pamphlet 'What is Independent Working-Class Education?',[59] and in 1921 'P.L.E.B.S.' praised the curriculum of a Russian workers' college in the following terms: 'It is interesting to note that there is no place in the Sverdlov curriculum for Philosophy. The students evidently are not forced to devote a disproportionate amount of their all too restricted time to a detailed perusal of the works of Dietzgen.' Persisting in the digression, 'P.L.E.B.S.' argued that the best way of honouring 'that energetic thinker' would be 'to substitute an illustrative introduction to exact scientific reasoning for the study of *The Positive Outcome*'.[60]

Meantime, Craik's projected Plebs textbook on Dietzgen had been replaced, provisionally at least, by a textbook on psychology by Eden and Cedar Paul. They, like Hogben, were part of the 'sandals and flowing hair' set recruited to the movement at the time,[61] and they were determined to omit Dietzgen from their range of reference.[62] A few months later, *The Plebs* printed an interview with the American socialist L. B. Boudin who affirmed that 'there has been too much "Dietzgen-worship" in our movement'.[63]

This rather abrupt cold-shouldering of Dietzgenism in *The Plebs* was associated with the idea that Marxism was scientific, not philosophical, and that — as Eden and Cedar Paul argued in *Creative Revolution* (a book whose title makes a clever cross-reference to their philosophical guru, Henri Bergson, France's leading academic philosopher) — the Marxist doctrine of Historical Materialism did not in any way presuppose philosophical materialism.[64] Maurice Dobb, another Cambridge intellectual, used the authority of Benedetto Croce, the leading academic philosopher in Italy, to support the idea that Marxism should be considered 'the *realist* interpretation of history', the question of materialism serving only to confuse the issue. He commended the American Marxist Harry Waton who had stated that 'the philosophy of Marx is not an ontology', and concluded that the 'viewpoint of the communist' depends 'on a certain philosophical theory of social evolution' rather than on philosophy as such.[65]

Ordinary members of the Labour College Movement could not fail to notice the changes. The newly formed National Council of Labour Colleges, with its offices in Hampstead, had taken over *Plebs Magazine,* retitling it *The Plebs,* and this had given a central organizational base to intellectuals who, however deep and sincere their commitment to Independent Working-Class Education, already wielded an overbearing authority on account of their University affiliations, and intimidated and discouraged their provincial working-class seniors, particularly through their disdain for Dietzgenism and philosophy.

Correspondents began to protest at the conversion of *The Plebs* into 'a sort of tilting-ground for intellectuals', where 'the very ordinary and stupid worker' would not be of any account: 'I'm not in love with these intellectuals! As a matter of fact they are not a bit plebeian in spirit and would be regarded by an average crowd of workers as a lot of conceited asses I'm afraid', wrote one of them.[66] Others, however, drew comfort from the intellectuals' criticisms of Dietzgen: there must have been hundreds who had been browbeaten by Dietzgen's obscurity, and they were greatly reassured by the revelation that it might have been Dietzgen's fault and not their own. There was, wrote one correspondent from the provinces, 'a growing opinion here that he [Dietzgen] is an impostor, a quack of the Yankee type'. Craik's reply, an assertive pastiche of Dietzgenism, cannot have reassured these waverers.[67]

Craik, based in the Central Labour College, was persisting in his partisanship for Dietzgen, and the intellectuals began to gather for a final battle. Maurice Dobb, in a tone of exasperated reasonableness, wrote to *The Plebs* that if students wished to study philosphy, they should concentrate on the latest and best works of the 'modern scientific philosophers', such as Karl Pearson and Bertrand Russell.[68] In the next issue, another Cambridge man, Raymond Postgate — who was also noted as 'a connoisseur of wine and cookery'[69] — threw his weight behind Dobb. 'The question is', he said, '"Is Dietzgen and all Dietzgen stands for worth studying at all?" . . . I suggest that we abandon Dietzgen teaching altogether, and respectfully, but firmly, put old Joseph on the shelf.'[70] The anti-Dietzgenites seem to have had absolute assurance of their rightness and of the inevitability of their victory. An anonymous contributor to 'Notes by the Way' in 1925, noting a reported policy in the Soviet Union that 'less attention should be devoted to pure philosophy', was able to deliver the smug but distorted judgement that 'this seems to justify the line which *The Plebs* has taken in recent years in such matters'.[71]

The enthusiasts for Dietzgen, mostly older, and lacking in intellectual self-assurance, were infuriated by this condescension: they felt that the whole cause of Independent Working-Class Education was being betrayed. In the early stages of the attack on Dietzgenism, one Labour College tutor, referring to 'the findings of a proletarian philosophy', had boasted that 'any class-student who has grasped the ABC of Dietzgen can see his [Bertrand Russell's] errors as a philosopher'.[72] Another correspondent, enraged by Eden and Cedar Paul's habit of preferring Bergson to Dietzgen, wrote of Dietzgen's 'positive achievement and contribution to proletarian culture';[73] and a third uttered the following plaintive lament: 'Oh, why is Joseph Dietzgen ignored so much and when will he come into his own?'[74] Another mocked Dobb and Postgate, noting 'the orthodox ideology of the Universities still remaining in their heads', and demanded: 'Is not our educational movement based on the teachings of Marx and Dietzgen?'[75] And yet another remarked truculently: 'It's all very well for Bourgeois Thinkers like RWP [Postgate] to talk of putting "old Joseph on the shelf". That is just what most other bourgeois would like to do with Marx, Engels, Dietzgen, and all the rest of our Proletarian Thinkers.'[76]

Despite protests from the provinces, the National Council did manage to 'put Old Joseph on the shelf'; and, with him, the whole idea of a proletarian philosophy as the crown of Independent Working-Class Education. In the middle 1920s, *The Plebs* carried four articles on 'The Method of Science', by James Johnstone, a biologist and Professor of Ocean-ography at Liverpool University;[77] they would not have been out of place in a professional academic journal of philosophy. A decade later, in 1934, *The Plebs* ran another series on philosophy, done in the same academic style. It was written by Edward Conze, a German intellectual who had fled from Nazism and settled in England about 1933, throwing himself into hard work for both the NCLC and the Labour Party.[78] He was a fluent, civilized, and conciliatory writer, who began by lamenting the barbarity and difficulty of the existing texts on Marxist philosophy, and who therefore set himself the task of presenting it as 'nothing but a codification of common sense', arguing in particular that the phrase 'dia-lectical materialism' ought to be replaced by 'scientific method', since it could not really mean anything different.[79] From this point of view, there was obviously no sense in the idea of a specifically proletarian philosophy; and in a book published a year later, Conze gently disparaged Dietzgen, delicately suggesting that his 'lasting influence on some of the most advanced members of the British Working Class' was 'not all to the good'.[80] In spite of anguished protests from Casey,[81] the NCLC adopted Conze's articles as the basis for a correspondence course, and reprinted them as a book.[82]

So, in the space of a quarter of a century, the inspiration of a 'proletarian philosophy' in Britain had declined into an enfeebled and implausible technology of 'brainwork' and then withered, to be replaced by an academic study of scientific method shorn of intrinsically proletarian or socialistic ambitions. And Tommy Jackson — a militant proletarian educator of unequalled philosophical culture — took remarkably little interest in this process. He had temporarily resolved his chronic financial difficulties by working as a full-time Labour College organizer in the North East, and in 1920 he wrote a Plebs League discussion paper on 'The General Plan of Our Studies', placing dialectical philosophy at the centre of his ideal workers' education. Hegel, he said, was 'the Lenin of the professors', and the Hegelian treatment of change, interdependence, totality, and destiny, along with those of Heraclitus, Galileo, and others should be the foundation of all proletarian education, whose general theme must be 'flow' — 'flow . . . from the general universe in which human beings and their relations arise as special details of a general flux' towards 'the inevitable end dictated by its nature, the conscious co-operation of all for the commonweal'.[83] On this basis, Jackson endorsed the provision of Dietzgenite 'Science of Understanding' courses in the Labour Colleges.[84]

At this time, Jackson was popular for his bold and entertaining way with words. He called for earthiness and humour in textbooks ('T. A. Jackson's plea for "jokes in economics" was heartily applauded', as one conference report recorded[85]); for plain language ('If it be not profane to say so, I will affirm that Communism — or Communist Propaganda — needs only one thing to make it triumph, viz., translating into English, the English of the workshop. . . . Let us speak the tongue our class uses'[86]); and for humility amongst teachers ('a becoming humility . . . of those of us who are distinguished from our fellows merely by the fact that we have taken to books instead of to drink, or dogs, or football or religion'[87]). If he had put his mind to it, Jackson could have dominated the Plebs League's debates about philosophy, marking its teaching with his informed, humorous, humble, and exciting style — especially if he had taken up the job he was offered in 1921 as Lecturer in History, Economics, and Philosophy at the Central Labour College.[88] Instead, however — although he gave occasional lectures at the College — he chose to stand apart from the Labour College Movement throughout the 1920s. He had other things to do.

Chapter 4

British Communists and Dialectical Materialism 1920–1937

1 The Communist Party and the Labour Colleges

The first twenty years of the century offered British Marxists a confusing array of political alternatives. Apart from the non-Marxist organizations — Keir Hardie's Independent Labour Party (founded 1893) and the Labour Representation Committee (formed in 1900, reconstituted as the Labour Party in 1906 and dominated by Ramsay MacDonald) — there were three main Marxist parties: Hyndman's old SDF, which had become the British Socialist Party in 1911 (from which Hyndman seceded in 1916 and in which John MacLean, a stalwart of the Scottish Labour College, was active until 1920[1]); the de Leonite Socialist Labour Party, with close ties to the Labour College Movement (and including working-class intellectuals like Bell, Connolly, and Tommy Jackson amongst its leading members); and Sylvia Pankhurst's London-based Workers' Socialist Federation.

The Russian Revolution in October 1917 completely rearranged these political options. Suddenly, the profusion of discussions amongst Marxists became dominated by an absolutely commanding authority: Lenin — 'of whom, previously,' wrote Tommy Jackson, 'we had barely heard the name'.[2] Lenin's grasp of issues in British politics had always been imperfect, and was now, inevitably, growing obsolete.[3] He wrote patronizingly of the vigorous, youthful 'temper' of MacLean, Pankhurst, and Gallacher (whom he mistakenly associated with the WSF instead of the BSP[4]), insisted that Marxist revolutionaries in Britain should organize themselves into a single Communist Party, under the new (Third) International, and repeatedly advised them to support, and if possible affiliate to, the Labour Party. As he saw it, the danger for Britain lay not in reformism but in 'ultra-leftism' ('for', he said, 'every truth, if overdone (as Dietzgen Senior put it) . . . can be reduced to absurdity').[5]

Lenin gave the British Socialist Party his seal of approval, and it became affiliated to the International as the Communist Party of Great Britain. Most members of the SLP followed the Leninist flag and were therefore amongst the several hundreds of founder-members of the Party when it began life in July 1920. (Tommy Jackson was one of them, except that he was stuck in Newcastle and unhappily missed the foundation meeting.[6]) Consequently the Communist Party was an amalgamation of former SLP-ers and former BSP-ers, one of the main differences between the two constituencies being the importance which the former attached to the Plebs League, the Labour Colleges, and the ideal of Independent Working-Class Education.

The infant Communist Party was also joined by another group — universitarian intellectuals and writers, mostly without previous political experience, who were moved by the Russian Revolution — the same individuals, more or less, who involved themselves in the National Council of Labour Colleges, such as Francis Meynell, Raymond Postgate, Lancelot Hogben, Maurice Dobb, and Eden and Cedar Paul; and also by William Mellor, Ellen Wilkinson, Walton Newbold, Rajani Palme Dutt, and Robin Page Arnot.

In those days, when most Marxists were counting off the weeks till world revolution (afraid 'that the revolution would be over before we were ready to take a leading part in it'[7]), education — which takes years or even decades to bear fruit — was low on the agenda of socialist debate. Many Communists had reservations about the Plebs Leaguers, regarding them as cranky, old-fashioned (Second Internationalist), and ineffectual — but they were content to leave Marxist education in their hands. The Plebeians, for their part — despite all their splits and disagreements — emphasized a set of concerns which were clearly rather different from those which were rising to prominence in the Communist Party. Where the Party was political and pragmatic, they were cultural and theoretical; where the Communists wooed the Labour Party, the Labour Colleges — with their de Leonite, impossibilist background and their commitment to proletarian culture as a complete alternative to bourgeoisdom — were wary of it; and where the Party saw in Russia the growth of a workers' state, a dictatorship of the proletariat, the Labour College movement was apt to see the Soviet system as the dawning of anarcho-syndicalism, the beginning of the end of centralized state power.[8] On the other hand, of course, many Party members were individually involved in Labour College work; it provided, in fact, a kind of refuge for those who might be uneasy about some real or imagined aspect of the Communist Party line.

In August 1920, the weekly newspaper of the BSP, *The Call*, became the organ of the new party, and was renamed *The Communist*. At first it was dominated by pro-Labour Party statements, including some from the pen of Tommy Jackson; but soon it came under the control of Party members with Labour College connections. The high-born Francis (later Sir Francis) Meynell had been called in to redesign the title, and was then asked to become editor — in spite of the fact, as he said later, that he 'knew no Communist dogma, had read no Marx or Engels, and had never heard of dialectical materialism'.[9]

Under Meynell, *The Communist* was progressive about sex, children, and culture; it tried to encourage open debate, and it overlapped considerably with the revamped *Plebs*. During 1920, it welcomed the enlargement of *The Plebs,* describing it as 'a journal which no thinking communist can afford to miss';[10] it delighted in a statement from the Executive Committee of the International Bureau of 'Proletcult', according to which 'it is not to gain power for power's sake that the proletariat fights. On the contrary, it aims at the suppression of all government . . .';[11] and Stella Browne lauded Eden and Cedar Paul's *Creative Revolution*: 'vibrating with revolutionary enthusiasm', she said, and a worthy offering to its dedicatee, N. Lenin.[12]

In the new year, Francis Meynell introduced a fresh format for *The Communist* — racier, jokier, and far more elegant: it was a fine achievement in graphic design. There were articles by Tommy Jackson, Raymond Postgate, Mark Starr, Eden and Cedar Paul, and J. P. M. Millar — all of them celebrities of Independent Working-Class Education. The authors praised each other's work, especially that of the Pauls, and spoke up for the Labour College Movement, particularly the NCLC. In spite of a police raid in the middle of May — as a result of which Tommy Jackson gave up his NCLC work in the North East and the Party Branch he had set up in Newcastle, and moved permanently to London in order to be a paid employee at Party headquarters and to work on the paper[13] — the atmosphere of *The Communist* remained cheerful, affirmative, and extremely welcoming. In July 1921, Francis Meynell, disappointed with communism, was replaced as editor by Raymond Postgate,[14] who sustained a vigorous paper, giving prominence to the Plebs League, carrying open-minded features on women,[15] even pausing for a quizzical moment to notice Carpenter's progressive views on nakedness.[16]

However, there were clouds on the horizon. At the first full Conference of the British Communist Party, held in London in March 1922, Jackson made a speech about the Labour Party in which he argued in favour of affiliation. But his sweetness had a kick in it: 'I would take them by the hand', he said, 'as a preliminary to taking them by the throat.'[17] This remark was not forgotten or forgiven, either by the Labour Party, or by its suitors, Jackson's fellow members of the Communist Party — especially as Comintern had just issued circulars to all its sections calling upon them to construct a 'united front', and had specifically told British Communists to make fresh overtures to the Labour Party in spite of having been rebuffed several times already. Postgate, himself disillusioned, made a quiet and unobtrusive exit from the paper in May 1922,[18] and Tommy Jackson was left as captain of the small, sinking ship.

In effect, Labour College supporters, with their love of education and their residually 'impossibilist' hostility to the Labour Party, were being made uncomfortable amongst the Communists. Tommy Jackson's remarks about the Labour Party were explained, somewhat unconvincingly, as having implied no criticism of the Third International,[19] and the complaint — not groundless — that *The Communist* had been rather more Patrician than Plebeian, began to be loudly voiced. A correspondent objected to the (actually very limited) concern with sex,[20] and the paper steadily became less concerned with culture, more with day-to-day politics— so much so, in fact, that it was actually published daily during the November 1922 election campaign, in which it obediently backed the Labour Party.

Behind the scenes, what happened seems to be that a group within the Communist Party, headed by an experienced militant, Harry Pollitt, and an able young intellectual, Rajani Palme Dutt, had managed to promote what might be called a 'more Plebeian than the Plebs' line. A monthly review, to rival *The Plebs,* was begun in May 1921,[21] and in 1922 Pollitt and Dutt got the CPGB to accept a 'Report on Organisation', based on a model proposed by Comintern the year before. This recommended, amongst other things, a more disciplined approach to education and propaganda, and called for *The Communist* ('a small magazine of miscellaneous articles with a Communist bias') to be replaced on the one hand by a party newspaper for factory workers[22] and on the other by a theoretical periodical, 'a review of party thought'. *The Communist,* now run by Jackson, was killed off in February 1923, but was immediately reborn as the *Workers' Weekly,* edited by Palme Dutt, who was already in charge of a nominally independent periodical of his own, *The Labour Monthly,* where his 'Notes of the Month' had established themselves as an indispensable bulletin of correct party thinking.[23] The *Workers' Weekly* was completely unintellectual, dealing only in politics and parliamentary affairs. It ignored the Labour Colleges and disdained the cultured socialism and socialist culture which they stood for,[24] and it pioneered a tense, grim, and stern-jawed rhetoric (about weaponry, battles, enemies, militancy, and above all 'struggle') in which there floated the assumption that the only theoretical light needed to guide the workers' movement was that provided by Lenin's writings on the Party and the State.[25]

Tommy Jackson, however — to whom this rhetoric was uncongenial — was not quite silenced. Indeed he complained forcefully about Harry Pollitt and his organizational schemes, which were accepted at the Party congress in 1924. Jackson asked whether the Party must now become a band of 'yes-men': 'is an ignorant membership necessary to the working of the plan of organisation adopted at Battersea?', he enquired.[26] But now that Ramsay MacDonald's Minority Administration (January–November 1924) was giving Britain its first experience of Labour government, Jackson's abiding hostility to

Labour leaders was becoming entirely acceptable amongst Communists. He became a member of the Party's Central Committee, with special responsibility for education and propaganda,[27] and was able to write passionately about politics in the *Workers' Weekly*.[28] He even took charge of the paper for a while in 1925-6, when its regular staff were imprisoned. (In May 1926 he spent a few weeks in Wandsworth gaol himself, held under the Emergency Powers Act.)

In March 1925 the Party launched a project to which Tommy Jackson was to be strongly attached — the *Sunday Worker*. The editors (first William Paul — no relative of Eden and Cedar Paul — then Walter Holmes) were Party members, but it was not intended to be a Party paper. Its readers were pictured as easy-going people, interested in sport, films, music, gardens, and books; not members of the Party, but perhaps willing to consider joining if approached with hale, smiling sincerity.

The *Sunday Worker* was particularly friendly to the Labour College Movement, the editor commending the 'splendid work' of the Plebs League[29] and giving space to such authors as Mark Starr, Eden and Cedar Paul, and even Fred Casey.[30] There were letters from readers calling for a Dietzgenite Workers' Freethinkers' Organization, and an article on Dietzgen was published on the occasion of his centenary;[31] Tommy Jackson wrote regularly on figures like Bunyan, Milton, Edward Lear, and Dickens, and advised workers to read Lewes's *Biographical History of Philosophy* and Fraser's *Golden Bough*; Henry Dobb contributed some notably sophisticated film criticism, and Rutland Boughton wrote prolifically on music; J. G. Crowther provided starry-eyed articles on the vigour of the scientific community in the Soviet Union; there were enthusiastic pieces on Meredith, Spinoza, and even Virginia Woolf. Moreover, this lively, accessible paper was associated with a broad political organization: the National Left Wing Movement, initiated by the Communist Party in December 1925,[32] which aimed to lead and co-ordinate any socialists who, for the time being, were still hesitating about joining the Party. The Left Wing Movement, and the *Sunday Worker* with it, and indeed the Labour College Movement too, rode on the crest of the wave

of the General Strike of May 1926. Then all three of them
were dashed down by the 'ignominious surrender of the
General Council', as Tommy Jackson put it,[33] and the
collapse of the strike.

After the General Strike, many readers began to dislike
the breezy interest in literature and culture which was
displayed on the pages of the *Sunday Worker*. There were
complaints about Henry Dobb and Tommy Jackson with
their 'sexual conception of history',[34] and by 1928 there
were regular letters in which a correspondent signing himself
'Clydebank Riveter' clamoured for down-to-earth 'working-
class language' in the ostensibly working-class paper. As a
manual worker who lived at the tough end of a hard working-
class streeet in Glasgow, he was unshockable, he claimed,
but 'the latest spasm about Lady Chatterley and some nut
called Lawrence is the absolute world's worst'.[35] The question
of 'working-class language', though, was not settled by such
bullying proletarian chauvinism, and some correspondents,
in the old autodidactic spirit, retorted that what they sought
was strenuous efforts for self-improvement, not a complacent
celebration of what they already had. According to them,
'Clydebank Riveter's' aggressiveness amounted to 'acquiescence in the cultural disinheritance which the bourgeoisie
had imposed on the working class'. And the riveter left
himself open to an obvious countercharge. 'Have we found a
new language?', readers enquired. 'May I ask if the language
employed by the Clydebank riveter is Gaelic?' The editors
commented acidly: 'We think he invented it under the
impression that that it is a peculiarly proletarian form of
expression',[36] and shrugged it off in the next issue with
a feeble joke: 'Gaelic', they said, was just a misprint for
'Garlic'.[37]

Jackson and the other exponents of the *Sunday Worker*'s
cultivated but never snooty style were evidently saddened:
support was falling away from them on all sides, and the
bland freshness of the year leading up to the General Strike
had gone sour. They were not, it seems, in much of a mood
to fight for their old vision of an educated and militant
working-class culture, or to protect their long-standing friendship with the Labour Colleges. The Communist Party had lost
its faith in the Labour Party, but at the same time the Labour

Colleges were forgetting their 'impossibilist' purism about working-class education and drawing closer and closer to the Trade Unions. From now on — a strange and complete reversal — the Communists would vilify the Labour Colleges as reformist compromisers and agents of the Labour Party.

In 1927, William Paul, editor of the *Sunday Worker* and member of the Executive of the Plebs League, slammed a Plebs League pamphlet on the General Strike for defending the General Council,[38] and at the beginning of 1928, Jackson returned to the attack, wondering whether the NCLC was 'lost for good'.[39] Jackson did not stay for an answer. He began to argue — very much against his usual convictions — that Marxism and Leninism had to be kept pure, and therefore should not be propagated outside the Party. Reviewing Lenin's recently translated *Materialism and Empirio-Criticism,* he wrote:

Now that the last stronghold (outside the Communist Party) of even would-be Marxism in Britain (the Plebs League) has been brought under the control of the official labour movement, there is no hope of a widespread popular assimilation of Marxism unless the Communist Party takes in hand this work of popularisation, conscious of its vital importance and acutely aware that literally Titanic efforts will be required to prevent a spurious substitute being palmed off upon the proletariate for the Marxism, by whose aid Lenin lived, fought and conquered.[40]

From then on, the *Sunday Worker*'s references to the Labour College Movement were few but barbed.[41] When the full-time Central Labour College closed down in 1929, the *Sunday Worker* cooed with pleasure. 'Those thoroughly acquainted with the laws of dialectical materialism', wrote its correspondent, would see that this was a victory, not a defeat, and that it would enable the teaching of Marxism to 'reappear on a more secure and higher plane . . . under the direction and control of auspices that are definitely and avowedly Marxian both in theory and practice'[42] — that is to say, of the Communist Party.

In arguing, however, against the Labour College Movement and in favour of firm party control of education and culture, the *Sunday Worker* was blighting the stock which it had been cultivating for the past three years. It was calling for its own destruction, a repetition of the painful history of the replacement of the *Communist* by the *Workers' Weekly* less than seven years before. By the end of 1929, the writing was on the wall, and the *Sunday Worker* was referring to a 'More than Usually Brilliant' analysis by R. Palme Dutt of the need for a workers' daily.[43]

According to Tommy Jackson, 'an inner crisis developed in the Party'. There was, he said, 'a plague of "deviation" hunting. . . . It was, in general (to borrow a phrase from *Hudibras*) "as if Divinity (read 'the Party') had catch'd the itch on purpose to be scratched!".' On the Central Committee, Jackson made it clear that he was 'dubious about the new line proposed', and opposed the 'drive . . . for a more militant and aggressive policy, especially towards the Labour Party, and for the immediate establishment of a Daily Party journal'.[44] To Jackson's dismay, the *Sunday Worker* was put to sleep by the end of the year, amidst plans for a *Daily Worker,* and somewhat unrealistic hopes for a *Workers' Illustrated News.* But these changes were not made without a well-aimed protest from Tommy Jackson, in a nimble *Sunday Worker* article diagnosing 'a double weakness in British Marxism': on the one hand, there was the teaching of the Labour Colleges, adhering 'more or less consciously to the standpoint of the Second International' and 'fixed in that pre-war stage in which Marx stood for a profound fundamental truth, but one which bore little or no relation . . . to the practical daily tasks of the Labour movement'. But at the same time — and here Jackson, a prominent Party member, had to pick his words with care — there was an equal, opposite danger in an uncouth, thuggish, and pragmatic attitude which had fashioned for itself the strange title of 'Leninism' or even 'Marxism-Leninism':

The section of British Marxists, on the other hand, which adhered to the Communist International became by the fact so occupied with practical concerns (for which Lenin was a more immediate and obvious guide than Marx) that Marx himself tended to be for them little else than a 'name of power'. . . . The all-too-eager 'Leninists' tend to relegate theory further and further into the background and become thereby increasingly empirical and hand-to-mouth in their ideology.

Having thrown this grenade, Jackson hastily ducked back into the trenches of orthodoxy, with the observation that 'the comrade who deliberately neglects Marx cannot possibly be a good Leninist'.[45]

Jackson's loyalty to his vision of a cultured and philosophical kind of socialist education had continually strained his relation with the Party of which he was a founder-member. In 1929, the dispute finally cost him his place on the Central Committee, and he lost his living as an employee of Party Headquarters. Subsequently he often felt that his fellow-Communists shunned him ('as though I had been guilty of a sin against the Holy Ghost'[46]), even though he repeatedly confessed that he had been wrong to oppose the creation of the *Daily Worker*. Henceforth he would describe himself ('in his lighter moments' at least) as 'loitering on the Party line with intent to commit a deviation'.[47] And the Party line itself was changing.

2 Education and the Party Line 1925-30

By 1929, the Communist Party's attitude to the Labour College Movement had become quite spiteful; and, as Tommy Jackson complained, 'there is a difference between scratching your arse and tearing the skin off'.[48] The hostility had, however, been accumulating for years, though concealed by the Party's policy of trying to form a 'united front' with the Trade Unions, the Labour Party, or any other organization representing Labour. There had been premonitions in the 1922 'Report on Organisation', and suggestions of seizing control in a circular issued in 1924.[49] However, it was only when various factions of the left began to fall out with each other following the General Strike and its aftermath that the Party — swamped with inexperienced new members — became seriously concerned with organizing its own programme of Marxist education, or rather — and the change in terminology was full of meaning — with what was now called 'Party Training'.

The *Party Training Manual,* first issued in 1926, was designed as a primer for experienced members training new recruits, and dealt in a piecemeal and fragmented way with recent economic and political events and with the constitutional organization of the Party. Even its author,

Tom Bell, had to admit that the result was both unhistorical and undialectical.[50] At the end of the year, the *Communist Review* began to make a regular monthly feature of 'Party Training Notes', seasoned always with sneers at the 'cultured intellectuals' of the Labour College Movement. (For instance: 'Leninist education addresses itself always to the studious workers and not to the cultured intellectuals who are "interested" in Leninism.') The aim of Leninist education was specified in political terms, not intellectual ones: 'giving to the militants who participate in the work the necessary knowledge to enable them to accomplish in the best way the tasks which fall upon them in the degree of the party where they find themselves placed.'[51]

In the winter of 1926-7, twelve Party members were given six months of full-time training in London. Their course dealt mainly with various aspects of Leninism, and with questions of Party administration, and gave no space at all to general history, still less to philosophy.[52] An article in *The Communist* (the new name for the *Communist Review*) congratulated the Party for having displayed an interest in political education without rival or precedent in the British Labour Movement. The SDF, it claimed, had merely encouraged familiarity with 'certain books and central ideas', failing to establish 'any connection of these with organised party activities'. And 'the coming of the NCLC did not improve matters . . . an arid, abstract kind of Marxism was cultivated with no definite political direction.'[53]

During 1927, *The Communist* featured various articles on education, including one by Andrew Rothstein on the importance of grasping 'Lenin's Method' so as to appreciate the need for 'party discipline' and 'analysis of the situation'; but still no reference was made to historical or philosophical questions.[54] In November, however, *The Communist* began a six-part series of 'Self Study Syllabuses', which promised to be broader and more liberal. The series was entitled 'Historical Materialism and the Tendencies of Capitalist Development', and the first instalment began with an introductory section on 'Dialectical Materialism' (quite a strange phrase to English readers at the time[55]), designed to show students that Marxism was originally formed in the context of nineteenth-century European philosophy. Next month, however, there was an abrupt but unexplained change of tack: the series was renamed 'Fundamentals of Leninism' and henceforth dealt exclusively with a subject defined by Stalin's formula as 'Marxism of the Epoch of Imperialism and the Dictatorship of the Proletariat', and seen through the prism of Stalin's essay 'Foundations of Leninism'.[56] A couple of months later, Tommy Jackson, at the same time as expressing his own bitterness about the NCLC, used the publication of Lenin's *Materialism and Empirio-Criticism* in English as an opportunity to recall that Leninism itself, however political, had a well-developed philosophical side too.[57]

The Party's growing hostility to the Labour College Movement had, up to this point, coexisted with a continuing commitment to a united front with all the organizations of Labour. In fact a long Central Committee statement reaffirming the Party's loyalty to the doctrine appeared in *The Communist* for February 1928.[58] The next issue, however, gave prominent publicity to outspoken and influential dissent: from Dutt and Pollitt.[59] And within a few days, it was revealed that these two unlikely deviants, if they had strayed from the British Party Line, had exactly anticipated that of Comintern. The message of the International was that the class struggle had pushed Western societies to the brink of collapse, that it was time for Western Communist Parties to abandon all alliances, to destroy all 'Social-Fascist' (i.e. non-communist) Labour organizations and to intensify the struggle of 'class against class'. The National Left Wing Movement was discouraged and then closed down in March 1929: the Party had to be sailing resolutely in its new direction in time for the General Election in May, supporting parliamentary candidates against the Labour Party now, instead of within it.

The Party could now detonate all its stockpiled hatred of the Labour Colleges, and *The Communist* let rip, especially against the NCLC activist Raymond Postgate — himself a former member of the Party, and editor of the first incarnation of the Party paper, which had also been called *The Communist*. In an exceptionally ugly contribution, Harold Heslop gleefully speculated that Postgate might have dropped dead. Postgate's death would be a blessing to Communism, because, with smarmy bourgeois ease, he had attempted 'to make fun of

Marx, and continue to masquerade as a Marxist'.[60] The next issue followed through with some vitriolic 'Further Jottings on R. W. Postgate', and sounded a note rather similar to that of the 'Clydebank Riveter' in the *Sunday Worker* — a self-righteous proletarian scholar-bashing, offensive not only to universitarian socialist intellectuals, but also to the older generation of working-class socialist autodidacts. The choice, it was announced, was simple — between 'the outlook of the scholar Postgate and the non-scholar Marxian member of the Communist Party'.[61]

Comintern, however, did not allow this abusive anti-intellectualism to continue unchecked. The foundation of training in the British Party — the *Party Training Manual* — was relentlessly and unanswerably criticized: it contained 'no mention of the theory of Marxism-Leninism as the scientific basis of our programme', and 'the absence . . . of the Marxist world-conception, the attitude to religion, etc' was, Comintern continued, with cutting understatement, 'a serious omission'.[62] The Party had derided and dumped the seemingly impractical and unproletarian philosophizing which it considered to be promoted in the Labour Colleges, but it was now being required by Comintern to produce a philosophical education of its own. For various reasons, it hesitated, and it was only in 1930 that a permanent educational system was installed.

At its eleventh Congress, in October 1930, the British Communist Party resolved, not for the first time, to try harder at education. As a result, it set up a dual system, with district schools for the training of experienced members, and, in order to remedy 'our greatest weakness', a network of 'workers' study circles', based on local branches or branch groups, for the education of ordinary Party members and selected sympathizers.[63] Study circles consisted of about twelve people, meeting one evening a week for a minimum of two or three months. Each district had a panel of tutors, who might give lessons on basic concepts of Marxism: A. L. Morton recalled that 'You learnt all about what is a class, what is value, or what is surplus-value in a rather catechism-like way. It was probably quite good.'[64] But although 'you would always hope that there would be a tutor',[65] study circles were often left to their own devices — in fact it had

always been the Party's policy to encourage 'self-study' as
opposed to 'barren lecturing of the Labour College type'.[66]
In the absence of a tutor, the Workers' Study Circles would
do collective reading — 'to say we studied texts makes it
sound too like a University'.[67] In theory, the members of
a study circle would all take turns at introducing a section
of the chosen reading at the weekly meeting — although the
timidity of some, or the disproportionate confidence of
others, might prevent this from working out smoothly in
practice.[68]

It was up to each study circle to decide what texts to use,
and, in the early thirties, their choices fell into two groups.
There were the 'classics', headed at that time by Lenin's
State and Revolution or *Left-Wing Communism,* Stalin's
Leninism, and the *Communist Manifesto.* And then there
were 'Study Outlines' and 'Study Courses', specially produced
by the Party for the use of study circles. These consisted of
structured sequences of substantial pamphlets on such
topics as 'Political Economy' and 'Working Class History',
divided into short sections to facilitate class discussion, and
equipped with 'test questions' to check that the lessons were
reaching their targets.[69]

The Communists believed that through this educational
system, they would be able to contest the structure as well
as the content of bourgeois knowledge. They would avoid
dividing knowledge into separate subjects, and would instead
teach everything from the unifying point of view of the
unique theoretical possession of 'Marxism-Leninism' —
namely the philosophy of Dialectical Materialism. Tommy
Jackson was to claim that 'the term "dialectical materialism"
began to trickle into use after the Russian Revolution';[70] but
in the early thirties the trickle became an incantatory flood,
and the words came to be written, more often than not, with
a respectful capital D and M. Flaunting this monopoly of
philosophical fundamentals, the Communists intensified the
attack on their rivals in socialist education, the 'Plebs Leaguers'
in the Labour Colleges — directing against them many of the
weapons which the Plebs themselves had been using for years
both against the WEA and against the Communist Party itself:
the Labour Colleges (said the Communists) had compromised
with reformism and were now peddling the poisonous quack

medicines of bourgeois culture, especially by depriving their students of a clear philosophy with which to fight back. 'Marxian economics cannot be separated from philosophic materialism', as Olive Budden wrote in 1930, quoting Lenin's characterization of Marxism as 'a view of the universe'. The NCLC, she claimed, had failed through neglecting philosophy and presenting economics 'as something separate and distinct.'[71]

The Communists could hardly get away with the claim that the Labour Colleges had totally neglected philosophy, however. If anything, the boot was on the other foot. But they could and did argue that the mainly Dietzgenite philosophy taught in the Colleges was dangerously defective because it was not genuine Dialectical Materialism. One of the many Communists who had been associated with the Labour Colleges in the twenties was S. Knight of Bury — and in 1930 Knight was deputed by the NCLC to teach courses on Fred Casey's *Method in Thinking.* In the new 'class against class' atmosphere, Casey and Knight did not find it possible to collaborate. Knight apparently believed that, under the influence of 'Caseyism', the leadership of the NCLC was 'heading more and more towards Social Fascism', even though the 'rank and file' were obviously 'moving to the left'.[72] Casey, meanwhile, was disgusted by the Communist Party's antagonistic new line, and argued that it was a terrifying example of the dangerous consequences of incompetence in dialectical logic. The Party, he thought, had

failed because of its rigid non-dialectical view that it should be antagonistic in all ways to all Reformist parties. . . . A splendid chance . . . was missed by the Communist Party of Great Britain in 1929, when it refused to take the opportunity of putting the Labour Party in overwhelming power and thus producing an object-lesson on the impossibility of a purely reform party being able to bring in the new order of Socialism.[73]

Knight provoked a show-down with Casey at the Manchester Tutors' Council in which he attempted to prove that Casey was a deviationist who had treacherously accused Marx of 'slips' and insolently categorized Lenin as a specifically 'practical' dialectician. Knight concluded that 'these contrasts between the teachings of dialectical materialism and Caseyism show most decisively that Casey is an exponent of idealism.'[74] Casey himself, always wary of the amoralism of 'Bolshevists', came to the conclusion that Knight 'was the dirtiest double crosser I ever met'.[75]

The *Communist Review,* perhaps unaware of Casey's own grievances about the slighting treatment of Dietzgen by the NCLC, alleged that 'the leading districts of the NCLC have regarded it as vital to have within easy reach a trained *"Dietzgenian"* (whatever that may mean).' Apostrophizing Casey as 'the Chief prophet of Dietzgenianism', they exhumed his old book, *Thinking,* and alleged that his '"Dietzgenian logic"' was in 'the centre of the stage' amongst 'the "courses" prescribed by the pseudo-Marxist NCLC'. Contrasting Casey's 'mass of muddle-headed confusion and crude "idealism"' with the purity of neat Leninism, they called on readers 'to combat the dangerous ideas propounded by Casey and the NCLC' and to engage in 'a persistent exposure of the pseudo-Marxist position of the NCLC'.[76]

Then, in 1932, there was a translation of a series of articles from *Under the Banner of Marxism*, depicting 'Social Fascism' as a 'struggle against dialectical materialism'.[77] This was followed by an attack on the 'castrated Marxism' of the Labour Colleges, and an exhortation to develop 'broad Marxist schooling activity on the initiative of the party as a counter to the NCLC'.[78]

The Party's commitment to Dialectical Materialism grew with its revulsion against the NCLC. Caseyism could only be defeated 'by definitely equipping ourselves with a knowledge of the Marxian philosophy as contained in the classical works of the revolutionary leaders — Marx, Engels, Lenin — on dialectics'.[79] And the time was ripe now for teaching dialectics to the proletariat: 'Just now, when many hundreds of thousands of workers *want to know,* the movement for developing revolutionary theory has the brightest prospects.'[80]

But what was this Marxist philosophy, this Dialectical Materialism, if the Labour Colleges, which took themselves to have been teaching it for twenty years, had proved to be traitors to it, and the bourgeoisie had no knowledge of it either? Even established party intellectuals, like Maurice Dobb — who had played his part in combating Dietzgenism in the Labour College Movement a decade before — apparently didn't know. Comrade Dobb had 'vulgarised' Marxism, it was alleged, by failing to recognize the supremacy of Dialectical

Materialism — the philosophy of the working class and of the future: 'When the world has been changed by the philosophers of Dialectical Materialism — the working class — they will enter into the widest possible discussions of Dialectical Materialism, as they are doing today in the Soviet Union.'[81] It was as though the British Communist Party had traded its quite rich inheritance of miscellaneous old-fashioned theoretical devices — the cosmic evolutionary world-views of the autodidacts, the potentially tiresome panaceas of the Dietzgenites, or the urbane philosophies of scientific method favoured by the University intellectuals — for a brand-new set of 'Leninist' slogans alleging their monopoly of a new philosophy, a Dialectical Materialism so 'pure' that you could hardly open your mouth without calumniating it. Belatedly, in 1932, the British Communists turned to the Soviet Union hoping to have their slogans filled up with some intelligible meaning.

3 Soviet Philosophy in the Twenties

Before the Revolution, most progressive political discussion amongst Russians and other East Europeans had been rooted in philosophical soil, communism being seen as the outcome of a cosmic evolution, interpreted in bluntly atheist, materialist, or monist terms.[82] They might be vague about what 'socialism' and 'science' meant, but they would be sure that essentially they meant the same. Georg Plekhanov, for instance — who was largely responsible for introducing Marxism to Russian readers during the 1890s — described Marxism as 'Darwinism in its application to social science'.[83] And his term 'Dialectical Materialism'[84] proclaimed, epigrammatically, the idea that Marxism is embedded in the fabric of Western philosophical traditions.

The young Lenin saw Marxism through Plekhanov's eyes, and regarded Plekhanov's philosophical writings as 'the best there is in the whole international literature on Marxism'.[85] In fact his hostility to the ostensibly 'scientific' philosophy of 'empirio-criticism' was essentially a reaction in favour of Plekhanov's scientific materialism.[86]

The taste for philosophy amongst educated and cosmo-politan revolutionaries was not always shared by Russian peasants or proletarians, or by natural scientists, as represented in the Academy of Sciences. After the Revolution, it was argued by some — not without plausibility — that if you wanted to purge the Socialist Republics of bourgeois culture, you should give no quarter to philosophy. So an influential article appeared in 1922, blazoning the proposition that 'PHILOSOPHY IS A PROP OF THE BOURGEOISIE':

Not idealist, not metaphysical philosophy only, but precisely philo-sophy as such. . . . In a word the proletariat retains and must retain science, only science, but no kind of philosophy. SCIENCE TO THE BRIDGE — PHILOSOPHY OVERBOARD.[87]

In the same year, there was a move to abolish professorships in philosophy and replace them with posts in 'History of World Conceptions',[88] and in 1927 Stepanov wrote that 'the Marxist recognises no special field of "philosophical activity" distinct from that of science; for the Marxist, materialist philosophy consists in the latest and most general findings of modern science.'[89] In the following year, Academ-ician V. I. Vernadskii led a strong and initially successful campaign to exclude philosophers from the Academy of Sciences, on the ground that philosophy was always and inevitably 'antagonistic to the science of its time', Dialectical Materialism in particular being no more than a 'survival of Hegelianism'.[90]

These anti-philosophers were in open disagreement with Lenin, who had believed that philosophy was a — perhaps the — most important weapon in the proletarian revolutionary's theoretical arsenal. It was not general philosophical culture, however, which Lenin tried to promote. It was, on the contrary, *partiinost* — partisanship or 'partiness': philosophical positions, especially materialism and idealism, seemed to Lenin to correspond directly with class positions; politics was a continuation of class struggle, and philosophy a continuation of politics. Hence proletarians should be taught, not the classics of philosophy, but the doctrines of materialism.[91] And when, during the war, Lenin began to read Hegel, he became convinced that revolutionaries should be educated in 'dialectics' too. In 1922, Lenin provided a theoretical manifesto for the philosophical journal *Under the Banner of Marxism*. He referred appreciatively to the example of Joseph Dietzgen, and recommended that the journal should in the first place promote 'militant atheistic literature of the end of the eighteenth century' and so become 'the organ of militant atheism', and secondly, pursue research into Hegelian dialectics:

> The contributors to *Under the Banner of Marxism* should organize systematic studies of Hegel's dialectics from the materialist standpoint — the dialectics applied by Marx in his *Capital* and in his political and historical works with such great success . . . .
> To be sure, the study, interpretation and propagation of Hegelian dialectics, in the manner suggested, is not going to be an easy task. . . . Taking the materialist application of the Hegelian dialectics by Marx as a basis, we can and should make it ours in all its phases, publishing in the magazine extracts from the most important works of Hegel. . . .[92]

The effect of this article, however, was not quite what one might have expected. Karl Korsch, a Marxist of considerable philosophical learning and sophistication and a member of the German Communist Party, responded in 1923 with a fine essay on 'Marxism and Philosophy'. In it, he respectfully quoted Lenin's article, and concentrated on criticizing Lenin's targets — 'vulgar Marxism' and 'reformism'. At the same time, however, with adroit footnotes[93] and by his own example, Korsch showed his dislike for Lenin's belief in the political centrality of philosophy and his habit of insisting on a direct correspondence between political and philosophical partisanship. In the same year, another philosophically learned Marxist, the Hungarian Georg Lukacs, published 'What is Orthodox Marxism?',[94] which, with its own implicit rejection of Lenin's view of philosophy, can be regarded as a 'companion volume'[95] to Korsch's 'Marxism and Philosophy'.

Lenin died in January 1924, and this instantly gave the recently published essays by Korsch and Lukacs an air of audacious impiety or even sacrilege. An old friend of Lukacs, a comrade from the Hungarian communist movement named Laszlo Rudas, quickly composed a lengthy denunciation of 'What is Orthodox Marxism?', condemning its 'idealism' and its unpoliticalness.[96] At the Fifth Congress of the Communist International, held in Moscow at the end of June, the main item for discussion was 'Lenin and Leninism: On the Foundations and Propaganda of Leninism'. Zinoviev threw his weight behind Rudas, saying that 'we' could not tolerate the theoretical deviations of 'our Hungarian Comrade Lukacs . . . in the domain of philosophy and sociology':

I have received a letter from Comrade Rudas, one of the leaders of this [i.e. the Hungarian] fraction. He explains that he intended to oppose Lukacs, but the fraction forbade him to do so; thereupon he left the fraction because he could nto see Marxism watered down. Well done Rudas! We have a similar tendency in the German Party . . . Korsch is also a professor — (Interruptions: 'Lukacs is also a professor!') If we get a few more of these professors spinning out their Marxist theories, we shall be lost. We cannot tolerate such theoretical revisionism of this kind in our Communist International.[97]

Korsch was expelled from the Communist Party in 1926[98] and Lukacs — fearing isolation from the Communist movement — recanted and tried to keep out of further trouble.[99]

During the 1920s, the Leninist conception of philosophy was developed and defended inside the Soviet Union by A. M. Deborin. Deborin was a professor of philosophy, a former Menshevik, who had published a Plekhanovite 'Introduction to Dialectical Materialism' shortly before the Revolution, and was quick to denounce Lukacs for his 'deviation' into dualism,[100] and to formulate a Leninist philosophical orthodoxy after Lenin's death.[101] From 1922, he presided over the group of philosophers who ran *Under the Banner of Marxism,* in which particular emphasis was placed, first on Hegel's 'dialectical method', and then on Engels's *Dialectics of Nature,* which they published for the first time in 1925. The main polemical target of the Deborinites was, not unnaturally, the scientific anti-philosophers, whom they condemned as 'mechanists'.

The chief of the mechanists (as far as the Deborinites were concerned) was Nicolai Bukharin — a cosmopolitan and highly intellectual Bolshevik who had been close to Lenin during the revolution.[102] It would be wrong to classify Bukharin himself as an anti-philosopher, though. Like Dietzgen and Plekhanov, he believed that Marxism had originated in philosophy but grown beyond it, rendering Hegelianism, in particular, completely obsolete. But Marxism, for Bukharin, was essentially a scientific theory of historical change as resting on economic development, and it left little room either

for the effective operation of political will or for the jurisdiction of an independent intellectual discipline called
'philosophy'.

In 1928, the difference between the 'mechanists' and the
Deborinites became politicized as Russia, under Stalin's
leadership, steeled itself for the complete transformation of
agriculture under the Five Year Plan. Bukharin, appalled by
the arbitrary radicalism of the policy, protested and got
himself denounced as a 'Kulak agent' and a right-wing
deviationist. The Deborinites argued, not without justification,
that Bukharin's gradualist attitude towards land reform was
all of a piece with his 'mechanist' philosophical outlook, and
were able therefore to profit from Stalin's campaign. By the
beginning of 1929, everything was going their way: they had
extensive power over academic appointments and over
philosophical contributions to the *Great Soviet Encyclopaedia*;
they secured a resolution from the Second Congress of
Marxist-Leninist Institutes of Science to the effect that
Mechanism was 'inconsistent with the tenets of Marxist-
Leninist philosophy';[103] and they acquired enormous kudos
by publishing, for the first time, Lenin's exceedingly complex
'Notes on Hegel's Book *The Science of Logic*'.[104] They even
got the august Academy of Sciences to reverse its decision
to blackball Deborin and in February 1930 he was able to
introduce a completely new note into the Academy's hitherto
unphilosophical proceedings with his discourse on 'Lenin
and the Crisis of Contemporary Physics'.[105]

Certain foreign observers saw the accession of the Deborinites
as heralding the dawn of a cultural renaissance in Russia,
based on a 'new interest in Hegel'. It was excitedly reported
that

the mechanistic conception of reality and the crude materialism found
in the works of Bukharin, Plekhanov, and other 'pillars' of orthodox
Marxism is being sharply criticised by the new generation of red 'philosophers'. . . . The significant thing is that at least they have begun to
think for themselves, and to attack the very doctrine they had been
taught to regard as gospel truth. The glimpse of Hegel's philosophy
that they have had through Lenin and Engels has led them to suspect
that there may be other kinds of reality than that of sensuous objects
in space and time.

The blinkers of crude materialism — or so it seemed — had fallen from communist eyes, and there was, reportedly, an effervescence of philosophical creativity in the Soviet Union. A smuggled shorthand transcript suggested that the shackles of dogma had been destroyed, with one Russian philosopher plaintively commenting that 'one used to feel so much more comfortable in the old days — one called oneself a dialectical materialist, and that was the end of it — but now it's nothing like enough!'[106]

These enthusiastic reports, however, were drastically confused, for what was in fact occurring was a comprehensive closure of the whole Deborinite enterprise — an event which shortly came to be known as 'the New Turn on the Philosophical Front'.[107] The 'New Turn' resulted from a seizure of philosophical power by a new generation of indignant young radicals — Raltsevich, Yudin, Mitin, Adoratsky, and others — all of them proletarians educated mainly since the revolution. Russian educational apparatuses, as they had experienced them, were conspicuously non-proletarian and unpolitical — very few academics were in the Communist Party,[108] and in spite of well-publicized efforts, hardly any students were from working-class families.[109] Recognizing this, the Institute of Red Professors expanded its intake and excluded nearly all non-proletarians. The philosophical section, where Deborin's curriculum had concentrated on the study of Spinoza, Kant, and Hegel, was now filled, as one of them put it later, with 'young comrades, free of any "specific" philosophical tradition, educated in conditions of our country's civil war and class struggle, who have no special medals in philosophy but in the political field, on the other hand, have served the Party and the working class well'. To these proletarian radicals, the Deborinites appeared as 'a sort of philosophical sect, very small, indrawn and barred against those who are not initiated in the secrets of their philosophical guild'.[110]

By the end of 1929, the students were straining to outdo Deborin in offering philosophical backing to Stalin against Bukharin. On the occasion of Stalin's fiftieth birthday on 21 December, Adoratsky wrote a panegyric to 'Stalin as Theorist of Leninism'.[111] Six days later, Stalin himself gave an address to a Conference of Marxist Agronomists, and although it said nothing about philosophy, it was to be a decisive philosophical event. It announced the persecution of 'Kulak agents', forcible 'dekulakization', and the liquidation of the kulaks as a class', and included the fateful remark the 'theoretical thought is not keeping pace with our practical successes . . . there is a certain gap between our practical successes and the development of theoretical thought.'[112] This manifesto gave the young proletarians of the 'New Turn' space in which, during the coming year, they could stake their own claims: the Deborinites, they would argue, had been faint-hearted and 'formalistic' in their attacks on Bukharinite 'mechanism',[113] and Deborin himself had slanderously described Lenin as a practical politician, in contrast to the theorist Plekhanov.[114] Now Stalin had called for 'a struggle on two fronts' — against rightist podkulakniks and Trotskyite leftists. Bukharin's 'mechanism' had been identified as the philosophy behind the right deviation — so far the Deborinites had been correct; but, according to the New Turn radicals, it must now be revealed that the philosophy behind the left deviation was none other than Deborinism itself. The radical students were opposed by most of the staff of the Institute, with the exception of the twenty-nine-year-old Mitin, who had graduated the year before;[115] and they were attacked in *Under the Banner of Marxism* and by the Agitprop department of the Communist International.[116] From June 1930, however, they had access to the official newspaper *Pravda,* and by October they had routed Deborinism completely.[117] In December, Stalin gave his ruling on the great philosophical debate, denouncing Deborin as an instigator of the Trotskyist left deviation, the counterpart in the 'war on two fronts' to the Bukharinite right deviation, and adding that Deborin was also a 'menshevising idealist'.[118] This position was later confirmed in a decree from the Central Committee of the Party.[119]

The New Turn had been led by Yudin, aged thirty, a former journalist and party official, who now became head of the philosophy section in the Institute. Mitin gained influence, and became a member of the board of *Under the Banner of Marxism* and editor of what was now the supreme Russian philosophy journal, *Problems of Philosophy.*[120] Riazanov, creator and director of the Marx and Engels Institute (now the Marx-Engels-Lenin Institute) was replaced by Adoratsky, having been accused of crypto-menshevism and mishandling some of the correspondence of Marx and Engels. By the beginning of 1932, Yudin reported that 'almost all the old philosophical "Gods" had to be dismissed from the Institute and it is primarily young comrades, new cadres, that carry on the work'. Mitin looked forward to an era of unprecedented philosophical creativity: 'Rallying all our forces, under the leadership of our dear and beloved teacher, Comrade Stalin, we will indubitably move forward the work on the philosophical front, and will create serious, fundamental works of research.'[121] But what did the new philosophers actually know or think about philosophy?

Negatively, it was clear that they would strive to avoid academicism or antiquarianism; they would be 'political', concentrating on 'applied dialectics', not the dusty philosophical classics, and studying recent congress resolutions, not old texts by Kant or Hegel.[122] They would side with Lenin, and for that matter Deborin, in affirming the autonomy of philosophy, and its sovereignty over all other enquiries; they would make a sharp distinction between 'dialectical materialism' ('diamat') and 'historical materialism', respectively the 'philosophy' and the 'science' founded by Marx and Engels. And in philosophy, they would — following the lead of Lenin's *Philosophical Notebooks* (of which they produced a new full edition in 1933[123]) — develop positive enquiries into dialectics. In this project, their starting-point would be the three 'laws' to which Engels, in the recently published *Dialectics of Nature*, had claimed that dialectics could, 'in the main', be reduced:

The law of the transformation of quantity into quality and vice-versa;
The law of the interpenetration of opposites;
The law of the negation of the negation.[124]

Moreover, they would emphasize that these laws, the proper object of philosophical enquiry, governed the objects of all other disciplines, from history ('historical materialism') to the natural sciences. In other words, they would assert (against Korsch and Lukacs) that there must be a 'dialectic of nature', and (against the mechanists) that the sciences were subordinate to philosophy. Their own chief task would be the codification of the 'dialectical laws'.

The 'dialectical laws' were supposed to explain how progress arose from 'contradictions'. The main conceptual innovation introduced by the 'New Turn' was a distinction between 'antagonistic' and 'non-antagonistic' contradictions,[125] based quite unconvincingly on the authority of a mystifying remark said to be a quotation from Lenin.[126] The political point of this innovation was plain: if 'dialectical laws' proved that contradictions exist everywhere, then socialist society itself must be contradictory; but the new distinction enabled it to be explained that the contradictions of socialism were harmless because they were of the non-antagonistic variety. In philosophical as distinct from political terms, however, the distinction never lost its makeshift and arbitrary air. Hegel and other dialecticians had certainly tried to produce a conception of progress as arising from 'contradiction'; but they had not theorized any distinct concept of 'antagonism', and it would have taken hard philosophical argument (such as the 'New Turn' did not provide) to show that the idea of 'non-antagonistic contradiction' meant anything at all,[127] or was more than a euphemistic way of describing contradictions in Soviet society. In spite of the new philosophers' official belief in the sovereignty of philosophy, this was not a case of philosophical reflection leading to political practice, but rather the other way about.

The philosophers of the 'New Turn' attempted to justify this disconcerting shuffle between 'the political' and 'the philosophical' by adopting, reiterating, and reinterpreting a slogan about 'the unity of theory and practice'.[128] The words had no direct authority in the writings of Marx or Engels, but were approximately derived from Marx's posthumously published 'Theses on Feuerbach', together with the recently issued *German Ideology*.[129] The new philosophers did nothing to remedy the histrionic ambiguity of the phrase, but they used it liberally in order to make a short cut to the Leninist doctrine of 'partisanship' in philosophy, by implying that it was possible to derive philosophical 'positions' directly from political ones, and conversely. It became absolutely indiscernible, as a result, whether they supposed that party policy was to be determined by philosophical argument, or whether it was the opposite way round. And this instability had its uses, as was displayed by Mitin in 1932:

The further development of Marxist-Leninist theory in every department, including that of the philosophy of Marxism, is associated with the name of Comrade Stalin. In all Stalin's practical achievements, and in all his writings, there is set forth the whole experience of the world-wide struggle of the proletariat, the whole rich store-house of Marxist-Leninist theory.[130]

Deborin, perhaps the most cultured philosopher in the Soviet Union, found the argument persuasive. He acknowledged that he had given support, unwittingly, to 'Menshevising Idealism', and thanked the Party's Central Committee, 'and especially the leader of our party, Comrade Stalin', for having 'restrained him just in time'.[131]

4 The British Communist Party and Dialectical Materialism

After 1927, the British Communist Party had made repeated efforts to institute an effective educational system to counter-act the Labour College Movement, and by 1931 the system of workers' study circles was functioning well, though it was relatively small.[132] Dialectical Materialism had been mentioned repeatedly as the foundation of Party education, but no one seemed to know anything about it except that it was deeply important, and that Soviet thinkers were expert in it. The situation was complicated by the fact that when, in 1927, Comintern had criticized the *Party Training Manual* for its lack of philosophy, it was directed by Bukharin, who had resigned a few months later[133] and been denounced as a 'right-deviationist' in politics and a 'mechanist' in philosophy. His accusers, the Deborinites, had in turn been humiliated during the 'New Turn' in 1930.

It was not till the end of 1931 that the dust settled in the philosophical battlefields of the Soviet Union, and British readers were at last able to learn what had been going on about Dialectical Materialism. D. S. Mirsky, a Russian émigré sympathetic to the revolution, reader in Russian Literature at London University, gave a detailed account of 'The Philosophical Discussion in the CPSU' in *Labour Monthly,* presenting a pleasingly symmetrical tale of how the bold young proletarians, led by Stalin, had smitten the craven foes of Communism to the left and the right.

Mirsky's article contained no theoretical arguments what-soever: ascriptions of class position and party allegiance had to deputize for them. For Mirsky, the philosophical inadequacy of the Deborinites followed from their class position: they were 'an intelligentsia, democratic to be sure, but by no means proletarian'. This had made them scholastic and idealistic and incapable of grasping 'the unity of theory and practice':

Deborin, by unduly emphasising Dialectic as distinct from Materialism tended to substitute for dialectical Materialism a dialectical scholasticism that was devoid of material content and was thus virtually idealistic. . . . The great philosophical achievement of the last years, said the anti-Deborinites, is contained not in the treatises of a small group of professional dialecticians, but in the policy of the CPSU and the Comintern, embodied in their theses and resolutions, and in the writings of such leaders as Stalin.[134]

In the following months and years, *Labour Monthly* gradually added to the English reader's knowledge of the 'New Turn' of Dialectical Materialism, with further articles by Mirsky, a few translations from the writings of the new philosophers, and tantalizing references to the new, but unavailable, classics — *The German Ideology* and Lenin's *Philosophical Notebooks,* especially his list of sixteen characteristics of dialectics.[135]

The importation was supervised by Clemens Dutt, brother of the editor of *Labour Monthly,* and compiler, with the New Turn philosopher Adoratsky, of an English anthology of Lenin's writings. Clemens Dutt was a zealous guardian of philosophical purity — of materialist health and dialectical hygiene. 'The viewpoint of dialectical materialism', he wrote, 'represents the class theory of the proletariat', and 'the task for Marxists in this field is, as Lenin emphasised, to conduct an irreconcilable struggle against idealism in general and all its manifestations in natural science . . . to fight for the purity of Marxist theory against mechanist distortions and conciliations to idealism.'[136] The first systematic attempt to expound the new philosophy to English readers was made in the winter of 1933, with a two-part article by Laszlo Rudas — the Hungarian whose opposition to Lukacs had been praised by Comintern in 1924[137] and who was now employed at Adoratsky's Marx-Engels-Lenin Institute in Moscow. Rudas described 'Dialectical Materialism' as the 'ideology' of communism, an ideology whose appeal, he felt, was bound to grow as the Soviet Union steamed ahead into unheard of prosperity, while the capitalist world, shaken by economic crises, sank forgotten and unlamented into abject poverty. Dialectical Materialism, Rudas explained, comprised universal a priori 'laws':

Dialectics . . . is a still more general law than that of the conservation of energy, which latter is only a physical special case of general dialectics. . . . The dialectics of society is only a special case of the *general dialectics* of the world, since society, in the last resort, is also part of nature and is developed from nature.[138]

Brusquely, Rudas stated Engels's three 'laws' of dialectics and laid down the distinction between antagonistic and non-antagonistic contradictions. He realized that this procedure would not recommend itself to intellectuals, especially those who were acquainted with the classics of Western philosophy, particularly the works of Hegel. But, taking into account the principle of the unity of theory and practice, Rudas was not the least bit discouraged:

Dialectical materialism is only recognised and expounded by Marxist revolutionaries. The pre-requisite for understanding dialectical material-ism is . . . the *revolutionising* of thinking, and also sooner or later — enrolment in the ranks of the revolutionary party. . . . Dialectical materialism is the consciousness . . . in the heads of the members of the vanguard of the revolution: the Communists. How can the objective movement and the consciousness of it not be inseparably connected? How can one conduct a fight *correctly* with incorrect consciousness? And how could a non-communist be a dialectical materialist? . . . Only those who take their part in the struggle to change the world can rightly understand the theory of the world's dialectical development.

There could be plenty of objections to this tight little circle of reasoning — for instance, it is obviously possible to fight correctly without a correct consciousness, and vice versa; and if understanding Dialectical Materialism is strictly equivalent to joining the Party, then it is hard to see how philosophy could be either use or ornament to militants — they would do better to stick to practical Party work and leave thinking to take care of itself. In fact, by Rudas's account, political effectiveness was the only criterion of philosophical merit. However, with unblushing inconsistency, Rudas went on to assert that Dialectical Materialism must in some way be the basis of Party policy:

What Marx predicted by the aid of the dialectical method has been
verified almost word for word. . . . The Communist Party is the only
party which can truly forecast the course of events of capitalist society,
and which predicts and also realises the inevitable social revolution
which it is able to do thanks to dialectical materialism. . . . With the con-
tinual application of the dialectical method, the Soviet Union is celebrating one triumph after another in the construction of socialism. The
plan, on the basis of which the construction is carried on, is done on the
basis of the dialectical method. . . .[139]

Rudas's article — being the only available account of the new
philosophy — gained immediate popularity in Britain, and
was soon issued in an expanded version as a pamphlet.[140]

A year later, it was joined by the work of his colleague
Adoratsky. His was in a way an even more baffling essay than
that of Rudas. Adoratsky started from the premiss that
Dialectical Materialism is the philosophy of the proletarian
vanguard party, and that it must be defended against the
'distortions' of Bukharinism on the right and Deborinism on
the left. But then he found it impossible to move beyond this
starting-point, and avoided any attempt to state or explain
what Dialectical Materialism actually propounds. 'The
dialectic is difficult and complex, "cunning" as Hegel expressed
it: it is very hard to master', he wrote. He mentioned the
three 'laws' of dialectics, identifying the 'unity of opposites'
as the most important of them, but he deprecated all such
schematisms. Dialectical Materialism, to him, was simultaneously an extremely exacting creed, and also one of almost
unlimited elasticity: 'Materialist dialectics does not tolerate
the use of stereotyped and ready-made schemes. It demands
the profound study of concrete circumstances; the precise
formulation of the real process of development; it also
demands revolutionary action.' At this rate, it came to seem
that philosophy, by definition, meant Party membership.
'Philosophy must be completely party philosophy', he
remarked, but whichever way he turned, he left the conundrum
of the New Turn untouched: was the party to be philosophical,
or was philosophy to be subordinated to the party; or, which
came first, philosophy or the party? 'Theory must be placed
at the service of the proletarian revolution and adapted to the
practical class struggle', Adoratsky declared — inviting, but
not confronting, a doubt as to what difference 'Theory' was
supposed to make to the practice it served, and implying that

'service to the revolution' could automatically and univocally dictate the correct party line, without 'Theory' having to be consulted after all.[141]

Considering how vociferous the British Communists had been about basing their theoretical and educational work on 'Dialectical Materialism', the flimsy pamphlets by Rudas and Adoratsky constituted a pathetic and weedy evasion: where readers might seek precision, they made a blur, and where doors needed to be opened onto philosophical traditions, they were slammed shut and firmly bolted. The deficiences of these perfunctory texts were to some extent remedied with the translation in 1937 of a three-part *Textbook of Marxist Philosophy* (one part on each of the 'laws') which had been prepared by the Leningrad Institute of Philosophy.[142] But this book was not published by the Communist Party, and was not intended as a sectarian attack on 'pseudo-Marxism' in non-communist Labour organizations. For the political season had changed again, and from 1933 on, with Hitler's accession to power in Germany, Communist antagonism was directed towards Fascism, and overtures were once more made to those who had, in the class-against-class period, been reviled as 'Social Fascists'. Dialectical Materialism ceased to be a hot issue, and the Communists even supported the Labour Party in the November 1935 General Election, again reapplying (unsuccessfully of course) for affiliation.[143]

The *Textbook of Marxist Philosophy* was published by the Left Book Club, a determinedly non-party organization founded in 1936. It sold books to individual members, of whom it had 50,000 in 1937, and also organized 'Study Groups' (1,500 of them) and rallies (they overflowed the Albert Hall in 1937).[144] All this was a conspicuous victory for Popular Frontism, but a resounding defeat for the idea of partisan Party teaching based on an exclusive Party philosophy.

Thanks to local Labour Colleges, to the Left Book Club, and indeed to local Communist Party groups and various unclubbed individuals, a steady bass note of socialist education, which had begun to sound before the First World War, was sustained throughout the 1930s, indifferent to the shrill staccato of the Communists' debates with themselves and everyone else. Tommy Jackson, for instance, now in his late fifties, carried

on with broadminded educational work, a popular lecturer
both to Party Education classes and in the Labour Colleges,
always keeping clear of divisive partisan debates. And Lawrence
Daly — a boy growing up in a Communist miner's family
near Fife in 1930s and 1940s — received a political and
philosophical education which cut across all the lines laid
down in Central Committees and capital cities. He and his
family revered Tommy Jackson, who would occasionally
lecture in Fife; and the library of the local Miners' Welfare
Institute provided a range of reading much of which was
inevitably out of date in terms of any changing party line.
Although he was a Young Communist, Daly took NCLC
correspondence courses in English Grammar, Social History,
and Trade Unionism, and read *The Plebs*. Encouraged by his
father, and with no sense of unorthodoxy, he also got to
know Fred Casey's textbook of Dietzgenism, *Thinking*. His
father would talk about the book:

about phenomena appearing, growing, developing, declining and dying;
and in the process, within the particular phenomenon . . . there was a
struggle inside between the old and the new — the unity of opposites
and the struggle of opposites. He (my father) used to talk about this.
I didn't get the impression that he was a reader, but he was a very
good listener, and — in the 20s — he'd heard people in the Party talking
about dialectics and so forth. His understanding came from going to
classes in the CP.[145]

Daly's education in dialectics, then, owed nothing to the
celebrated 'New Turn' in Russia, but leapt over the decades
to join with the illumination received by people like Shanley
in the 1920s, or Casey in the early years of the century, or
indeed Jackson in the 1890s — a conviction that change and
struggle, so far from being opposed to the natural order of
things, are actually intrinsic to it.

Nevertheless, the Party's promotion of the 'New Turn' in
philosophy may have made an impression on some activists.
Edward Upward's *alter ego* Alan Sebrill, for instance, 'liked'
Adoratsky — though it had been Plekhanov who first got him
interested in philosophy.[146] But most of the testimony is
extremely negative. In 1932 a Labour College student argued
that the main task of the Labour Colleges was to teach English,
recalling the 'super-pedant' who had

contended that Dialectical Materialism was of the first importance, probably forgetting that the two words 'dialectical materialism' were enough to completely put the wind up workers having just completed a shift in the mine, a day on the foot-plate, or nine hours in the factory.[147]

And one of my informants recalled that, in the Party in the thirties, 'Theory' was regarded as something originating in the Soviet Union. The attitude was that

'This is something that they can do, over there, but we can't . . .'. . . . In the ordinary branch, you didn't get any conscious concern about a philosophy so abstract as Hegel. People called themselves Marxists because they were in the CP — with no knowledge of Theory.[148]

This judgement is borne out by the recollections of the Plebs Leaguer and Upholsterers' organizer Jock Shanley, who eventually left the Party in 1936:

The party had become completely sectarian [following the General Strike]. They had created a world which was reality for them, and didn't want to go outside it. . . . It meant that people like myself were isolated. . . . There was a cleavage between intellectuals and the party. Palme Dutt became a predominant influence . . . to me, an evil influence. You got a stage where, instead of getting down to studying basics, people waited for Palme Dutt's 'Notes of the Month'. And so, you got a period when you didn't have a mind-searching, you didn't have a seeking for knowledge of fundamentals, you got a period of acceptance of the commandments laid down by the high priest. . . .

You got into parrot phrases: 'theory divorced from practice is sterile, practice divorced from theory is blind' — and this became a *formula*. And they immediately went on practising blindly, and uttering the magic formula.[149]

A very similar experience was recalled by Dudley Edwards, another lifelong Marxist, who left the Party after the thirties, and who said that in reality Dialectical Materialism 'reduced itself to the parrot-repetition of certain things — like the combined unity and antagonism of opposites.' Nevertheless, militants considered that their Party was distinguished by its Theory:

They'd simply say that the Communist Party is the only body which has a scientific theory of the development of human society — and that covered the point. . . . Very often, when discussing something like a strike or a housing campaign, during the discussion someone would get up and say, 'Oh well, that's not dialectical'. I don't think anyone really understood what they meant when they said it 'wasn't dialectical', but that was enough to more or less carry the day. . . . The two were probably interchangeable, but probably they used the word 'dialectical' more than the word 'materialism'. But not very much effort was made to explain what the dialectical process was. . . . It just corresponded with what you agreed with. . . . The tactic that you wanted — that was the dialectical process operating.

But above all, as Edwards recalled, the promotion of Dialectical Materialism in the 1930s was associated with a growing divide between workerist workers and intellectualist intellectuals.

It was a philosophy for the élite. . . . You were told, 'Well, you don't want to spend a long time doing the dialectic theories — they won't understand it anyway . . . the main thing is to get on with the job. . . .' So it became a sort of stamping ground for intellectuals. . . . I don't think that many of the workers were very much interested. . . .[150]

The story was, then, taking a most curious turn. The 'Dialectical Materialism' which had been promoted in the British Party in the early thirties had been formulated in the Soviet Union during 1930 as a proletarian alternative to the academic philosophy of the middle-aged Deborinite professors, and it had been imported into Britain as part of the Communist Party's campaign against the allegedly impractical and dilettante Marxism of the Labour Colleges. It had been advertised as the philosophy of the proletariat, and as unintelligible (in Rudas's words) to 'the intellectual, who does not come to the theory of dialectical materialism by way of revolutionary practice, but from the ordinary school philosophies'. ('Dialectical materialism is only recognised and expounded by Marxist revolutionaries', he wrote.[151]) Some workers thought they understood it, though their comrades might harbour a disloyal doubt; but most simply left it to the intellectuals — the very group against which it had officially been devised and deployed in the first place. And some of the intellectuals, in the event, showed a keen appetite for it.

Chapter 5

Dialectical Materialism and the Scientists

1 Biology and Scientific Socialism

You may remember how, in the early twenties, a number of youthful University intellectuals, mostly associated with the embryonic or new-born Communist Party, started a philosophical quarrel within the Labour College Movement by mounting a campaign to 'put old Joseph on the shelf'.[1] In shelving Dietzgenism, they wished also to abandon dialectics, which, so far as they were concerned, was a throw-back to Hegel, whose pre-scientific ideas had been decisively superseded by the technical and apparently 'scientific' philosophical work of the past twenty years, notably that of Bertrand Russell. Of this group, Maurice Dobb appears to be the only one to remain long in the Party, refusing to be provoked by taunts about his incapacity for Dialectical Materialism. Eden and Cedar Paul stayed at least till the late twenties, willing to criticize the Labour Colleges but extremely irritated by the Party's regressive attachment to 'the rather unhappy term "dialectics"'.[2] Raymond Postgate, meantime, had come to the conclusion that 'the dialectic' was 'out of date',[3] and in the early thirties he began co-operating with G. D. H. Cole, Frank Horrabin, and J. T. Murphy (just separated from the Communist Party)[4] in a campaign to assert an open and empirical kind of Marxism within the Labour Party.[5]

But it was Lancelot Hogben who had cast the first stone at Dietzgenism back in 1919. He and his wife Enid Charles had worked for Sylvia Pankhurst's Workers' Socialist Federation, and for the ILP; during the 1920s he had taught biology in South Africa, and written extensively on mathematical genetics, voicing a rude professional scepticism about allegedly scientific and biological arguments in support of eugenics, social darwinism, racism, and sexual inequality. In 1929 he returned to England to take the chair of Social Biology at the London School of Economics. He then made a new entry into philosophical debate, of a much more constructive kind than his Dietzgen-knocking of ten years before. Hogben's treatise was called *The Nature of Living Matter*; it was dedicated to Bertrand Russell and contained numerous mottoes from Hume. Its central thesis was that political ideals cannot be derived from scientific biology, and that the scientific pretensions of eugenics are bogus. In particular, Hogben criticized the 'holistic' philosophy of biology advocated by J. S. Haldane, who believed that life could not be explained in 'mechanistic' terms, or in other words that biology could not be reduced to physics, and who concluded that biology pointed the way to theology, to 'scientific deism'.[6]

Hogben tried to undercut the holism–mechanism controversy by means of a general philosophy of knowledge which owed much to Bertrand Russell, and which was essentially the same as the 'empirio-criticism' which had taken root in pre-revolutionary Russia, and in which Lenin had perceived merely a disguised, socialized, subjective idealism. Hogben's philosophy was spun out from the two basic categories of 'privacy' and 'publicity'. Everyone lives — so Hogben's argument ran — in both a private world of subjective feelings and values, and an intersubjective world of publicly testable facts. Knowlege of the public world, as Hogben saw it, was derived from and dependent upon knowledge of the private world; in Russell's terminology, he saw the public world as a 'logical construction' out of private worlds. Science, from this point of view, was the attempt to define factors common to different private worlds so as to incorporate subjectivities into an ever-expanding public world. Hogben's 'publicist standpoint' (as he was unwary enough to call it) implied that neither physics nor biology dealt with an objective 'real world', independent of how people experience it; like the other sciences, they were concerned only with the 'public world', and 'the public world is the world of socialised belief'.[7] A 'real world' distinct from the 'public world' was a myth. Hence, Hogben concluded, the controversies about holism, mechanism, and the true nature of matter were meaningless irrelevances.

The Nature of Living Matter was an academic treatise, and refrained from any comment on specific social or political issues. In particular Hogben did not draw attention to the incompatibility of 'publicism' with the Dietzgenite and Plebs League conception of independent proletarian culture and education: for — so it would seem at least — if scientific claims were to be checked against 'socialized belief' rather than against the objective world, then — and this had been the whole impetus of Lenin's fury against 'empirio-criticism' — oppressed groups could never be justified in contesting the opinions of 'publicly' acknowledged experts. Minority beliefs would be by definition unscientific.

However, there was a socialistic, if not revolutionary, way of interpreting Hogben's publicism, and this was seized upon by Hogben's near-contemporary, the Cambridge scientist and benign Christian socialist Joseph Needham. Needham found that Hogben's theory provided the materials for proving the unity of science with socialism, which he conceived as jointly forming a coherent alternative to individualism and irrationalism:

> If we are individualists, we think the private incommunicable worlds most important, most real; if we are — what? Communists? — we think the public communicable world most important, most real. And it is just here that we encounter the peculiar importance of his [Hogben's] whole position, namely, the emphasis which it lays on the social group, the community of observers, the body of workers. This emphasis confers upon it the character of a communist philosophy, a point of view fitted to answer in the theoretical world to communism in the practical world. For this reason, the importance of publicism is potentially very great. In the course of time world-communism will certainly acquire a philosophy other than the Hegelian dialectic of the Russian Marxists, and it would be possible to conceive of several worse ones than that whose germ is contained in Hogben's book.[8]

Needham's airy tipstering about the future philosophy of 'world-communism' indicates a rather surprising apathy on his part (and Hogben's too) towards the actual development of what he called 'communism in the practical world', and especially towards the development of science in the Soviet Union during the 1920s. The enthusiasm of other scientists, however, easily compensated for this neglect.

2 British Scientists and Soviet Science in the Twenties

For socialists all round the world, the Bolshevik revolution
has been more than a historical event, over and done with in
weeks, months, or years; it is also a sign and a portent, a
permanent possibility of interpretation. It has proved full of
ambiguities, the crux being the idea, or rather different ideas,
of the State. Lenin's *State and Revolution,* composed just
before the revolution, affirmed that the Bolsheviks had the
same aim in view as the anarchists — the complete abolition
of the State. But it argued that this destination could be
reached only by going through a 'phase' in which the State,
commandeered by the proletariat, would impose 'factory
discipline' with unabashed authoritarianism, so that the
'whole of society' could be organized 'like a single office and
a single factory'. The country would be managed on the lines
of a national postal system, but purged of idle bureaucrats.
('The mechanism of social management is here already to
hand . . . a splendidly equipped mechanism . . . which can
very well be set going by the united workers themselves. . . .
To organise the *whole* economy on the lines of the postal
service . . . this is our immediate aim.'[9]) Under the slogan
'electrification plus soviets', Lenin (followed by Trotsky)
went so far as to advocate the methods of factory discipline
associated with American 'scientific management' and time-
and-motion study, as developed by F. W. Taylor:

> The task the Soviet Government must set the people in all its scope is —
> learn to work. The Taylor system, the last word of capitalism in this
> respect, like all capitalist progress, is a combination of the refined
> brutality of bourgeois exploitation and a number of the greatest scientific
> achievements. . . . The Soviet Republic must at all costs adopt all that
> is valuable in the achievements of science and technology in this field.
> The possibility of building socialism depends exactly upon our success
> in combining Soviet power and the Soviet organisation of administration
> with the up-to-date achievements of capitalism.[10]

Stalin, faithful to this programme, defined the two 'characteristic features' of the 'special Leninist style in work' as
'a) Russian revolutionary sweep and b) American efficiency'.[11]
And with the introduction of his first Five Year Plan in 1928,
a new interpretation of the revolution was licensed: the Soviet
Union stood, above all, for the application of scientific

expertise to technical problems of production: in a word, it stood for planning, and the dictatorship of the proletariat turned out to be the dictatorship of science, the Soviet Union a harbinger of a new social order — not socialism exactly, but rather what you might call 'scientocracy'.

During the 1920s, a novel kind of intellectual subculture grew up in many Western countries, a 'scientific community' which prided itself on its hard-headed, down-to-earth, unsentimental factualness. In Britain, it was at home in the industry-linked institutions of technical education in London or in midland and northern cities, or, in another way, in the eccentric scientific dynasties of Cambridge University — the Needhams, the Huxleys, the Darwins, and the Keynes's. At all events, these scientists were quite out of sympathy with the sort of classical literary education in which Oxford specialized, and which remained an almost indispensable qualification for office in British State institutions. Whether high-born or low, their advocacy of science, especially in its applied forms, inevitably led them into conflict with traditional British political educational arrangements. In the unscientific past, as Julian Huxley saw it, 'a general humanistic education was a good, and indeed perhaps the best possible, preparation for statesmanship'. But in the twentieth century, things were altered, and 'the professional politician and the scientific expert had come into their own'. To such scientists, the most important aspect of the Bolshevik 'scientific experiment' (as they liked to call it) was the scope it seemed to give to expert scientific planning.[12]

Hyman Levy learned about British society from his experience in Edinburgh as the child of a poverty-stricken German Jew and her Russian Jewish husband. In the 1900s, the teenage Levy listened to the propaganda of rival socialist speakers at the Mound, and resorted to reading Marx in a heroic attempt to disentangle their disagreements.[13] By 1920, however, he had climbed educational 'ladders' to Edinburgh University, then to Göttingen, and then to work as an applied scientist at the National Physical Laboratory at Teddington (where he got into trouble for organizing a Union of Scientific Workers), and finally to a lifetime job teaching mathematics at London's Imperial College of Science and Technology. Levy combined his professional commitment to

science with a political commitment to Labour, and in the
1920s he began the attempt to bring the two — 'two movements so clearly destined to change the nature of society' —
into a fruitful union. On the one hand, he urged his scientific
colleagues to interest themselves in the social dimension of
industry, as well as the technical, and to recognize that 'the
present stage of society, which utilises the wage system as a
means of effecting distribution, with its million unemployed,
is . . . from the scientific point of view utterly indefensible'.
On the other hand he hoped that traditional politicians
would make way for professionals with 'a true scientific
training', experts who would introduce 'scientific method'
into government and administration, even if this meant
discarding the democratic scruple of consulting the opinions
of an unscientific electorate.[14] Levy urged this perspective
within the Labour Party throughout the 1920s, until he was
expelled for his links with the Communists; then, in 1930,
he officially became a member of the Communist Party.[15]

John Desmond Bernal was another Communist scientist,
who hoped, like Levy, to use science to liberate the oppressed.
He was an Irish Catholic, born in 1901, whose ambitious
American mother arranged for him to be educated in an
English Protestant public school — an awkward predicament
in those spectacular years of Irish revolutionary activity.
At school, Bernal came to the conclusion that 'science
offered the means, perhaps the only means, by which the
people of Ireland could liberate themselves.'[16] As an undergraduate at Cambridge he read Marx, Engels, and Lenin,
and in about 1923 he became a member of the Communist
Party, to which he remained loyal till his death in 1971,[17]
combining Communism with professional work as a scientist
in Cambridge and later at Birkbeck College in London. He
wrote unsigned articles for *The Communist* in 1927,[18] and
presented his vision of socialism in his not quite tongue-in-
cheek essay *The World, the Flesh and the Devil,* in 1929. The
future of 'the rational soul', as he presented it there, lay in
the cultivation of scientific 'brains', scooped out of their
inconvenient human bodies, surviving hundreds of years
in ever-increasing scientific knowledge, and dispensing with
language, not to mention personal frictions and friendships,
by means of direct electrical hook-ups with other brains.

Eventually the plugged-in brains of the universe would function as 'multiple organisms', a 'more or less permanent compound brain' would come into existence, and consequently 'death would take on a different and far less terrible aspect'. (Bernal does not pause to consider whether life would still be worth it, without livers.) Space travel would enable these communicating brains to distribute themselves across the universe. And the boring old way of life — brains encumbered by bodies, with sexual difference and all sorts of other tiresome distractions from science — could even be retained on earth as a kind of archive for the edification or delight of any celestial superbrains which happened to have a sentimental or antiquarian disposition:

Mankind — the old mankind — would be left in undisputed possession of the earth, to be regarded by the inhabitants of the celestial spheres with a curious reverence. The world might, in fact, be transformed into a human zoo, a zoo so intelligently managed that its inhabitants are not aware that they are there merely for the purpose of observation and experiment.

This Utopia was penned by a member of the Communist Party — in fact few had been in the Party longer than him, though many had been more active — and Bernal, loyally enough, stuck this bizarre tail onto the Soviet donkey: a dictatorship of the mandarinate — or indeed of 'science' itself:

In a Soviet state (not the state of the present, but one freed from the danger of capitalist attack), the scientific institutions would in fact gradually become the government, and a further stage of the Marxian hierarchy of domination would be reached. Scientists in such a stage would tend very naturally to identify themselves emotionally rather with the progress of science itself than with that of a class, a nation, or a humanity outside science, while the rest of the population would, by the diffusion of an education in which the highest values lay in a scientific rather than in a moral or a political direction, be much less likely to oppose effectively the development of science. . . . From one point of view the scientists would emerge as a new species and leave humanity behind; from another, humanity — the humanity that counts — might seem to change *en bloc*, leaving behind in a relatively primitive state those too stupid or stubborn to change. . . .[19]

Bernal's support for the Soviet Union as a pioneering scientocracy became less fanciful but not less fervent when he made his first visit two years later.[20]

Levy and Bernal were probably the most prominent scientists associated with the Communist Party in the 1920s. The scientists who were best informed about Soviet Science, however, had nothing to do with the Party at all: J. B. S. Haldane and J. G. Crowther. Haldane was the son of the philosophical biologist and 'scientific deist' J. S. Haldane (the target of Hogben's criticisms in *The Nature of Living Matter*), and nephew of Lord Haldane, a philosophical follower of T. H. Green's public-spirited Hegelianism, and a barrister who became a minister in the first Labour government in 1924. J. B. S. Haldane (like Needham, Bernal, and Hogben) was primarily a geneticist, and was fond of shocking public opinion with his hard-headedness (not to say hard-heartedness) about the possibility of eliminating defective strains of human beings by applying scientific breeding techniques, and of using scientific means to determine the rights and duties of individuals. ('Some day', he wrote, 'it may be possible to devise a scientific method of assessing the voting power of individuals. . . . In the remote future mankind may be divided into castes like Hindus or termites.'[21]) It was this vision of a 'scientific State' which appealed to Haldane when he visited Russia, on the invitation of the geneticist Vavilov, in 1928.[22] He came back proclaiming that the chief point about the Soviet Union was that a serious attempt was being made there to incorporate scientific ideas into politics. Still, it was not yet 'a scientific state':

It purports to be a scientific state in the same way that the states of medieval Europe purported to be Christian. . . . The test of the devotion of the Union of Socialist Soviet Republics to science will, I think, come when the accumulation of the results of human genetics, demonstrating what I believe to be the fact of innate human inequality, becomes important.

At that point, said Haldane, it would be up to the scientific socialist state to jettison all the 'sentimental and unscientific views often associated with Socialism'.[23]

Haldane's anti-sentimentalism was fanatical, indeed sentimental; J. G. Crowther, by contrast, was — in spite of his evangelism about science — a relatively dispassionate observer. His father was a pioneer of technical education in Bradford, and he himself climbed through Bradford Grammar School to Trinity College, Cambridge, whence he graduated in 1922. He spent a few years working as a school science teacher, and then as a science editor for Oxford University Press, and at the same time became involved in the Labour College Movement. But from 1927 on, he devoted himself to creating the role of 'scientific journalist' and got a job with the *Manchester Guardian* in that novel capacity. In the summer of 1929 he visited Leningrad and Moscow with a friend from his school-days in Bradford — Ralph Fox, a leading Communist Party intellectual, and member of the staff of the *Sunday Worker*.[24] On his return, he appeared as 'our scientific correspondent' in the *Sunday Worker*, where he claimed that the intellectual vitality of modern scientific Russia was comparable only to that of Renaissance humanistic Florence. However, Crowther was no Communist, and the *Sunday Worker*'s eclecticism was in evident conflict with the new class-against-class line of the Communist Party. Crowther had written: 'How is it that capitalistic civilisation should contain a diseased literature [D. H. Lawrence] and a healthy science side by side? Because science is the same under all conditions. . . . except insofar as improved opportunities for research allow a much greater rate of expansion of the sciences under Communism.' The same issue of the paper contained a plaintive request from a reader for an explanation of the baffling phrase 'Social-Fascist' and its application to the leaders of the Labour Movement. In this atmosphere Crowther's idea of science as 'above politics' did not go down well with *Sunday Worker* readers: 'a heap of bourgeois rubbish', wrote one, and another requested that the *Sunday Worker* should try to popularize 'the writings and discussions on scientific philosophy published in the USSR' and should dump non-party correspondents like Crowther, who had 'only the haziest notions about Dialectical Materialism'. Ralph Fox tried to defend his friend, but it is hardly surprising that Crowther's full story of the wonders he had witnessed in Russia was reserved for the consumption of readers of the *Manchester Guardian* during the following month.[25] In the thirties, the intellectual and literary culture of British scientists and intellectuals, however enthusiastic they might be about Communism and the Soviet Union, was almost entirely separate from the activities of the British Communist Party.

3 Intellectuals and the British Communist Party

When, towards the end of the 1920s, the British Communist
Party began to scourge the Labour College Movement for
being too intellectual, it was turning its back on an alliance —
between love of knowledge and a yearning for socialism —
which went far back into the nineteenth century, and which
still meant a lot to many members of the Party: not only
to old-timers like Tommy Jackson, but also to certain young
intellectuals, like Freda Utley, a London University graduate
who joined the Party in 1927 after a visit to Russia.

In 1930, Freda Utley reviewed a recent volume of translations of Lenin's writings of 1900-2 in the *Communist
Review*. Her review quoted copiously from *What is to be
Done?*, in which Lenin had stressed the need for 'Theory'
and argued that bourgeois intellectuals had a distinct and
indispensable part to play in the working-class movement —
contrary to the philistine errors of 'economism', according
to which the economic predicament of the working class
would automatically induce socialist conviction in it. The
true voice of the working class, according to Lenin, spoke
as follows:

We are not children to be fed on the sops of 'economic' politics alone;
we want to know everything that everybody else knows. In order that
we may do this, the intellectuals must talk to us less on what we
already know and tell us more about what we do not know and what
we can never learn from our factory and 'economic' experience. . . .
You intellectuals can acquire this knowledge and it is your *duty* to
bring us that knowledge.[26]

Freda Utley commented: 'Might not Lenin have addressed
this speech to the British Communist Party today?':

I am of course aware that our present day economists will indignantly
dispute this assertion. But comrades it is not enough to repeat the
slogan 'Down with the Social-Fascist Labour Government' and 'A
Revolutionary Workers' Government' and feel that in so doing you have
fulfilled the whole of your task of raising the political consciousness of
the workers. . . .
   Does the *Daily Worker* bring to the workers the 'political knowledge'
they are waiting for? . . . Very rarely does it do this, if it did its circulation
would be mounting rapidly. . . .
   We have hardly any intellectuals worthy of the name and this is
clearly one of the primary reasons for our weakness. Those in our

movement who could be the 'revolutionary socialist intelligentsia' are for the most part only anxious to show that they are as good as anyone else at 'bowing to the spontaneity of the masses', especially those of bourgeois origin who try to pose as proletarians instead of fulfilling their revolutionary duty of acquiring and propagating knowledge of Marxian science and method. . . .

On the whole most comrades despise theory. Party training is treated as of secondary importance or is non-existent and as far as real theoretical study and hard application to the science of Marxism and Leninism few even dream.[27]

Comrade Utley was roundly and self-righteously criticized in the coming months,[28] and the debate was closed with a statement from the Political Bureau of the Party, which condemned her for 'falling into the bog of left sectarianism' but suggested that if she paid more attention to Comrade Stalin's reflections on 'theory' and 'practice' then her 'theoretical deviations' might be cured.[29]

But the Party could not really afford to be so rude. Membership had reached five thousand in 1922, and after collapsing in 1924, climbed to ten thousand during the General Strike, though much of this disappeared within months if not weeks. By 1930 the Party had only two and a half thousand members — fewer, probably, than at any time since its formation, and covering only about one ten-thousandth of the population it proposed to lead.[30]

Whilst languishing in this bitter unpopularity, the Communist Party found quite large numbers of students, teachers, and scientists clamouring for admission. There was even an elaborate plan within the Party for a 'Section of Intellectual Workers', directly responsible to the Central Committee, with subsections of Marxist Biologists, Marxist Physicists, Marxist Historians, and so forth. When the scheme was firmly and finally rejected in 1932, Palme Dutt wrote a long and thoughtful explanation. He referred to 'the best elements of the younger scientists, technicians, writers, who are . . . beginning to realise that the future of all they care for lies with Communism, with the Proletarian revolution, and who are anxious to take part in this world historic process. . . . It is essential that the best of these should join the Communist Party.' Within the Party, however, the intellectual would have no special rights or duties: 'First and foremost, he should *forget that he is an intellectual* (except in moments of necessary

self-criticism) *and remember only that he is a Communist. . . .
like any other Party Member.*' At first sight, this might seem
to involve the impostion of irksome discipline on such
intellectual recruits. But really, it was rather the reverse:

> We have not the slightest concern to combat the desirability of Com-
> munists who are competent to do so entering into polemics and
> theoretical work in special fields of their interest, biology, physics,
> etc. . . . They will naturally discuss with one another, or with non-Party
> specialists who may approach our outlook in this field, without any
> need to be specially organised by the Party to do this. *But this is not
> their decisive work, nor their main work, as revolutionary Communists.*[31]

From the point of view of the intellectuals, this was something
of a Bill of Rights. It meant that joining the Party need not
interfere with intellectual and literary projects, nor indeed
with academic or scientific careers — except, of course, to
the extent that Party work might leave no time for reading
and thinking. In the Communist Party's view, joining the
Party and being a Marxist intellectual were disparate activities,
occasionally pursued by the same individual, but normally
not.

An example of this type of Marxist intellectual in the
Party was David Guest, a mathematical logician and one of
Wittgenstein's students at Cambridge. In 1930 the nineteen-
year-old Guest interrupted his undergraduate studies in order
to work with Hilbert at Göttingen. He was horrified by what
he observed of Nazism, and spent a miserable and frightening
fortnight in gaol, much of it in solitary confinement, following
a demonstration on Easter Sunday 1931.[32] On his return to
England, Guest came across Lenin's *Materialism and Empirio-
Criticism.* He went to a meeting of the Cambridge University
Moral Sciences Club, 'bubbling over with excitement about
it, and kept reading passages aloud, especially those parts
which deal with the class basis of philosophy. Some of the
students were rather shocked, others thought he had gone
crazy, but he took no notice.' Guest soon joined the newly
founded University branch of the Communist Party in
Cambridge, taking several fellow-students with him.[33] In
1932, he took a First in Moral Sciences, and then worked in
the student movement, co-ordinating Communist student
groups in London, Cambridge, and Oxford.[34] He then spent
a year teaching at an Anglo-American school in Moscow,

and subsequently gave lectures on Philosophy at the Marx
Memorial Library in London, which had been founded in
1933 as part of the Party's ever-new hope of making its mark
in education. (His course ranged widely over the history of
philosophy, and presented clear cases against Russell, Conze,
and Casey in the name of a measured and undogmatic
materialistic dialectics. It was worked up by Tommy Jackson
into a brief book which came out in 1939.)[35] In 1937 he
began a conventional academic career in the mathematics
department of University College Southampton. But he
found that it 'required an incredible effort to concentrate
on mathematics when the world seems on fire',[36] and he
devoted all the time he could spare to ordinary Party work.

'It was all a very high moral tone', said Vivien Morton,
remembering the London University Student Group which
she joined in 1932. 'No larking about or anything.' She
remembered being criticized for her appearance ('a Grecian
tunic and a cloak, and sandals and bare legs . . . they took me
to task and said I'd never get anywhere in the Party if I wore
such bizarre clothes'). These student groups, and also the
University Branches which now existed alongside town
Branches in London, Oxford, and Cambridge, were not in
any way interested in challenging the intellectual values of
the University. They saw the education system as a repository
of objective knowledge and expertise, rather than as a propa-
gator of ruling-class ideology. Academic distinction was to
be cultivated and revered. 'I always remember David Guest
saying,' (said Vivien Morton), 'we've really all got to go for
first-class degrees . . . nothing else is really good enough.'
However, the influence of Guest, and of many others who
tried to combine the roles of Marxist intellectual and Party
member — such as John Cornford, Ralph Fox, and Christopher
Caudwell — was abruptly curtailed: 'they nearly all went off
and got killed in Spain'.[37] 'Guest himself went, and after a
few weeks of organizing and training — and working on
mathematics in his spare moments — died there, shot through
the heart, in 1938.

4 The Russian Invasion of British Science

The majority of Marxist intellectuals, however, kept clear of
the British Communist Party. Levy was almost alone amongst
the Marxist scientists, for example, in maintaining his
membership through the thirties. Bernal left in 1933 — not
at all because of disagreement with the Party, but, on the
contrary, because it was thought that he would serve it
more effectively from outside, as an independent, a 'fellow-
traveller'. So the question of joining did not trouble the
Marxist scientists, and if they had an acute or exacting sense
of political duty, it was likely to be satisfied in the promotion
and pursuit of scientific research, and the popularization
of its results, preferably in a reduced, angular, scientific,
'Panoptic' English, ruthlessly shorn of adverbs, rather than in
directly political work.[38]

At the same time, the Marxist scientists were interested in
the formation of a new professional discipline for the historical
study of the sciences. Hogben and Needham, in fact, co-
operated in the planning of the second International Congress
of the History of Science and Technology, a four-day event
scheduled from Tuesday to Friday, 30 June to 3 July 1931.
Although a session was planned on 'The Sciences as an
Integral Part of General Historical Study', the main tenor of
the congress was to be specialized and uncontroversial. There
would be one participant from the Soviet Union — Professor
Zavadovsky, who was to give a paper on evolution and genetics
in the session on 'Interrelationships of the Physical and
Biological Sciences'. But then there occurred a quite unexpected train of events.

Exactly a week before the conference was due to open,
Stalin officially relaxed his harsh 'proletarian' hostility to
bourgeois intellectuals, and decided to try and gain publicity
in the West for the industrial and scientific triumphs of the Five
Year Plan. And the first step in his programme was to send
a delegation of eight high-powered scientists and historians to
the London Congress. The delegates (apart from Zavadovsky)
had only three days to prepare their papers, to pack, and to
fly to London, where they met with a rather bewildered
organizing committee and began bargaining for some time in
the already full Congress proceedings. The best offer they

could get from the President of the Congress — Professor Charles Singer — was an extra half-day session, on the Saturday after the official closure of the conference. The delegates were reconciled to this by Hogben's suggestion that, in the five days that remained, they could translate, print, and circulate all their papers. This they did, and what's more the translations appeared as a well-produced book, entitled *Science at the Crossroads*, at the beginning of the following week — a fortnight after Stalin's remarkable and indisputably creative decision.[39]

This frantic hyperactivity was a marvellous testimonial to the ubiquitous over-achievement which was supposed to be characteristic of the Five Year Plan. Several of the papers were unashamedly propagandistic, extolling the unhampered joint development of science and technology in the Soviet Union, compared with its obstruction and perversion in capitalist countries, or celebrating the application of science to planning and the premature completion of the Five Year Plan, or advocating electrification and the 'conveyor system of production' as the basis of socialism.[40]

However, the Russians did also make some substantial intellectual contributions to the Congress. Zavadovsky's paper on biology was of course the only one to have been carefully prepared specifically for the conference. He addressed the very problems in which Bernal, Haldane, Needham, and Hogben were particularly interested — the relation of life to mechanism, of biology to physics. Zavadovsky surveyed a range of conflicting attitudes to evolution amongst Western biologists, from 'idealistic vitalism' to 'vulgar materialism', and asserted that this disarray was due to the biologists' ignorance of philosophy, or at least to 'their inability, in virtue of the class limitations upon their general train of thought, to adopt the only correct philosophical positions of dialectical materialism'. In harmony with the radical young philosophers of the 'New Turn', he referred to the three 'laws' of dialectical materialism, which were 'binding on all forms of motion of matter', and asserted that these entailed a rigorous philosophical conception of the *'relative autonomy* of the biological process'.[41]

At the special Saturday session of the Congress, the Russians presented two weighty contributions, which raised questions about the theoretical foundations of the whole project of constructing a 'history of science and technology', by considering the nature of science, of ideologies about science, and the choice of approaches to the study of its past.

In an exceptionally learned and supple address, only slightly disfigured by a pompous verbiage, Bukharin outlined a powerful and imaginative criticism of 'capitalist theories of cognition' — by which he meant empiricisms like Carnap's and Russell's (or for that matter Hogben's) — for which the object of science was not the material world but the sensations of individuals or communities. All such theories, Bukharin pointed out, depended on the supposition 'that "I" have been "given" only "my" own "sensations"' and this, he argued, was ridiculous because the crucial terms — 'I', 'given', 'my', and 'sensations' — took on meaning only in the context of social practice in a material world, where 'the interaction of theory and practice, their unity, develops on the basis of *the primacy of practice*'. Bukharin went on to some adventurous remarks about the dangers inherent, not in science as such, but in the 'fetishising' of it, and the 'deification of the corresponding categories'. By this circuitous route, Bukharin was able to arrive at a homily on the achievements of the Socialist Five Year Plan. Planning was the process by which society freed itself from subjugation to incomprehensible necessities, making the future a matter of scientific will, not blind fate: 'the future lies ahead as a plan, an aim: *causal* connection is realised through social teleology.' This planning applied not only to economics, but to knowledge of the natural world: 'the principle of planning invades the sphere of "mental production", the sphere of science, the sphere of *theory*.' Science would be tamed by planning, its mystery would be removed, and science and socialism would surge forward together.[42]

Bukharin's somewhat speculative description of science and its history was complemented by an enormously detailed paper by B. Hessen, a junior member of the delegation. Hessen began with a clear summary of 'Marx's theory of the Historical Process', indicating that, for Marx, the ideas of an epoch should be explained in terms of the prevailing forces and relations of production, and not just in terms of other ideas. He then gave an astonishing display of what, in application to a particular case, this approach might mean. With full though rather lifeless documentation, he tried to show how all the themes of Newton's *Principia* could be related to the technical exigencies of material production in that particular phase of the transition from feudalism to capitalism.[43]

The members of the audience were at first unsure how to respond to Bukharin and Hessen. It may have occurred to them that the advocates of the planning of science ought to be able to organize conference delegations more than a week in advance, and might have shown rather more respect for the planning done by the official organizers of the Congress. And many of them were completely bewildered by the idea that Marxism — which they had supposed to amount to little more than the clamorous ravings of nihilistic Slavic vandals — could even claim to throw light on the nature of science; and they were put off by the vocabulary of Marxism, which struck them as ugly, barbaric, and opaque, and by the attitude to the writings of Marx, Engels, and Lenin, which struck them as 'medieval' in its reverence.

Bukharin and Hessen had, however, made some forthright pronouncements about undeniably fundamental issues that most of them would have to admit they had never bothered to think about before. Some were offended that Hessen — a young man from a backward foreign country — should have attempted to dissipate the genius of Newton, the national scientific hero, in a series of sordid explanations about the requirements of transport, production, and warfare in the 'epoch of the rising bourgeoisie'. The industriousness of Hessen's scholarship, which none of them could rival, only aggravated the offence.

Others in the audience were more receptive. David Guest, the precocious undergraduate recently returned from Germany, just recruited to the Communist Party, was prompted by Hyman Levy to break the embarrassing silence by making a nervous speech about the history of mathematics, which he felt confirmed the conclusions of Bukharin and Hessen,[44] and in the coming days and months the other leaders of the scientific left — Hogben, Haldane, Levy, Bernal, Needham, and Crowther — were all, in their different ways, to realize that this Russian invasion had completely altered their views of science, philosophy, and politics.

5 British Marxist Scientists in the Thirties

Amongst the chaos of impressions left behind by the Russians'
visit to London, the one that went deepest in the minds of
the Marxist scientists was made by Hessen's address about
Newton. It became, in Bernal's words, 'the starting point of
a new evaluation of the history of science'. The chief point
was that it presented science as all tangled up with the
noisy needs and emergencies of everyday life, instead of a
languid and elegant aristocratic contemplation of Nature and
her Laws. Levy found that it made most existing work on
the history of science obsolete;[45] Crowther was inspired to
undertake a new interpretation of nineteenth-century British
science;[46] Needham criticized his own book on the history
of embryology and hoped that 'further historical research
will enable us to do for the great embryologists what has
been so well done by Hessen for Isaac Newton',[47] and in the
fifties became the dauntingly prolific historian of Chinese
science; Hogben launched his popular historical studies of
mathematics and science;[48] and Bernal eventually began
work on his *Science in History*.[49] The authors of this massive
new orientation towards the history of science all acknowledged the example given by Hessen's address to the London
Congress.

What none of the Marxist scientists seems to have realized,
was that the glimpse they had had of Russian philosophy of
science was deeply eccentric, even heretical. After all, the
leader of the delegation, and protector of the young Hessen,
was Nicolai Bukharin, the right-wing deviationist Kulaknik,
the supposed leader of 'mechanism' in philosophy, now
removed from his positions as editor of *Pravda* and Chief of
Comintern, though still active in the Academy of Sciences.[50]
The Marxism which he had offered the British had more in
common with old fashioned, Plekhanovite, evolutionary
historical materialism than with the newfangled 'Dialectical
Materialism' which was now the touchstone of Marxist-
Leninist orthodoxy in the Soviet Union. The only one of
the eleven addresses which took seriously the 'New Turn'
idea that the empirical sciences came under the jurisdiction
of Engels's three laws was Zavadovsky's — the one which
had been arranged before Bukharin's delegation had even

been thought of. This apart, *Science at the Crossroads* actually concealed Dialectical Materialism from British scientists.

Lancelot Hogben, in fact, wishfully believed that the Russian delegation at the Congress demonstrated that Communist thought had moved decisively away from 'metaphysics' and towards 'empiricism' and faith in the untrammelled autonomy of science. Russian Dialectical Materialism, as he now understood it, seemed to be an enormous reinforcement in his long and lonely battle against Joseph Dietzgen, whose 'textbooks of "proletarian philosophy"' were still being 'peddled in this country by Marxist propagandists who are not communists'. With gleeful optimism, but little accuracy, Hogben wrote:

To those who are familiar with the history of communist philosophy a not insignificant feature of Lenin's *Materialism and Empirio-Criticism* is that it laid quietly to rest the ghost of Joseph Dietzgen. It thus relieved communist philosophy of a spectre which had haunted it for half a century.

The Russian Dialectical Materialists, to judge by the London Congress, were now simply re-enacting the exorcism:

The philosophers of communism are busy repairing the breach between natural science and Marxist philosophy made by Dietzgen's writings....

Marx's true theoretical soul-mate, Hogben argued, was Darwin: if the *Origin of Species* had been written thirty years earlier, Marxism might never have tangled with Hegelianism at all. And it was solely because of the spurious sociology misnamed 'social Darwinism' that no intimate relationship had sprung up between Marxism and natural science. Hogben's only criticism of the Soviet Union's delegates at the Congress was their insularity: 'They did not seek to establish any rapprochement between the standpoint of dialectical materialism and the empirical temper of our own tradition', he said. Yet once this 'rapprochement' had been made, it would be easy to see that Marxism was essentially a bold step in the emancipation of empirical science from the 'yoke of scholastic philosophy', enabling 'the social sciences' to pass 'from the hands of the metaphysician to those of the expert'. So Hogben concluded that 'essentially the epistemology, or in the Russian terminology, the *dialectic* of communism is empiricist.'[51]

Before long, Clemens Dutt, on behalf of the Communist Party, shattered Hogben's ecumenical illusions. With plenty of menacing references to 'irreconcilable struggle' and what 'Lenin emphasised', Dutt denounced Hogben's love of science as absolutely incompatible with Dialectical Materialism.[52] On the authority of his acquaintance with Adoratsky and the Moscow line, he condemned Hogben for displaying 'the natural scientist's scorn of philosophy', and for neglecting the all-important battle with idealism:

In regard to this fundamental philosophical struggle, the viewpoint of dialectical materialism represents the class theory of the proletariat. It is a viewpoint which necessarily comes into conflict with the representatives of contemporary bourgeois science. . . . Bourgeois science and bourgeois philosophy represents an important prop of decaying capitalism, an instrument for sowing confusion and demoralisation, a basic ideological buttress for reaction.[53]

Forced by this rather hollow intimidation to choose between the achievements of science and those of Dialectical Materialism, Hogben did not hesitate — he permanently dumped the Communists and the philosophers in complete exasperation, and proclaimed what he had really been inclined to believe all along, that Dialectical Materialism was really no more than 'a confusion of terms'.[54]

The rest of the scientists, however, showed much more patience, and did their very best to combine what they learnt about the Dialectical Materialism of the New Turn from *Labour Monthly* with the beliefs they already held about science. Hyman Levy, for example, in a lecture delivered in May 1933, was cautious but quizzical, examining the new Dialectical Materialism rather like an old craftsman evaluating a new gadget. In the first place, Levy made it clear that he had no time for philosophical jargon. 'The almost medieval language' of Engels's three laws must be 'repellent to the scientific man', he said. 'The language in which the so-called laws of the Dialectic are framed is still precisely the phraseology which Marx and Engels themselves naturally took over from Hegel.' Levy suggested that the essence of the dialectical materialist philosophy was that it was 'developmental', 'historical', and 'practical', and offered his own word to make it scientifically precise as well: 'Isolates'. The world, according to Levy, consists of infinitely complex relations between processes. In order to understand it, however, we have to proceed by

separating out, in thought, certain partial processes — aspects such, for example, as society, the means of production, changing objects, words. These we will call Isolates. An isolate is something that has been dragged from its environment in space, time and matter. . . . Science is almost entirely concerned with the formation and discovery of useful isolates . . .

Dialectical Materialism, Levy thought, was the philosophy which reminded scientists of this fact about science.

As far as it went, this approach to science was not in conflict with Plekhanov or Dietzgen, Bukharin or Deborin, Rudas or Adoratsky, or indeed with most bourgeois philosophies of science. It came down to no more than a platitudinous, but not pointless, reminder that science involves not just a passive transcription of experience, but the active construction of theories or 'models' with which to arrange it artificially: it did not venture into the territory where different philosophies might seriously diverge. Consequently, in spite of his wish to be loyal, Levy effectively obscured the main point of the new Dialectical Materialism — the belief in the sovereignty of philosophical 'partisanship' over science. He fumblingly asserted that

the so-called laws of the dialectic, couched as they must be in very general terms, must have their principal application in the field of social and economic development. They appear to add little or nothing to the detailed methods of analysis that scientific workers have produced during the past century or so.

Levy concealed this unorthodoxy from himself by a small verbal evasion: science, he stated, must 'fit in' with Dialectical Materialism, and Dialectical Materialism could do no more than 'interpret' science:

Pure and applied science, technology, and all the social changes that have stimulated and been stimulated by them, must, however, fit into the philosophical outlook of Dialectical Materialism. For science, therefore, it is primarily an interpretative method rather than a method of detailed investigation.[55]

Over the next few years, Levy wrote several philosophical books, all designed to explain scientific thought for the benefit of the general public.[56] Although Clemens Dutt, guardian of Dialectical Materialism in Britain, was rather condescending towards Levy's propagation of 'a British approach to dialectical materialism that ignores what has been done by the great international contributors in this field',[57] his work was allowed to stand as a homespun vindication of Dialectical Materialism and hence of the policies of the Soviet Union which were reputedly derived from it.

Eventually, in 1957, after what was to be the last of his visists to the Soviet Union, Levy became convinced that he could no longer dismiss charges of anti-Semitism as anti-communist propaganda.[58] The revelation brought him to the verge of complete mental breakdown. Lawrence Daly, who knew him at the time, recalls that he was 'shattered . . . in a very bad state . . . he was going through a deep emotional crisis'.[59] It is hardly surprising that this should have been so: he was sixty-seven years old, and recently retired; his father had been a Russian Jew; he had been in the Party since 1930; and he had been loyally defending the party by means of philosophical arguments whose inconclusiveness and gappiness he could not now deny, nor even wish to conceal. A lifetime's selfless work was ruined.

Other scientists were no less trusting than Levy, if rather less thoughtful. J. D. Bernal, in an evangelical lecture following Levy's explanation of his philosophy of isolates, tried to bear witness to the revelation that 'it is only in revolution and revolutionary activity that Dialectical Materialism can really be understood' (which, in consistency, ought perhaps to have been taken as an oblique admission that he didn't understand it himself). Certainly he fudged the basic issue, and was unwilling to give unambiguous support to Dialectical Materialism's claim to authority over the sciences. He affirmed, on the contrary, that 'Dialectical Method can be derived from that cooperative struggle with the material world which we call science'and warned, evasively, that 'Dialectical Materialism is not a formula to be applied blindly either in the natural or human world.'[60]

One reason for the extraordinary imprecision of these scientific enthusiasts of Dialectical Materialism, and their unreceptiveness to Clemens Dutt's repeated reminders that Dialectical Materialism claimed to be superior to 'bourgeois science', was their innocence about the inveterate opposition of Dialectical Materialism both to Deborin's alleged impracticality and to Bukharin's reverence for science. They continued, through Crowther, to maintain friendly relations with Bukharin, and to mistake his views for orthodox Dialectical Materialism. In fact, when Crowther visited Bukharin in 1934, in his office at *Isvestiya,* of which he was now editor, he was advised to arrange for the translation of a book of essays which had just been published by the Academy of Sciences to commemorate the fiftieth anniversary of Marx's death. Ralph Fox's translations appeared in 1935: the two leading articles were by Academicians Bukharin and Deborin respectively[61] — that is, by the leaders of the 'deviations', to left and to right, which Dialectical Materialism was intended to destroy.

By 1936, however, the truth about Dialectical Materialism was beginning to filter through. Crowther gave a fair and scrupulously non-committal account of it in a book on Soviet Science which came out in 1936,[62] and Bernal, writing in a new American Marxist quarterly, significantly entitled *Science and Society,* began to claim that Dialectical Materialism was a positive guide for scientific inquiry — 'indicative', as he put it, and 'not merely critical'.[63]

The last and biggest convert to New Turn Dialectical Materialism amongst the British scientists was J. B. S. Haldane. His regular visits to Russia from 1928 on, and his friendship with top biologists there, had made him vaguely interested in Marxism, and in 'the prevalence of this philosophy in the Soviet Union, and the successful attempts which were being made to apply it in different fields, including my own field of biology'. He even discussed the matter with his uncle, the Hegelian Labour Government Minister, just before the latter's death in 1928. Lord Haldane had, it seems, warmed to the Hegelianism of it, though he was distressed by its materialism.[64] In spite of this encouragement, J. B. S. Haldane pursued his highly satisfactory career as University Professor, amusingly impudent broadcaster, and Fellow of the Royal Society for nearly a decade, without paying much attention to Dialectical Materialism; in fact it was not till 1936 or 1937 that he began to call himself 'a Marxist'.[65] His conversion was due to the facts that he found the Communists hospitable to his view of science (he began to write a science column for the *Daily Worker*) and alone in recognizing and fighting the menace of Fascism, particularly in Spain. Also, he got on well with Harry Pollitt. Haldane concluded that the Communists and the Soviet Union must be on to something in the field of 'philosophy'. ('As a result of my scientific and political experience, I had to accept Marxism as the best available philosophy. . . . The Marxist Philosophy is called dialectical materialism.'[66]) As he told students at Birmingham University at the beginning of 1938, most people didn't even know of the existence of 'Marxist philosophy'. Haldane struck out energetically to annihilate this ignorance.[67] The classic texts of Marxist philosphy, for him, were Engels's *Ludwig Feuer-bach, Anti-Dühring,* and *Dialectics of Nature,* with Lenin's *Materialism and Empirio-Criticism.*[68] With this equipment, Haldane began to evangelize for the tabloid philosophy of the New Turn. His expositions were always arranged under three headings — Theory and Practice, Materialism, and Dialectics. Of theory and practice, he preached that they were in 'unity', but with 'the primacy of practice' — which he seems to have interpreted chiefly as a warning against impractical, academic ratiocination;[69] materialism he defined as 'the acknowledge-ment of the temporal priority of matter over mind and the belief that there are unperceived events';[70] dialectics consisted of Engels's three laws, conceived as applying uniformly to all kinds of events and processes[71] — biological, cosmological, physical, mathematical, etc. As applied to society, they yielded 'historical materialism', of which the basic text was Engels's *Origin of the Family.*[72]

In the twenties, Haldane had liked the prospect of the Soviet Union as a 'scientific state', whose citizens would relish science and respect scientists.[73] Now, his enthusiasm was redirected towards philosophy and philosophers, and he became an advocate of what might be called 'philosophism'. Philosophy, he declared in 1938, was 'a subject of very general interest in the USSR'. ('Plato said that the ideal state was only possible when a philosopher became a king. Lenin was, amongst other things, a philosopher.'[74]) The new Russia, as Haldane now saw it, would have delighted his deceased Hegelian-politician uncle, or his scientific-deist father, both of whom had deplored the young Haldane's impatience with philosophy, and his belief in the self-sufficiency of science. Haldane now proclaimed the deposition of science by philosophy within the field of the his own special scientific expertise, evolutionary genetics. His first 'dialectical materialist' publication began with an 'apology' which was really a rather boastful conceit: being written behind enemy lines in Spain (Haldane was there on a brief visit) it was composed without benefit of reference books, except Lenin. And, after some pious remarks about 'theory' and 'practice', Haldane then asserted, at considerable length, that the theory of evolution was somehow implicit in Dialectical Materialism, from which it was possible to deduce 'mutation' as the 'antithesis' of 'heredity', and 'variation' as the 'synthesis' of the two; and similarly with selection, variation, and evolution. [75]

Whatever Haldane may have achieved in unifying 'theory' and 'practice', this performance leaves some doubt as to his ability to unify theory and theory. Adapting an argument of Maurice Dobb's, the economist A. P. Lerner claimed that Haldane's apposition of dialectics and evolution was only a literary artifice:

in his scheme dialectics is used not as a weapon or method of scientific research or discovery — as is usually claimed for it — but merely as a kind of pigeon-hole into which, with much ingenuity (and a little pressure) he fits biological principles discovered by scientists who were in the main quite innocent of dialectics. [76]

It was a very good point, and Haldane realized that if he conceded it then all his claims for philosophy and Dialectical Materialism would collapse. The only way to defend his new attitude to philosophy would have been by deducing some valid new science from the principles of Dialectical Materialism and showing that it could not have been arrived at otherwise. But all he did was to offer some lame anecdotes from personal experience, rather like testimonials to a patent medicine, to the effect that since he had started reading Engels and Lenin, his ability to solve scientific problems had improved miraculously. [77]

Haldane's conversion to Dialectical Materialism led him into loyal work for the Communist Party, particularly during the embarrassing period from September 1939 to June 1941, when the Soviet Union and Comintern were trying to remain neutral in the war against Fascism. Haldane supported the banned *Daily Worker* by serving as chairman of its board in 1940; two years later he joined the Party, and two years after that, he was on its Executive Committee.[78] In 1948, however, he became intolerably embarrassed by the action of the Soviet Academy of Sciences in closing an unfinished debate on genetics (in which Haldane himself was interested) by means of an appeal to the authority of Dialectical Materialism. This case — the 'Lysenko affair' — cost Haldane his faith in Dialectical Materialism and the Soviet Union; and he slowly extricated himself from the Party — a painful separation completed only in 1956 — bewildered, disappointed, and, so he felt, obscurely betrayed.[79]

Haldane's general view of science — as the practical attempt by social individuals to improve the available concepts of the real world — had not been altogether insubstantial, especially at a time when it was fashionable to believe that science dealt with 'sensations' or 'perceptions' rather than with reality itself. But, as a Marxist, Haldane had pinned his hopes on doing much more — deriving Marxist scientific results from 'Dialectical Materialism' and demonstrating the gap which separated these from the undialectical science promoted by the ruling classes of the West — and in these attempts, he had failed utterly. The robustness of his belief in Dialectical Materialism, following his tardy conversion to it in 1937, coexisted with a complete inability to give theoretical arguments in its defence; and the more plausibly he elaborated it, the less definite and exclusive it became. In a characteristically excellent phrase, he had written that 'Marxists are the only intelligent people who preserve their grandparents' belief in progress';[80] and as the years passed by, it became clearer and clearer that his own philosophy, though nominally revolutionary, was actually quite similar to the reformist Hegelianism of his late uncle, and to the scientific deism of his late father. (There was an inevitable suspicion of a kind of Oedipal plagiarism, especially as Joseph Needham's respectful obituary of J. S. Haldane in 1936 — which argued that J. S.'s pre-war philosophy of biology was, essentially, identical with Dialectical Materialism — appeared alongside an article in which J. B. S.

claimed personal credit for pioneering the application of Dialectical Materialism to biology, a quarter of a century later; and his father's ashes scarcely yet dispersed in the ancestral highlands home![81]) J. B. S. Haldane sometimes recognized the family affinities of his views;[82] and although the likeness may be wholly to the credit of his own philosophy, or, conversely, of theirs, it certainly casts doubt on the supposed revolutionary proletarian partisanship of his 'Dialectical Materialism'.

Chapter 6

Dialectical Materialism and the Philosophers

1 The Embarrassment of the Professionals

When the Marxist scientists fixed the seal of their professional approval on the philosophy of Dialectical Materialism, they must sometimes have felt a twinge of queasy discomfort. They could not be unaware that they were, as Haldane put it, 'trespassing on the professional philosopher's ground';[1] but yet, the philosophers themselves — the hundreds of teachers and researchers in the philosophy departments of Universities — seemed completely indifferent to the intrusion. The scientists rushed in to offer a helping hand to their philosophical colleagues, some of whom, at least, they expected to find toiling over Dialectical Materialism in the great philosophical engine-room of Revolution; but the place was quite deserted, and filled with an eerie quietness. And this could hardly be put down to the unproletarian class position of the philosophers, since the scientists themselves were at least as handicapped in this respect.

If it was disconcerting to the scientists, it was painfully embarrassing to the philosophers, puzzling away at rather abstruse problems in the privacy of their studies, whilst outside a clamour went up about the urgency of rallying to dialectics and materialism in a philosophical defence of Communism. To the professionals who were devoting their lives to it, philosophy might be compelling, perhaps the finest distillation of the entirety of human intellectual effort; but even if they sympathized with the Soviet Union, it still seemed to them an implausible flattery to nominate their own discipline as the vengeful sharp sword of Revolution. Notoriously, the philosophers found the great philosophical traditions which they had inherited deeply perplexing, constantly trapping those unwary enough to seek simple, or profound, or clear-cut answers. They saw themselves not as evangelists of philosophical enlightenment, but as shy acolytes of meticulous technique, dazzled by the awful elusiveness of any philosophical conviction at all.

To the professionals, the points which the exuberant amateurs were taking up — dialectics versus metaphysics, materialism versus idealism, theory and practice — were neither clear nor particularly interesting, and certainly did not provide the only (let alone 'eternal', as Engels would have it) way of looking at philosophy. To them, it was much more important to cultivate a certain philosophical agility and suppleness of mind, than to 'take sides' on a predetermined roster of points of philosophical doctrine. Moreover, it must have seemed mere impudence to encourage people to enlist for 'materialism' and 'dialectics' when they hadn't even opened any of the great volumes, let alone engaged in any of the elaborate discussions, in which, if anywhere, such terms were quickened with meaning.

There was another embarrassment too. Whilst the Dialectical Materialists flared with gallant declarations of respect for Philosophy, they persistently insulted it with quite horrifying solecisms. For instance, they assumed, gratuitously, that political differences were always rooted in philosophical ones: it was a point that might perhaps be demonstrable in particular cases, but which could hardly be assumed to be valid across the board. And, as Bertrand Russell had observed in his book on Bolshevism back in 1920, 'the mixture damages both philosophy and politics'. ('Political theories are both supported and opposed for quite irrelevant reasons, and arguments of theoretical philosophy are used to determine questions which depend upon concrete facts of human nature', he wrote.) Russell mentioned, in particular, the confusion of philosophical materialism (the doctrine that nothing exists except matter) with historical materialism (the belief in the fundamental role of production in human history): in truth, as he pointed out, there was 'no logical connection either way' between the two.[2] And if it was drudgery to go over such distinctions with each year's new batch of opinionated or obtuse students, it was much worse when, by the end of the thirties, the same mistakes were being magisterially propagated by Fellows of the Royal

Society and occupants of some of the most dignified scientific chairs in the land. When, in 1938, Hyman Levy's concept of 'Isolates' was presented to members of the Left Book Club under the title *A Philosophy for a Modern Man,* and Harold Laski claimed that the book showed how it was 'rationally possible to look upon the universe in a way that validates the philosophy of the Left', Bertrand Russell could not repress his impatience at such quackery — 'the mutterings of the pale ghost of Hegel' — masquerading as professional philosophy;[3] and Susan Stebbing, Professor of Philosophy at London University, took the trouble to deliver Levy a condescending but not unwarranted lesson about the importance of linguistic fastidiousness in philosophical prose.[4]

The professional philosophers could add several more to Russell's and Stebbing's complaints about the Communists' exaggerated faith in the power of philosophy, their amateurishness, and their confusion of historical and philosophical materialism. For instance: Lenin's arguments against empiriocriticism are, at most, a vindication of philosophical realism, and it is a mere misnomer to associate them with 'materialism';[5] again, 'dialectics' had been devised as a way of conceptualizing the self-fulfilling activity of 'spirit' (Hegel) or of 'Humanity' (the young Marx), never of matter in itself, so Engels's three laws, whatever their status (and the scientists had thoroughly muddied this question), scarcely deserved to be called 'dialectical';[6] thirdly, it was very doubtful whether any sound theoretical basis could be found for the distinction between 'antagonistic' and 'non-antagonistic' contradictions;[7] and finally, the doctrine of the 'unity of theory and practice', if it was to be worthy of philosophical consideration at all, could not be interpreted as a norm which 'revisionists' should be blamed for flouting, but would have to be taken as implying that the theoretical and practical aspects of human activities, of whatever political tendency, could never be separated from each other anyway.[8] The validity of such criticisms was hardly deniable, even if it might be argued that Dialectical Materialism could be reformulated so as to survive them. The interesting point is how reluctant the philosophers were to give them voice, let alone to insist upon them. They mumbled their criticisms to themselves, as if they hoped not to be noticed.

One reason for the philosophers' reticence had to do with the changes which had recently overtaken their profession and their discipline. Fifty years before, it might have been generally agreed that philosophy was no less than a brave effort to 'see things as a whole', and that, therefore, nothing in human knowledge was alien to it: it was not one of the special sectors of knowledge, but the complete circuit of them all. And in the hands of 'Hegelians' like T. H. Green, (who really owed as much to Plato as to Hegel) this conception led, it may be remembered,[9] to the zealous conviction that one could not be fully a citizen, participating in the life of the community — let alone a politician, guiding it in the corporate interest — unless one was inspired with philosophical culture.

This inclusive notion of philosophy was not at home within the new educational organizations that grew up after 1870; in Universities organized into separate but equal departments offering specialized courses, no discipline could lightly claim jurisdiction over any other. At the same time, the younger generation of philosophers, in England and America, like Russell, Moore, and Perry, found theoretical faults in the free-wheeling style and the idealistic arguments of their 'Hegelian' masters, and repudiated the affiliation of philosophy with public affairs. Both intellectually and institutionally, then, the Golden Age of grand philosophizing had closed, and the new professionals looked back on its pretensions with a combination of perplexity and regret, and set about constructing a new discipline, which would compensate in rigour for what it had forsaken in scope.[10] For many of them, such as Stebbing, philosophy became little more, indeed, than linguistic continence, practised to avoid the illegitimate and unwanted 'metaphysical' conceptions which had over-populated the nineteenth-century philosophical world. 'Whatever else a philosopher should do, he must surely learn to avoid talking in abstractions', she declared, probably unaware of how perverse and astonishing this ruling would seem to anyone unacquainted with recent changes in the philosophical profession. Hyman Levy, she concluded, 'is utterly mistaken with regard to the nature of philosophical thinking, and is wedded to an outworn conception of metaphysical reality'.[11] As far as the professionals were concerned,

Dialectical Materialism and 'Marxist Philosophy' were throw-backs to the bad old days of 'Platonism' and 'Hegelianism', which had now been left behind by the progress of the discipline.

2 The Philosophers' Overtures

There were some British philosophers, however — such as Joseph and Lindsay — who harked back to the Grand Style, and who were prepared, in the teens and twenties, to lecture and write about Marx's economics, or even his transformation of Hegel's Dialectic.[12] In the United States, the twentieth-century survival of the old conception of philosophy was represented by John Dewey, and it was his brilliant pupil Sidney Hook who, in 1928, at the age of twenty-six, first tried to draw the attention of English-reading professional philosophers to 'dialectical materialism'. He called upon his 'incredulous' colleagues to look to the example of the Russian revolution, where philosophy had a prestige and influence it had now lost elsewhere:

I know of no more impressive evidence in recent times of the *power* and *importance* of the philosophic *idea* as such, than the political and social history of Russia from 1875 down to the present day. . . . One might well say that the Russian revolution of November 1917 was due in part to Lenin's belief that Marxism must be interpreted as a voluntaristic humanism rather than as the teleological fatalism embraced by Social-Democrats everywhere else.

Drawing on a wide and perceptive reading of the recent Russian editions of Marx's formerly little-known early works — the *Critique of Hegel's 'Philosophy of Right'*, the *Holy Family,* and especially Part One of the *German Ideology* ('the most important single source') — Hook argued that Marxism ought to be accorded an honoured place, not just in the annals of socialism, but in the pantheon of 'technical philosophy' too. He constructed a definition of knowledge in terms of people's active and practical relations to the physical world, and attributed it, quite plausibly, to the young Marx and thence to 'Marxism' as a whole. Unde-terred by the cumbrous multiplication of philosophical 'isms', he described this 'dialectical materialism' as an 'emergent naturalism' involving a 'striking anticipation of the *instrumentalist* [i.e. Dewey's] theory of knowledge', and found that it was also really identical with Roy Wood Sellars's 'critical evolutionary naturalism'. Dialectical materialism, Hook concluded, was in fact 'a philosophy held under other names by many who disavow political interests altogether'.[13]

In 1928, Sidney Hook smoothed over the philosophical differences between the young Marx, the mature Marx, Engels, and Lenin (though he criticized the latter's carelessness), considering that they could all be combined as 'dialectical materialism', which was 'the philosophic expression' of 'modern socialism', and which stood opposed to the 'fatalism' of Social-Democracy. Soon, however, in working on two books on the young Marx, Hook became aware of fissures within this edifice. In the spring of 1929 he met Karl Korsch in Berlin and attended his lectures there, and in the summer, as he explored the archives of Riazanov's Marx-Engels Institute in Moscow, it was borne in on him that Soviet Communism, though 'avowedly Marxist in inspiration', might not conform to the doctrines which he thought he had discovered in Marx's own writings.

In 1933, Hook — now a Professor at New York University — defined himself as 'not . . . an "orthodox" Marxist' (a trait which he believed he shared with Marx), and he went out of his way to express his gratitude for the attention given to dialectic and human activity in Lukacs's *History and Class Consciousness* and Korsch's *Marxism and Philosophy,* which had of course been condemned by Comintern several years before.[14] Then, in the name of anti-Fascism, workers' democracy, and 'the principles of Marxism', Hook published several articles criticizing the policies of Comintern, and especially the pretence that these arose from a coherent philosophy of 'dialectical materialism' — 'the tissue of absurdities that Mr Rudas and others [are] attempting to palm off on the world as the "official" state philosophy of Russia'. Sarcastically but efficiently demolishing Rudas's works, Hook concluded that the 'whole philosophy of Marxism' was being

made ridiculous by a person who lacks the slightest qualification to open his mouth on any philosophical subject. . . . Mr Rudas is simply practising a fraud on the workers who are subsidising him. Instead of his charlatanries being exposed for what they are, he is sent forth to expound them to the English-speaking world with the official sanction of the Third International. Explain it who can![15]

Hook's criticisms of Rudas had little circulation and less influence in Britain, where only Rudas's side of the argument was published.[16] And before long, Hook ceased to regard 'the orthodox brand of dialectical materialism as represented by Mr Rudas' as a distortion of a still salvageable truth. In his second book on Marx, in 1936, he made a point of acknowledging his debt to Riazanov 'whose recent death in a Russian concentration camp was a heavy blow to Marxian scholarship'.[17] Subsequently, Hook worked on technical philosophical questions, and turned completely against the idea of dialectical materialism, which, he concluded in 1955, was an enemy to rational enquiry and whose practical implications had become 'apparent in all their enormity under the régime of Stalin'.[18] Even so, he remained loyal to some of his early enthusiasm for the young Marx, regarding his own 'experimental naturalism' as 'a continuation of what is soundest and most fruitful in Marx's philosophical outlook upon the world'.[19]

In the period of the popular front against Fascism, a number of British philosophers, all more or less nostalgic for the former glory of their discipline, began to cast longing glances towards Russia, hoping to find there a society with a sense of purpose — with a philosophy, in the grand old sense, to live by: a philosophy which, they hoped, might somehow supply the deficiencies they suspected in modern Christianity. So in 1933, John MacMurray, Grote Professor of the Philosophy of Mind and Logic in the University of London, wrote admiringly, not of Dialectical Materialism, but of 'the Philosophy of Communism', which he saw as chiefly Hegelian, and as based on the affirmation of freedom. Communism, to MacMurray, was 'the necessary basis of real freedom'.[20] His conviction that the Communist Movement was based on this benign, post-Christian philosophy was reinforced by his friendship with Julius Hecker, a Russian-born philosopher educated in America who had returned to Russia after the revolution to become a teacher at Moscow University, but who had remained, in MacMurray's words, 'a patently Christian character'. In 1933, MacMurray organized the English publication of Hecker's *Moscow Dialogues* — a long discussion, in dialogue form, of the 'philosophy' behind the Russian revolution. Hecker argued that this 'philosophy' was implicit in Lenin, although no one had yet spelt it out, and whilst expounding with approval the philosophers of the New Turn — favouring especially their insistence that philosophy 'must not only be independent of natural science, but must also lead it on to new discoveries' — Hecker also referred lavishly to its roots in nineteenth-century Russian philosophy, and in European philosophy from Spinoza to Feuerbach.[21] In a later essay, Hecker described the role of Christian churches in the Soviet Union and cheerfully claimed that all that was best in Christianity was about to find 'a new life in the ascending Communist spiritual culture'.[22]

MacMurray's bland Christian Communism led to the formulation, in 1933, of a plan for a collection of essays by Christians and Communists exploring any philosophical ground which they might hold in common. The unwieldy project was eventually brought to a successful conclusion by a lecturer in Social Philosophy in the Extramural Department of Cambridge University — a Christian, a Plebs-Leaguer, and enthusiast for the Boy Scout movement named John Lewis.[23] He professed himself astonished, at first, to find that Communism had a spiritual purposefulness which Christianity all too often lacked, and he wrote an agitated essay on 'Communism the heir to Christian tradition', in which he claimed that 'We live in the apocalyptic times foretold by the New Testament, the Day of the coming of the Son of Man. Religion is faced with the alternatives of fulfilment or apostasy. Fulfilment means the carrying over into Communism of the age-long struggle to sanctify the common life and concretise the Divine ideal.' If reactionaries were smug enough to argue that 'Communism is not a religion at all', then so much the worse for their religion:

If it is no longer the gospel of the Kingdom, it is wholly of the decadence, it is world-denial, delusion, and the cult of death, 'the opium of the people'. It may well be that the time has come for religion to dissolve like an insubstantial dream and leave not a wrack behind, dying to be born again as the Holy Spirit of a righteous social order.[24]

Shortly afterwards, Lewis became secretary of the Left Book Club, and his anthology was reissued in a Club edition in 1937, with a new preface in which Lewis, appalled by the prospect of the Pope backing Fascism and Nazism in an anti-Red alliance, issued a 'plea for a united front' between Communists and the Church.[25] By this time, Lewis had begun to phrase his arguments more in terms of his profession as a philosopher than of his vocation as a preacher, producing a thorough historical introduction to the Left Book Club's translation of a Russian textbook on dialectical materialism, continuing to present this doctrine as the culmination of the whole historical development of philosophy, and relishing the prospect of a philosophical state, just as T. H. Green would have done. 'If rulers must be philosophers that means that in a State where the workers rule the workers must themselves be philosophers. . . . This is why [in the Soviet Union] thorough training in dialectical materialism is universal.'[26] John Lewis shortly became a member of the British Communist Party, and was later to become its leading philosophical authority.

John Lewis's philosophical path to the Communist Party was, however, one which he trod almost alone. A far more typical, indeed emblematic, experience was that of E. F. Carritt, a mild and rather unpolitical philosophy don at University College, Oxford, and a devotee of the collegiate and tutorial systems as the begetters of true philosophy. He was also, however, attracted by socialism and the Soviet Union, and in the early thirties he began to investigate the 'philosophy' that was supposed to lie behind them — though, as it happens, he relied on somewhat out-of-date sources — Plekhanov, the young Lenin, Bukharin, Deborin, and Riazanov. He treated their project as a serious and intelligent attack on the problem of the relations between matter and organism, and praised Bukharin for his particularly sensitive handling of the concept of 'dialectical moments'. But he concluded that, as philosophers of nature, the Dialectical Materialists had only stated the problem, without actually solving it:

The temptation is to rest satisfied with a couple of words each of which states one side of the apparent contradiction, and to suppose that we have thus solved it. Matter is what is not conscious or even organic, dialectical is what behaves as organised (and especially as conscious) beings do. The two words are really thesis and antithesis requiring a higher synthesis than mere juxtaposition.

And while Carritt was tentative, even pedantic, in weighing the philosophical virtues of Dialectical Materialism, he was intransigently sceptical about the claims made for its relevance to Communism or to any kind of politics. He was baffled and not a little plaintive:

> Finding myself in sympathy with the objective of Communists (though not usually with their strategy or tactics) I am disturbed to hear both from many Communists and from many of their bitterest opponents, that Communism is inseparable from a philosophy which I find it hard to understand and, so far as I understand it, impossible on philosophical grounds to accept.

And after close consideration, he said, he was still unable to detect 'any inconsistency in being a Communist without being a dialectical materialist or a dialectical materialist without being a Communist'.[27]

Carritt presented these conclusions as a series of University lectures in Oxford in the summer of 1933; and although the lecture title — 'Dialectical Materialism' — caused the Waynflete Professor of Metaphysical Philosophy, J. A. Smith, to expostulate with Carritt for having 'invented such a fancy title which nobody had ever heard of', the lectures brought Carritt the largest audience he ever had, overflowing the Hall of his College.[28] The substance of the lectures was even printed in *Labour Monthly* — as a 'discussion article', though, and with the promise that Carritt's errors would be demonstrated in due course.

3 The Rebuff

So Carritt now became — rather to his surprise — the British philosophical expert on Dialectical Materialism, and before long found himself drawn into debates of a kind for which his forty years in Oxford had ill prepared him. Hyman Levy prevailed on him to discuss the virtues of Dialectical Materialism with J. D. Bernal, under the chairmanship of J. B. S. Haldane, in a symposium organized by the Society for Cultural Relations in London in February 1934.[29] Bernal, a fine public performer, spoke first, offering a great profusion of sage remarks about 'the permanent impossibility of separating compromise in ideology from compromise in politics', and about the conspiracy of priests and philosophers with the ruling classes of all ages to separate pure thought from real action, in defiance of the dialectical 'unity of theory and practice' which proved, Bernal claimed, that 'it is always a sign of misunderstanding and of leaning towards reaction when critics and revisionists wish to separate the Dialectical Materialism of Marx from his political programme'.[30] Carritt's response was feeble in everything except philosophical intelligence. 'It is impossible to say without qualification whether one accepts Dialectical Materialism or not', he began with unblushing donnishness, going on to say that there were numerous versions of dialectical materialism, none of which — he had to confess — he could fully understand. (But Sidney Hook's *Towards an Understanding of Karl Marx,* which had just come out, was 'a more patient and lucid attempt to expound Marxism than any previously published', said Carritt — 'though I understand he is considered a Trotskyite'.)[31] He listed fifteen philosophical propositions which he thought might belong to dialectical materialism and which might, in his professional opinion, be true; then he ran rings round Bernal (and he brought in Levy and MacMurray too) for their fraudulent trade in the ambiguous slogan 'the unity of theory and practice'; next, he showed that those who claimed that 'dialectics' was necessary because 'traditional logic' could not explain change, merely demonstrated their own ignorance of elementary logical theory; finally, he argued that dialectical materialism had nothing in common with the materialist conception of history except a name. Bernal replied to Carritt's arguments with uncomprehending self-confidence, rhetorically wiping the floor with his philosophical opponent.[32] Edward Conze, the German-trained philosopher who was now preparing a Labour College correspondence course on philosophy, though critical of Carritt for being poorly informed about the claims currently advanced by dialectical materialists (hardly surprising, given the sources Carritt had used) agreed that Carritt might be philosophically in the right.[33]

The philosophers' serenades to 'the philosophy guiding the practice of Modern Russia'[34] were thus not receiving a very encouraging hearing. And later in the series, Ralph Fox — apparently forgetting about his own Oxford University education — gloated over the prospect that the Russian revolution would replace the bespectacled bourgeois book-worms of the University with muscular proletarians:

> The socialist society growing up in the USSR is the revolutionary creation of the working class, not the abstract 'experiment' of a dictatorship of the chosen few in horn-rimmed spectacles. . . . Hundreds of thousands of fitters, foundry-men, turners, locomotive drivers, miners, train-conductors, agricultural labourers, simple shepherds, have made this revolution, and are building the new society, filling its leading places. . . . The theoretical leader and organiser of the literary forces of the USSR is the young director of the Institute of Philosophy in the Communist Academy, Paul Yudin, a Communist. He is by origin a turner in a railway machine shop, became a soldier in the Red Army, and is now a professional philosopher, literary critic and an arctic explorer, as well as an active member of the Moscow Committee of the Communist Party. He represents, we must admit, a quite different type of philosopher from Professor MacMurray.[35]

For less atheticist responses to the philosophers, the British Party had already referred their writings to Moscow — not, indeed, to Yudin, who does not seem to have found much time for philosophy, but to the 'man-eating' Laszlo Rudas.[36] Rudas's first article — which I have already noted as the first full exposition in English of the 'New Turn' — was designed as a denunciation of Carritt. Rudas asserted that 'everyone who merely casts a glance at Marx's works can see' that Marx's social theory depends on Dialectical Materialism: but he also said, rather inconsistently, that

> The pre-requisite for understanding dialectical materialism is a decisive break with the traditional mode of thought, the *revolutionising of thinking,* and also sooner or later enrolment in the ranks of the revolutionary party. . . . Dialectical materialism is only recognised and expounded by Marxist Revolutionaries. . . . If now Mr Carritt reproaches us with recognising only the expositions of Marx, Engels, and Lenin as unexceptionable . . . then every sensible man will see that . . . Communists could not do otherwise without doing the greatest damage to the revolutionary movement by blunting precisely the sharpest weapon of revolutionary struggle. . . .

The philosophy of Dialectical Materialism, Rudas concluded contemptuously, as 'our sharpest weapon in the struggle for the liberation of the proletariat', could obviously 'neither be measured by the standard of the schools nor understood by them.'[37] In the same issue of *Labour Monthly*, Communists were warned against Hecker's *Moscow Dialogues,* in a review which observed that 'many bourgeois thinkers are coming over to the revolutionary programme, many are writing books about philosophy', and which concluded that, in the circumstances, 'we must . . . conduct an even sharper struggle to show that no bourgeois influences enter our philosophy . . .'.[38] A year later, Rudas raised his hefty philosophical 'weapon' to slay Conze, following a (rather favourable, as it happens) two-paragraph notice which Conze had given to Rudas in *The Plebs.* Conze had called for 'deeper analysis', and this, Rudas noted with italicized consternation, was just a euphemism for '*the revision of the teaching of Marx, Engels and Lenin*'. Challenged by Conze to explain the philosophical distinction between antagonistic and non-antagonistic contradiction, Rudas frothed that it was obvious that while contradictions would persist under communism, antagonism would not, and drew attention to 'the *practice of the Soviet Union* where this development can already be observed'.[39]

Conze's reply expressed astonishment at 'the sterility of philosophical research in the Soviet Union', in spite of the large resources at its disposal: 'If Mr Rudas demands self-criticism he might begin to think about the causes of the unsatisfactory state of dialectical materialism in the Soviet Union which is, visible to everybody, reflected in the insecurity of the Western socialists in the question of dialectics.'[40] Rudas refused to be drawn into this discussion,[41] but in response to Sidney Hook's quite convincing demonstration that he was a 'philosophical illiterate' he took up his 'sharp weapon' once more, fulminating about the impossibility of being a dialectical materialist outside the Communist Party, and even quoting Marx as a kind of clairvoyant support.

However, in the end, Rudas let up. The Communist Party, he said smilingly, was not too severe in matters of philosophy:

The fact that even though a leading theoretician of the rank of Comrade Bukharin was a mechanical materialist, he was in no way prevented from continuing in the party shows that the hypocritical lamentations of Mr Hook about the 'ruthless censorship' in the Communist Party are nothing else than — a ruthless calumny.[42]

Bukharin was in fact arrested, tried, and shot in 1938.

That same year, work was completed on an official history of the Russian Communist Party, designed to be used for educational and propaganda purposes throughout the International Communist Movement. Nominally, it was written by Stalin, but it is said[43] that Stalin was personally responsible only for a single brief chapter — the crucial chapter, though — the one which explained the philosophy of Communism, the 'world outlook of the Marxist-Leninist Party': Dialectical Materialism. In it, Stalin gave a brisk four-point summary of the dialectical (as opposed to metaphysical) 'method' (nature is not an agglomeration, it is not static, or smooth, or harmonious) and a three-point summary of the materialistic (as opposed to idealistic) 'interpretation of phenomena' (the world is material, matter is primary, and nature is knowable). This exposition (which occupied, in any case, less than three thousand words) could do nothing to allay the doubts of professional philosophers, but Stalin was unhesitating in drawing practical lessons from this philosophy by 'applying' it to history and politics. The dialectical method, he found, proved a whole range of points which must be followed 'in order not to err in policy'. It showed that nothing lasts for ever, and that therefore 'in order not to err in policy, one must look forward, not backward', which meant that 'in order not to err in policy, one must pursue an uncompromising proletarian class policy', because the proletariat is the class of the future, and that 'in order not to err in policy, one must be a revolutionary, not a reformist'. And materialism, Stalin then found, implied that society was governed by laws which could be the object of 'as precise a science as, let us say, biology', so that 'in order not to err in policy, in order not to find itself in the position of idle dreamers, the party of the proletariat must not base its activities on abstract "principles of human reason", but on the concrete conditions of the material life of society'.[44]

Thus briefly, in the first, smaller, part of his short chapter, did Stalin summarize the Dialectical Materialism with which the proletarian radicals had initiated the New Turn ten years before.[45] It boiled down to very few pages; and an intellectual mess. It did not occur to Stalin that the seven philosophical theses he had collected might be an incoherent jumble, for all that three of them were associated with the word 'materialism' and the rest with the word 'dialectic'; he did not perceive the paradox of seeking revolutionary policy orientations by teasing out the meanings of the two worn-out words, 'dialectical' and 'materialism', used to designate some traditional categories of Western philosophy; and he made no attempt to give arguments in support of his theses, or to confront any of the difficulties people might have in understanding or accepting them. Nor, finally, did he explain how any of the seven points of Dialectical Materialism could guide policy: even if dialectics were proved correct in seeing change as the outcome of a struggle of the old with the new, this would not make it absolutely irrational to side with the old; and if it were demonstrated that dialectics was right to say that quantitative changes lead to revolutionary rupture, that could be an argument for reform as much as for revolution — and so on right through this pitiful chapter. Its incompetence is equalled only by its self-confidence. It is hard to know where to begin a critical assessment, hard not to wonder whether it is not one's own fault if one finds it incomprehensible. It is easiest to accept it in silence, and hope never to be asked searching questions. The silence of incomprehension, which sounds very like the silence of unshakeable conviction, was almost the only possible response to this remarkable piece of prose.

Stalin's *History of the CPSU (B)* was soon translated into all the main languages of the world; and, distributed in extremely cheap editions, it became the basic text of Communist education in the 1940s. Its few pages on Dialectical Materialism were by far the most eagerly awaited philosophical statement ever, and undoubtedly the most widely published, at least until the promotion of the philosophy of Mao during the Chinese Cultural Revolution. They were often issued as a separate pamphlet and, in Britain at least, they became the only pretext for philosophical discussion amongst Communists.[46] They may have been sternly, plentifully, and unyieldingly incomprehensible, but they capped the whole argument which had shuttled back and forth amongst the autodidacts and the Dietzgenites, the Plebeians and the universitarians, the scientists and the philosophers. As far as proletarian philosophy in Britain was concerned, they were the Last Word.

Chapter 7

Farce and Tragedy

1 Loitering on the Party Line

T. A. Jackson — the self-educated socialist whose mind had been prepared for Marxism in the eighteen-nineties by a youthful passion for philosophy — has made no appearance in my story since the point when he tried, without success, to oppose the 'militant and aggressive' line which the British Communist Party adopted in 1929. His exit was marked by two articles, in one of which — as you may remember — he gave readers of the doomed *Sunday Worker* a warning against substituting Leninism for Marx.[1] In the other, which appeared in the *Communist Review* under the title 'Self-criticism', he expressed concern about 'some incidental phenomena' at the 1929 Party Congress, and especially about the distorted and cliché-ridden language that was coming into use at the time. 'Some forms of sentence-construction,' said Jackson, 'have so conquered the imagination of comrades that we are fast ceasing to be an English-speaking party.' With growing exasperation, he denounced the use of 'set phrases', such as 'agit-prop', 'the next task', 'politic', or, especially, 'the Right danger'. The effect of these was to yield power to the 'Inquisition Complex' so that 'the oldest and most reactionary passions — the Fear of the Unauthorized — is dressed up with brand-new "ultra-Leninist(!)" phraseology till it acquires the lustre of the highest revolutionary virtue.' The phrase which annoyed Jackson most was 'self-criticism':

During the early stages of the Conference we heard the *phrase* 'self-criticism' repeated so often that I was carried back in memory to my choir-boy days in the Church of England. . . . Just as in the Church of England the nice young ladies who lisp so prettily that they have done 'those things' they 'ought not to have done' would sue you for slander if you repeated outside the church, and as statements of fact, the self-accusations to which they have so glibly assented, so, it is to be feared, few of those worthy comrades who talk at conferences of the 'need for self-criticism' would be other than enraged if the need were brought home to them personally.

The Party, Jackson felt, was now filled with a clamour of 'heresy hunting', where criticism meant condemnation, and the spirit of open inquiry and philosophical reflexiveness was being annihilated.

For 'criticism' rightly so-called does not necessarily mean 'condemnation' at all. . . . Comrades should really learn that a 'judgment' in philosophy is something quite different from a 'judgment' in a police court. . . . All possibility of thinking dies in such an atmosphere; and as the thinking dies the Communism dies with it. . . .[2]

Suiting its action to his despairing words, Comintern condemned Jackson's heresy, pronouncing that 'we must put a stop to all this philistine twaddle about self-criticism, a good example of which is the . . . article by Comrade Jackson'.[3] Shortly after this he was removed from his position on the Central Committee and from his job at Party headquarters.

The vitality which, for nearly a decade, had been absorbed by political emergencies could now be applied again to the cultural and educational tasks which had occupied Jackson before the formation of the Party. He moved to Three Bridges, a few miles south of London, and became involved once more in the work of the Labour Colleges, lecturing regularly, marking essays for the Correspondence Department, and participating prominently in conferences.[4] It was an awkward predicament, because he was fiercely loyal to the Communist Party, and the Party and the Labour Colleges were constantly at each other's throats. He often found himself under attack from both sides.[5]

The result was that Jackson became marginalized, cast in the role of brilliant but obsolete bibliovore. His appearance was much remarked — unkempt hair, rummaged by his grubby hands; clothes crumpled, and pockets distended with books. Lawrence Daly's father was offended by Jackson, lecturing in Fife, 'standing there with his trousers held up by an old tie. . . . He thought this was letting the Party down. . . .'. Jackson was treated, according to one informant, as a 'historic figure', but 'a bit of a bad boy'; or, as Dudley Edwards said, he was 'a bit of an old eccentric who had to be tolerated, but kept in order'. No doubt, though, Jackson deliberately played up to the eccentricity which was expected of him; it enabled him to maintain, throughout that period, a vigorous dignity which is, in retrospect, quite conspicuous. The labour movement was a battlefield, but, as Jock Shanley put it, it was as though 'Tommy Jackson was above it all'.[6]

Jackson was now able to concentrate on writing. Back in 1904, he had conceived the ambition of composing a history of Ireland. But it was another fourteen years before, thanks to the guidance and encouragement of William Paul,[7] he learned to write fluently enough for publication. Throughout the twenties he had produced articles and reviews not only for the *Communist,* the *Communist Review,* and the *Sunday Worker,* but for the *Clarion* and the *Daily Herald* too. Now, in the thirties, he was able to embark on larger works, and he returned to the idea of a book about Ireland. But he also got drawn back into philosophy. For wherever he looked, he found the philosophical inspiration which had led him to socialism despoiled: no one, it seemed — neither the proletarian Dietzgenites (like Casey), nor the bland university philosophers (like MacMurray), nor the dogmatic translated Muscovites (like Rudas) — seemed able to resuscitate that urgent vision in which the imperatives of socialist morality had been integrated into a systematic and hopefully scientific understanding of nature, humanity's place in it, and the scope of human knowledge.

In 1933, Jackson, who was temporarily laid up with neuralgia at his home in Three Bridges, received a complimentary copy of Fred Casey's new book *Method in Thinking.* He had been publicly generous to Casey in the past,[8] but had also taken a private dislike to him, and after meeting him at his watch-making shop in Bury, had concluded ('much to my amusement', he said) that Casey was 'more completely devoid of humour than any human being I had ever met'.[9] Casey's 'Dietzgenism' now seemed to Jackson to be on a par with his jocularity. Dietzgen himself had 'had undoubted merits', but he 'was not in the least responsible for the Dietzgen cult which was worked up long after his death', and which claimed that the work of Marx and Engels 'was not completed until Dietzgen *added* the philosophy'.[10]

Casey's 'neo-Dietzgenism' sent the convalescent Tommy Jackson 'into a frenzy of disgust and indignation', and so he began to compose a critical assessment. It grew, though, till it was too long for a review or even an article. Eventually Jackson submitted the essay to Lawrence and Wishart for publication as a book. The editor, Henry Parsons, felt that Jackson's draft would have to be 'toned down', and sent the manuscript to Moscow for advice. ('In those days . . . we deemed nobody an "expert" who did not live in Moscow,' wrote Jackson.) After several months' delay, the message came back from Comintern that the work must be rewritten as a positive exposition of the Marxist philosophy. Thus the original essay — a 'comic masterpiece' according to its author — was lost to the English-reading public, and a larger and more ponderous book was drafted. This in turn was sent to Moscow, and after the best part of a year, an expansion of the critical parts of the work was requested. The exasperated Jackson agreed reluctantly. ('The natural enemy of an author is the publisher's "expert", especially if there is more than one of "him" ', he wrote.) This third draft was accepted, but then, with tireless word-by-word editorial advice from Dona Torr, rewritten and expanded again.

Eventually, in 1936, the book was published under the title *Dialectics: The Logic of Marxism,* and Tommy Jackson, aged fifty-seven, found himself engaged in 'a new way of life' — embarked on the career which had seemed to him, when a child, the most exalted in the world: he was a writer of books.[11] Six more were to be published before he died,[12] but the best of them is the first. *Dialectics* is the most spirited and persuasive exposition of dialectical materialism ever written in English. It thrashes and sprawls over 642 pages, propelled by a strong sense both of literature and of politics: the composition, Jackson claimed, was modelled on a favourite novel, *Tristram Shandy,* and the whole project was, he wrote, 'a byproduct of my struggle to write a Marxist history of Ireland'.[13]

One of the main tributaries to dialectical materialism, as Jackson saw it, was a veteran militant-materialist scientific rationalism, celebrating the empirical natural sciences not only as majestic monuments of human intellect, but also as weapons against the conspiracies and delusions of priestcraft and natural theology, the allies of political reaction. The sciences, he believed, showed that the so-called 'Laws of

Nature' had to be seen as part of a contingent natural order, and not as the fiats of a mathematically-minded creator. From this point of view, Marx was an intellectual compeer of Darwin:

Marx and Darwin . . . achieved essentially similar feats: they achieved them by exactly parallel methods: and their common achievement made possible a higher synthesis of human knowledge than was ever attained before. No two men ever worked a bigger intellectual revolution. They abolished the distinction between Natural law and the facts of Nature.

Marxist materialism, then, was not abstruse, arcane, or sectarian: it was the implicit method of all who looked dispassionately and scientifically at the facts of nature. Thus G. H. Lewes, with his positivist hostility to metaphysical, a priori, or impractical modes of thought was really a material-ist, or at least a 'semi-materialist'; his 'appeal to objective empirical test — "verification" — goes directly to that which is essential [and] . . . decisively endorses the scientific character of the procedure of Marx and Engels'.[14] Referring to Robert Tyndall's famous Address to the British Association in 1874, in which Theology had been notified that it was time for it to yield place to 'science', Jackson commented: 'With the term Dialectical Materialism inserted in place of the euphemism "science" used by Tyndall, and idealism added along with theology, this affirmation could well stand as the Marxist challenge and defiance to-day.'[15] The direction of this argument, however, could easily be reversed. If 'science' was just a prude's word for dialectical materialism, might it not just as well be said that 'dialectical materialism' was only a pretentious and needlessly offensive way of referring to science? What was the advantage of the more cumbersome title, and, in particular, what was supposed to be conveyed by the word 'dialectical'? At first, Jackson was exceedingly evasive on this issue, rejecting other people's definitions but offering none to take their place. Dialectics, he said, was not an alternative to or a substitute for ordinary, that is, 'formal', logic; nor was it susceptible of formulation as a 'method' separate from its application; nor could it be codified into 'laws' like those of Engels; nor 'pelmanised' into mnemonic slogans about 'negation of the negation' or 'thesis-antithesis-synthesis'. It is not surprising, in view of these denials, that the few pages where Jackson attempted to explain dialectics in terms of logical theory were extremely unsuccessful.[16] However, Jackson was able to give a more serviceable explanation by referring to the concept of 'practice'. Dialectical materialism, he maintained, was essentially a philosophy of 'practice', formulated by the young Marx in the 'Theses on Feuerbach' and the recently published *German Ideology*.[17] In spite of his general hostility to slogans, Jackson was willing to formulate the 'primary canon' of Marxism in the celebrated phrase used and perhaps invented by Bukharin: 'the unity of Theory and Practice based on the *primacy of practice*'. The chief inference which Jackson drew from this formula was that 'for Marx and for Dialectical Materialism *Practice*, i.e. *what men do*, is the basis of all development in objective history, and in man's subjectivity likewise'.[18] This in turn meant that — contrary to almost universal belief — all kinds of 'economic determinism' were entirely foreign to Marxism: the so-called 'laws' of economics referred only to an artificially abstracted aspect of human practice, and could always be overruled by determined action: it was thus, indeed, that the Russian people had begun constructing socialism, swimming valiantly against the economic tide.

So Tommy Jackson filled the phraseology of dialectical materialism with a robust and substantial content; and on this basis he proceeded to flay a whole range of writers who seemed to him to be doing dishonest trade in 'Dialectical Materialism' — and especially the hapless Fred Casey, 'High Priest in Britain (if not in the Universe) of Neo-Dietzgenian "Monist"-Marxism'. In over a hundred pages of spirited (but sometimes tiresome) polemic, Jackson convicted Casey of betraying even his messiah, Dietzgen, in the first place by using the idea of 'dialectical unity' as a pretext for arranging a 'reconciliation' of materialism and idealism, and so trying to include both God and the bourgeois leadership of the Labour Party within Marxism; and in the second place by failing to see that dialectics has everything to do with 'practice', and nothing to do with logical formulas, and consequently falling into a kind of fatalistic economic determinism:

First they postulate a closed (and therefore fixed) system of nature, *into which* they proceed, as by a surgical operation, to *insert the dialectic.* . . . . The result of this eclectic Irish stew — a statistical average of philosophical mutton, pork, beef, veal, peas, onions, carrots and potatoes — is then decanted into three bowls in turn, labelled respectively Thesis, Antithesis and Synthesis, and the contents of the third bowl are then offered to believers as the Pure Marxian-Dietzgenian Balm of Gilead.

The same argument was deployed against the 'economic determinist' interpretations of Marxism propaged by Postgate and other Labour College luminaries, like Cole, and Eastman, and Middleton Murry, and, before them by Second-International Social-Democrats, like Hyndman, Kautsky, and de Leon — who had been 'almost impervious to the dialectic'.[19] In addition, Jackson poured scorn on the elegant intellectual Marxists, dandies ravaged by 'Bloomsbury disease', constantly trying to foist some unwanted 'supplement' on to Marxism, such as, in particular, Freudianism — a movement so generally derided by Marxists at the time that Jackson did not pause to give grounds for his own hostility.[20]

Jackson's vehement repudiation of so many enemies of the Communist Party was immediately welcomed by the orthodox. Palme Dutt himself gave *Dialectics* what Jackson considered an 'excessively laudatory' notice in *Labour Monthly*.[21] 'No review can do justice to this book', Dutt exclaimed: 'Compared to the works that have so far been appearing from English pens on the theory of Marxism and Dialectical Materialism, it is as sunshine compared to a noisome swamp.'[22]

However, it slowly began to appear that Jackson's book, with its constant references back to an old intellectual world, and its traditional English radical prose style, echoing Bunyan, Shakespeare, Sterne, and the Authorized Version, was not quite in tune with the etiquettes of cosmopolitan Communism. In an uncharacteristic lapse, Dutt had failed to notice that Jackson's book totally ignored the New Turn — and did not even mention Adoratsky, Yudin, Rudas, or their concept of the dialectical laws. His blind spot was noticed, however, in Moscow, where *Under the Banner of Marxism*, whilst deferring to Jackson's 'weighty and valuable book', attacked it for neglecting the philosophical work done in the USSR during the 'battle on two fronts' in 1930, and for omitting criticisms of the mechanists, especially Bukharin. Jackson, they realized, had contrived to appear orthodox whilst actually preferring his youthful enthusiasm for philosophy to the detached conclusions by which, they said, 'Lenin and Stalin raised the philosophy of Marxism to a new and higher level'.[23]

Dialectics was, as Jackson knew, an unwieldy book, 'as full of faults as a dog is of fleas'.[24] Its history, he thought, was 'either tragic, or comic, or both, as you choose to see it'.[25] In terms of its underground reputation not only in Britain but also in America and India, it may have enjoyed 'a pronounced success';[26] but it was not reprinted and it totally failed to shift the focus of Marxist debates about philosophy. Jackson's references to the 'Theses on Feuerbach' and the *German Ideology* were ignored, and his exemplary hospitality toward philosophical writing which was not explicitly 'Marxist-Leninist' found no imitators. His wish to overthrow what he called 'the habit of taking it for granted that only Germans or Russians — with perhaps an odd Frenchman — could ever write anything fundamental' was not fulfilled.[27]

Characteristically, Tommy Jackson responded to this 'tragicomedy', as he called it, with a flippancy which could express either bitter disappointment or buoyant good cheer. Since Comintern had called the book 'valuable', Jackson made up a 'fable' to prove their point. A volunteer in the International Brigade in the Spanish Civil War owed his life to it — so the story goes — because it stopped a Fascist bullet when he was carrying it in his knapsack. 'And do you know', the Brigader said, 'the damn bullet couldn't get through the bloody thing any better than I could!' Comintern had also called the book 'weighty', so Jackson put a copy on the scales at his local Co-op. '"A weighty and valuable book?" I should think so. It weighed two pounds on the scales, and was "valuable" to that Brigader anyway.'[28] With the publication of Stalin's *History of the CPSU (B)*, it sank like a stone, leaving hardly a ripple.

If Jackson felt any disappointment, he kept it to himself. Lawrence Daly's speculation was that

at top level, inside the CP, on the quiet, he was . . . a bit of a dissident. . . . He probably thought that Harry Pollitt and company knew nothing about dialectics anyway. . . . But a story I once heard about Jackson possibly illustrates it. A fellow told me that . . . he went down to see him for a weekend. . . . It was a moonlight night, and Tommy said: 'I'll show you my garden'. And at the bottom of the garden was a big bunch of thistles in a circle, and in the centre was a bleeding big thistle. . . . And Tommy Jackson said . . . 'That circle of thistles represents the Central Committee of the Party and that big one in the centre is Harry Pollitt. And every Sunday morning I come down here and have a piss on the whole fucking lot of them.'[29]

All the same, Jackson clung to the Communist Party and from 1943 (when he lost his second wife and also his home at Three Bridges) till 1949 he spent eight or nine months a year touring the country to speak for the Party, and if possible lecturing for the Labour Colleges as well.

In the last and blandest of the three unpublished versions of his autobiography — all of which were written in the few years leading up to his death in 1955 just before his seventy-sixth birthday — he described the idea of his 'proneness to deviation' as a myth, a fiction, and an annoyance, since he 'had never, in fact, been in disagreement with the Party leaders on any major theoretical issue'.[30] No doubt this profession is true, but in the first version the emphasis was different, and Jackson tried to sum up the story of his life by recounting his attempts to convince his daughters that he had never 'deviated from the Party line'. They would not believe it, and his stern retort was that 'I have stuck as tightly to the Party line as a limpet to a rock. Barring now and then, of course.' Even this did not satisfy them: 'your coincidence with the Party line has been purely fortuitous', they insisted[31] — a point which Jackson himself had made many years before: 'How in hell', he had asked, 'can a poor fellow deviate when the *line* will keep following him round like this!'[32]

As he looked back, in the second version of his auto-biography, over the seventy years of British Marxism which he had lived through, he saw them dividing into three generations. First, there had been the temporizing Hyndmanites, whose theoretical knowledge was derived entirely from the first nine chapters of *Capital*; then, in reaction, there had been the 'impossibilists', who were devoted to a deterministic 'Materialist Conception of History', and who believed that Marxism was 'a simple amplification of Buckle, and . . . a continuation of Darwin, Büchner and Haeckel'. This inter-pretation was then refuted by the unexpected occurrence of a socialist revolution in Russia, which led to the replacement of determinism by 'dialectics' and the installation of a British Communist Party willing and able to give a Marxist lead to working-class politics.[33]

The Party, however — as Jackson had put it in the first version of his autobiography — was subject to 'those recurring spasms of "growing pains" which are, I infer, phenomena that are always to be expected until a party reaches a certain degree of integration'. And there was one 'defect of the Party' that Jackson found particularly regrettable —

a lack of attention to and appreciation for general culture and especially creative-imaginative literature. . . . We claim, as we have a right to claim, that we are the inheritors and custodians of all the cultural achievements of the ages. It is high time that we learned to value aright what we have inherited.

The Labour Colleges might have been weak on politics, but in their great days, before antagonism to the Communist Party, they had shown a proper care for education. 'I do not despair', said Jackson, 'of seeing a return . . . of the days of which I have written.'[34]

2 Lost Hope

Back in 1843, Marx had imagined philosophy meeting up with the proletariat and at last being 'made a reality'.[35] And sure enough, in Britain at least, noteworthy members of several proletarian generations were indeed moved by high philosophical hopes, which beckoned them to a commanding and compendious prospect of a whole new socialist world of knowledge. The hopes were pinned on a succession of different figures: first in the universities — but it turned out that stirring idealist philosophies of the State could not be used to vindicate the aspirations of the proletariat; and then the philosophers of the 'analytic revolution' arrived, and made a vice of edification and commitment, immuring their discipline with a daunting barricade of technical professionalism. There was also the explicitly proletarian philosophy of Dietzgenism, which was courageously anti-universitarian, but which decayed, in educational practice, into rather tawdry and mechanical

exercises in 'brainwork', despised by the more educated
comrades, and baffling to the rest. And finally, there was
an announcement of the imminent arrival of Dialectical
Materialism, trailing the glamour of the still young Soviet
Union, and promising to be the long-awaited anwer to the
craving for a distinctive socialist philosophy. Unfortunately,
hard information about this fabulous philosophy was scarce,
and the intellectuals — especially the philosophers and
scientists in the universities — seemed incapable of agreeing,
or even understanding each other, when they discussed it.
Still, a conviction grew — a rumour, transmitted by a thousand
mouths but originating in none — that everything would be
clear when Dialectical Materialism eventually arrived. The
waiting came to an end, finally, with Stalin's feeble pages on
'Dialectical and Historical Materialism'. The appointment
had not been kept, and the wan crowd dispersed: proletarian
philosophical hopes had apparently been sheer misunderstandings. A farce?

The socialist philosophies of Jackson, the Dietzgenites, and
the Victorian autodidacts are over and done with. Professional
philosophers, wary of undisciplined pulpitry, may find little
to lament in that; and modern Marxists, intellectual arsenals
crammed with a century's acquisitions of sectarian derision,
may feel quite satisfied too — for surely these philosophies
were just various mixtures of economism, mechanism,
evolutionism, idealism, humanism, and revisionism, and
probably of 'Stalinism' too. But this vocabulary of com-
minatory '-isms' may not be a good instrument for measuring
what has been lost. The main point about these philosophies
is that they answered a need, not for a particular theoretical
orientation within philosophy, but for the cultivation of
unconfined and unrelenting reflection, for an opportunity to
try to sort out your most fundamental values and beliefs,
your sense of how your own initiatives and inertias may fit
in with the larger rhythms of life, human society, and the
universe as a whole. Philosophy, in this sense, is not just a
specialized and esoteric genre of theoretical writing. It
belongs with those distinctive, numinous episodes which
everyone experiences sometimes — waking in the still of a
bright winter night and foreseeing your death, or reaching
a wind-swept mountain top when a distant landscape

unexpectedly reveals itself — moments when you feel alone in the universe, and long for an explicit, clear set of principles, justifying your values, your beliefs, and your existence in a sort of unanswerable cosmic manifesto.

The desire for philosophy in this sense may be satirized — and no wonder; it may be hidden away in shame; or it may be muzzled with sophisticated irony; but it will hardly be exorcized or eradicated. Least of all for socialists — battling for the rights of unknown people, or for future generations which may never even be born, and doing so, moreover, whilst surrounded by the imperturbable smugness of the rest. It is not surprising if they seek opportunities to think connectedly about what they are exhausting themselves for, so as to be fortified against violence, neglect, or scorn. Now that the aspirations of the proletarian philosophers have been annihilated, it is not easy to believe that the search will succeed. A tragedy.

Notes

Introduction: Marxism and Philosophy

1. Marx's main philosophical publications were the Doctoral Dissertation (defended in 1841, republished in 1902, English translation 1975), 'Zur Kritik der Hegelschen Rechtsphilosophie: Einleitung' (1844, in H. J. Stenning, *Karl Marx: Selected Essays*, London, Leonard Parsons, 1926), *Die heilige Familie* (with Engels, 1845, a short extract translated in Stenning, 1926, the rest in 1956), and *Misère de la Philosophie* (1847, translated 1900). Then there is *Die deutsche Ideologie*, completed by Marx and Engels in 1846, but abandoned, following unsuccessful attempts to find a publisher, to 'the gnawing criticism of the mice'. Part One was published in an edition by Riazanov in 1926 (Marx-Engels Archiv, Vol. 1), and a complete text edited by Adoratsky in 1932 (translated 1964). (A short extract from the opening section was translated in *Labour Monthly*, Vol. 15, No. 3, March 1933, pp. 182-8, with a translation of Adoratsky's introduction (pp. 163-9); a shorter extract still in Emile Burns, ed., *A Handbook of Marxism*, London, Gollancz, 1935, pp. 209-213.) Marx's other philosophical writings were not intended for publication — the so-called 'Economic and Philosophical Manuscripts' (written 1844, published 1932, translated 1959), the 'Theses on Feuerbach' (written 1845, published in amended form in 1888 — see below, note 3 — translated 1903), and the relatively late 'Introduction' to the *Grundrisse* (written 1857, published 1903, translated 1904). With the exception of the 'Theses on Feuerbach', none of these works has ever acquired anything like the status of a 'classic' in the canon of Marxist texts. And except for the Doctoral Dissertation, they all argue for a break from, rather than a position within philosophy (see Georges Labica, *Marxism and the Status of Philosophy* (1977), translated Kate Soper and Martin Ryle, Brighton, Harvester Press, 1980, esp. pp. 353-69). On the reception of the 'Economic and Philosophical Manuscripts', see Perry Anderson, *Considerations on Western Marxism*, London, New Left Books, 1976, pp. 50-1.

2. *Herrn Eugen Dühring's Umwalzung der Wissenschaft: Anti-Dühring*, much of which first appeared in the form of articles in *Vorwärts* in 1877, was published as a book in Germany in 1878, English translation by Emile Burns, ed. C. P. Dutt, London, Martin Lawrence, 1935. An extract was published as a separate pamphlet, first in French and then in many other languages. The English translation of this extract, by Edward Aveling, appeared in 1892, under the title *Socialism, Utopian and Scientific*, London,

Sonnenschein; and many more extracts appeared in *Landmarks of Scientific Socialism*, Chicago, Charles Kerr, 1907. The introduction was published separately as a Socialist Labour Party pamphlet in 1908.

3. 'Ludwig Feuerbach' first appeared in *Neue Zeit* IV, 4–5, and an expanded version was published as a book two years later, along with (for the first time) Marx's 'Theses on Feuerbach' of 1845 (*Ludwig Feuerbach und der Ausgang der klassischen deutschen Philosophie*, Dietz, Stuttgart, 1888). An English translation by Austin Lewis was published by Charles Kerr in Chicago in 1903, and a new version, edited by C. P. Dutt, and with an introduction by L. Rudas, by Martin Lawrence, London, in 1934.

4. The German text, accompanied by a Russian translation, was published in Moscow in 1925; this was translated into English by C. P. Dutt (Moscow 1934), a new edition, with a preface and explanatory notes by J. B. S. Haldane, appearing in 1940 (London, Lawrence and Wishart).

5. This 'classical' conception of philosophy along with 'Histories of Philosophy' designed to equip it with a two-thousand-year pedigree seems to have come into being in the eighteenth century. See Jonathan Rée, 'Philosophy and Histories of Philosophy', in Jonathan Rée, Michael Ayers, and Adam Westoby, *Philosophy and its Past*, Brighton, Harvester, 1978.

6. 'Der moderne dialektische Materialismus weiss . . . besser als der Idealismus, das die Menschen ihre Geschichte unbewusst machen' ('Hegel's sechzigsten Todestag', *Neue Zeit* X, 1 (1891) p. 278). Plekhanov also used the phrase, in Russian, in a foreword to a Russian translation (1892) of Engels's *Ludwig Feuerbach*. But its popularity is due to Lenin, who employed it (but only casually) in 1894 (in Russian of course) in his pamphlet *What the 'Friends of the People' Are* (see V. I. Lenin, *Collected Works*, Moscow and London, 1960 ff., Vol. 1, pp. 129–332; pp. 181, 183), and used it extensively later, particularly in *Materialism and Empirio-Criticism* (1909) whose preface states boldly but quite falsely that 'Marx and Engels scores of times termed their philosophical views dialectical materialism' (*Collected Works* Vol. 14, p. 19; see also pp. 135–6). It was through the dissemination of this work (which became available in 1927 in an English translation by David Kvitko, with an introduction about 'dialectical materialism' by A. M. Deborin, as the first contribution to an abortive projected 'Collected Works', London, Martin Lawrence, 1927–46) that the phrase acquired, from the late twenties, both popularity and a specious aura of classic authority. The truth seems to be that the phrase was never used by Marx or Engels, though something like the concept it designates was indisputably present in the latter's thought. Edward Aveling's version of Engels's *Socialism, Utopian and Scientific* (1892) includes the statement 'Modern materialism is essentially dialectic' (p. 39), but Engels's own sentence does not contain a word for 'materialism'. (See K. Marx and F.Engels,

Werke, (MEW), Berlin, Dietz Verlag, 1957 ff., Vol. 20, p. 24.) The 1934 translation of Engel's *Ludwig Feuerbach* gives 'Dialectical Materialism' as the title of the Fourth Chapter, but this has no counterpart in the German original. See Z. A. Jordan, *The Evolution of Dialectical Materialism*, London, Macmillan, 1967, p. 3, p. 3n; Loren R. Graham, *Science and Philosophy in the Soviet Union* (1972), London, Allen Lane, 1973, p. 475, nn. 1–2; *Oxford English Dictionary*, Supplement, 1972, s.v. 'Dialectical'. See also below, p. 142, Notes to Chapter Three, n. 12.

7. There are several conventional philosophers' histories of Dialectical Materialism. See especially Gustav Wetter, *Dialectical Materialism: A Historical and Systematic Survey of Philosophy in the Soviet Union* (1952), Trans. Peter Heath, London, Routledge, 1958; Herbert Marcuse, *Soviet Marxism, A Critical Analysis*, London, Routledge, 1958; Guy Planty-Bonjour, *The Categories of Dialectical Materialism*, Dordrecht, Reidel, 1967.

8. Sebastiano Timpanaro, *Sul Materialismo* (1970), translated by Lawrence Garner as *On Materialism*, London, New Left Books, 1975.

9. Lucio Colletti, *Il Marxismo e Hegel* (1969), the second part of which is translated by Lawrence Garner as *Marxism and Hegel*, London, New Left Books, 1973.

10. Peter Ruben, 'Problem und Begriff der Naturdialektik', in Anneliese Greise and Hubert Laitko, eds., *Weltanschauung und Methode*, Berlin, 1969; 'Aktuelle theoretische Probleme der materialistischen Naturdialektik', *Deutsche Zeitschrift für Philosophie*, 1973.

11. To be more precise, Lecourt sees this period as begetting an 'ontological' (as opposed to 'methodological') version of dialectical materialism. But for most of its advocates, from Engels on, dialectical materialism has always been, for better or for worse, an ontological doctrine. Dominique Lecourt, *Lysenko*, Paris, Maspero, 1976; trans. Ben Brewster, *Proletarian Science, The Case of Lysenko*, London, New Left Books, 1977.

12. This applies, for instance, to the contributors to John Mepham and David-Hillel Ruben, eds., *Issues in Marxist Philosophy*, Brighton, Harvester Press, 1979–80, 4 vols. See Jonathan Rée, 'Le Marxisme et la Philosophie Analytique', *Critique*, 399–400, August–September 1980, pp. 802–17.

13. 'Contribution to the Critique of Hegel's Philosophy of Right: Introduction' (1844), MEW, Vol. 1, p. 391, translated in Marx and Engels, *Collected Works*, London, Lawrence and Wishart, 1975 ff., Vol. 3, p. 187.

14. MEW, Vol. 1, pp. 383–14; *Collected Works*, Vol. 3, pp. 180–1.

15. Some of these issues are discussed in Stuart Macintyre's *A Proletarian Science, Marxism in Britain 1917-1933*, Cambridge University Press, 1980. For some telling criticisms of Macintyre's approach, see Tim Putnam, 'Proletarian Science?', *Radical Science Journal* 13, 1983 pp. 73–82. The same problems have been posed, in relation to a different period, in Jacques Rancière, *La Nuit des*

Prolétaires, Paris, Fayard, 1981, and 'Proletarian Nights', *Radical Philosophy* 31, Summer 1982, pp. 10-13.

One: Socialists and Autodidacts 1880-1910

1. 'My favourite trick was to wait until the family were all in bed, then creep downstairs, light a candle and sit reading half the night.' Harry Pollitt, *Serving my Time*, London, Lawrence and Wishart, 1940, p. 34.
2. 'I taught myself to write in the pit by holding a white stone over the smoke of a lamp. When the stone became black I traced the characters on it with a pin.' Keir Hardie, *The Clarion*, 9 July 1892, cited in Dona Torr, *Tom Mann and his Times 1856-90*, London, Lawrence and Wishart, 1956, p. 26.
3. 'By propping up his book on his jenny gallows while working during the day he [Joseph Barker] managed to snatch glances at it, while all the time exercising his mind upon his Latin lessons.' J. F. C. Harrison, *Learning and Living 1790-1960, A Study in the History of the English Adult Education Movement*; London, Routledge, 1961, pp. 45-6.
4. J. A. Leatherland, *Essays and Poems, with a brief Autobiographical Memoir*, London and Leicester, 1862, p. 10; Thomas Cooper, *The Life of Thomas Cooper*, London, 1872 pp. 46-7; Joseph Gutteridge, *Light and Shadows in the Life of an Artisan* (1893), reprinted in V. E. Chancellor, ed., *Master and Artisan in Victorian England*, London, Evelyn, Adams, and Mackay, 1969, pp. 75-238; pp. 135-6, 152-3; Torr, *Tom Mann and his Times*, p. 79.
5. See E. M. Wright, *The Life of Joseph Wright*, Oxford University Press, 1932. Virginia Woolf revered Wright as a male feminist, depicting him as Sam Robson in *The Years* and *The Pargiters*. Cf. Mitchell A. Leaska, ed., *The Pargiters* (1977), pp. xi-xv. Wright was by no means unique: see for instance Albert Mansbridge, 'Some Workman Scholars' (1937) in *The Kingdom of the Mind*, London, Dent, 1944, pp. 187-99. Other notably successful autodidacts were Thomas Okey, basket-maker, who became professor of Italian at Cambridge University, and J. M. Dent, bookbinder, who became the autodidact's publisher, and creator of the Everyman Library. Both Okey and Dent were graduates of Toynbee Hall. See J. A. R. Pimlott, *Toynbee Hall, Fifty Years of Social Progress 1884-1934*, London, J. M. Dent, 1934, pp. 54-5.
6. See J. F. C. Harrison, *A History of the Working Men's College 1854-1954*, London, Routledge, 1954, p. 118.
7. Both remarks date from 1886, and are quoted in Torr, *Tom Mann and his Times*, pp. 185, 217. Torr writes of Mann that 'the privation most deeply felt, and which to the very end helped to fire his Socialism, was that of opportunity for learning' (p. 28, see also p. 35).
8. Pollitt, *Serving my Time,* p. 48.

9. Cf. David Layton, *Science for the People*, London, Allen and Unwin, 1973. Proletarian interest in science was by no means new: in 1844, Engels noticed 'in how great a measure the English proletariat has succeeded in attaining independent education' and stated that he 'often heard working men, whose fustian jackets scarcely held together, speak upon geological, astronomical and other subjects'. (*Condition of the Working Class in England in 1844*, Marx and Engels, *Collected Works*, Vol. 4, p. 528.) There is a fine survey of the intellectual and political affiliations of spiritualism, and its relations to autodidacticism, in Logie Barrow's 'Socialism in Eternity: The Ideology of Plebeian Spiritualists 1853–1913', *History Workshop Journal* 9, Spring 1980, pp. 37–69.

10. T. A. Jackson, Unpublished Autobiography, Second Draft, Part One, p. 23. (Jackson wrote his autobiography three times. The opening section of the final version was published as *Solo Trumpet, Some Memories of Socialist Agitation and Propaganda*, London, Lawrence and Wishart, 1953. Copies of the unpublished versions are held by the Marx Memorial Library in London.) On Jackson see further Vivien Morton and John Saville, 'Thomas Alfred Jackson 1879–1955', *Dictionary of Labour Biography*, Vol. IV, London, Macmillan, 1977, pp. 99–108, and Vivien Morton and Stuart Macintyre, *T. A. Jackson, A Centenary Appreciation*, Our History Pamphlet 73, London, Communist Party History Group, 1979.

11. Tom Maguire, writing in 1892, quoted in E. P. Thompson, 'Homage to Tom Maguire' in A. Briggs and J. Saville, eds., *Essays in Labour History*, Vol. 1, 1967, pp. 276–316, p. 294.

12. H. M. Hyndman, *England for All: The Textbook of Democracy*, London, Allen, 1881; G. Bernard Shaw, *The Unsocial Socialist*, first published in serial form in J. L. Joynes's *To-Day: A Monthly Magazine of Scientific Socialism* in 1884; Edward Bellamy, *Looking Backward 2000–1887*, Boston, Ticknor, 1888, and numerous British editions; William Morris, *News from Nowhere*, first published in serial form in *The Commonweal* in 1890; G. B. Shaw, *Fabian Essays in the History of Socialism*, London, The Fabian Society, 1890; Robert Blatchford, *Merrie England: A Series of Letters on the Labour Problem*, London, The Clarion, 1894; J. L. Joynes, *The Socialist Catechism*, reprinted, with additions, from *Justice*, London, Modern Press, 1884. See Henry Collins, 'The Marxism of the Social Democratic Federation', in A. Briggs and J. Saville, eds., *Essays in Labour History 1886–1923*, Vol. II, 1971, pp. 47–69; p. 52.

13. *The Poverty of Philosophy* was translated by the self-educated SDF Marxist Harry Quelch, who selected it because it was written in French, and he did not understand German. When his translation was in the process of being printed by the SDF's Twentieth Century Press, Hyndman tried to suppress its publication, but was too late to succeed. See T. A. Jackson, *Solo Trumpet*, p. 68, and Unpublished Autobiography, Second Draft, Part One, p. 25.

14. Cf. Dona Torr, *Tom Mann and his Times,* pp. 183, 326.

15. James Clunie, born in 1890, recalls the following elements of his early reading: Jack London's *Before Adam,* Tom Paine's *Age of Reason,* Robert Blatchford's *God and my Neighbours,* Darwin's *Origin of Species* and *Descent of Man,* Huxley's *Lectures and Essays,* and the poetry of Burns and Whitman. See *The Voice of Labour: The Autobiography of a House Painter,* Dunfermline, 1958, pp. 25, 30, 33. See also Harry Pollitt's account of his early reading in *Serving my Time,* p. 34, and the early pages of Raphael Samuel, 'British Marxist Historians 1880–1980, I', *New Left Review* 120, April 1980, pp. 21–96.

16. T. A. Jackson, Unpublished Autobiography, First Draft, pp. 26–7, 48; Second Draft, Part One, p. 9; *Solo Trumpet,* p. 24. Jackson continues: 'Lewes led me to see a new significance in Plato and Aristotle, led me to realise there was such a thing as philosophic method, led me to really study Bacon, Hobbes and Locke, and better still the mighty "God-intoxicated" "master atheist" Spinoza and thereafter Old Man Hegel and ultimately, and in consequence, Marx.' (Pp. 24–5.) G. H. Lewes's *Biographical History,* first published in 1845–6, was reissued in 1892 as one of Sir John Lubbocks's Hundred Books.

17. *Solo Trumpet,* pp. 21–2.

18. Unpublished Autobiography, First Draft, pp. 56, 64, 60.

19. *Solo Trumpet,* p. 59. The SDF organized study circles to read *Capital,* and Jackson acquired a remaindered copy of Volume I in a shop in Holborn; he also got hold of a copy of *Wage Labour and Capital* (though it was out of print), Quelch's recent translation of *The Poverty of Philosophy,* de Leon's translation of Bebel's *Woman,* Lafargue's *Evolution of Property,* and Engels's *Revolution and Counter-Revolution or Germany in 1848,* which was then thought to be by Marx. (See *Solo Trumpet,* pp. 59–60.)

20. *Solo Trumpet,* p. 58.

21. *Solo Trumpet,* pp. 58–9.

22. Unpublished Autobiography, First Draft, p. 27.

23. Cf. Chushichi Tsuzuki, 'The "Impossibilist Revolt" in Britain: The Origins of the SLP and the SPGB', *International Review of Social History I* (1956), pp. 377–97.

24. *Solo Trumpet,* pp. 64–9.

25. De Leon lectured in Scotland and England in 1904. See Raymond Challinor's history of the British SLP, *The Origins of British Bolshevism,* London, Croom Helm, 1977, p. 42. See also James D. Young, 'Daniel de Leon and Anglo-American Socialism', *Labor History,* Vol. 17, No. 3, Summer 1976, pp. 329–50; Bernard Johnpoll, 'A Note on Daniel de Leon', *Labor History,* Vol. 17, No. 4, Fall 1976, pp. 606–12; James A. Stevenson, 'Daniel de Leon and European Socialism 1890–1914', *Science and Society,* Vol. 44, No. 2, Summer 1980, pp. 190–223.

26. For the role of the bookseller Adolph Kohn and of the SLP in importing American books, see Robert Barltrop, *The Monument:*

The Story of the Socialist Party of Great Britain, London, Pluto Press, 1975, p. 42; see also Challinor, *The Origins of British Bolshevism*, p. 29.

27. Cf. Tsuzuki, 'The "Impossibilist Revolt" in Britain', p. 396, n. 3.
28. It seems that Jackson left the SPGB in the hope of getting paid to give lectures for the ILP. To a friend, he wrote: 'I will join the SDF, ILP and "Clarion" mobs and peg away — bleed the swines — till I am expelled.' See Barltrop, *The Monument*, p. 41. In his autobiography Jackson recalled taking the revolutionary socialist side in a debate in Leeds in 1916. The SLP claimed he was speaking on their behalf, and when he protested that he wasn't a member, he was told he had become one the night before. (*Solo Trumpet*, p. 128.)
29. Daniel de Leon, *Flashlights of the Amsterdam Congress* (1904), New York Labour News Co., 1906, new edition 1929, p. 135.
30. De Leon, paraphrasing a speech by the French socialist Chauvin, *Flashlights of the Amsterdam Congress*, p. 100.
31. This Report, signed by SLP National Secretary Neil Maclean, was submitted to the Congress of the Second International in 1904, and is reproduced as an appendix to de Leon's *Flashlights*, pp. 212–18.

Two: Dilemmas of Working-Class Education 1880–1920

1. The ambivalence is present, for instance, in Tommy Jackson, who regarded the two high points of his long and eventful life as his first view of the Red Flag flying over the Kremlin in 1923 and taking tea with the author of *The Golden Bough*, Sir James Frazer, and his wife Lady Frazer, in 1929. (Vivien Morton, interviewed 9 June 1978.)
2. See J. F. C. Harrison, *Learning and Living 1790–1960* and *A History of the Working Men's College 1854–1954*; Sheila Rowbotham, 'The Call to University Extension Teaching 1873–1900', *University of Birmingham Historical Journal*, Vol. 12, 1969–70, pp. 57–71; J. A. R. Pimlott, *Toynbee Hall, Fifty Years of Social Progress 1884–1935*; and G. Spiller, *The Ethical Movement in Great Britain: A Documentary History*, Farleigh Press, 1934.
3. T. H. Green, *Lectures on the Principles of Political Obligation* (1895), London, Longman, 1941, p. 122.
4. Evidence to the Oxford University Commission, p. 44, cited in J. F. C. Harrison, *Learning and Living*, p. 221.
5. See Jonathan Rée, 'Idealism and Education', *History of Education*, Vol. 9, No. 3, 1980, pp. 259–69; Peter Gordon and John White, *Philosophers as Educational Reformers: The Influence of Idealism on British Educational Thought and Practice*, London, Routledge, 1979.
6. See T. H. Green, *The Work to be done by the New Oxford High School*, Oxford and London, 1882, pp. 1–2.

7. Edward Carpenter, *My Days and Dreams*, London, George Allen and Unwin, 1916, pp. 79, 80.
8. Preface to the 2nd (1912) edition of *Jude the Obscure*.
9. See Paul Yorke, *Ruskin College 1899-1909*, Oxford, Ruskin Students' Labour History Pamphlets, 1977, pp. 3, 17, 11.
10. Albert Mansbridge, 'Co-operation, Trade Unionism, and University Extension' (1903), *The Kingdom of the Mind*, pp. 1-11; p. 7.
11. Quoted in W. Sinclair, 'A Note on Ruskin College, Oxford', *The University Review*, Vol. 5, No. 29, November 1907, pp. 396-404, pp. 403-4.
12. Quoted in Paul Yorke, *Ruskin College*, p. 35.
13. A. Sanderson Furniss, Ruskin tutor in economics, recorded in his autobiography: 'I was completely ignorant of Trade Unionism or of the Co-operative movement. . . . I had never read a line of Marx, I knew very little of the Socialist writers, and those I had read had made no impression on my mind. I had hardly ever spoken to a working man except gardeners, coachmen and gamekeepers.' *Memories of Sixty Years*, London, 1930, pp. 83-4, cited in J. P. M. Millar, *The Labour College Movement*, London, NCLC Publishing Society, 1979, p. 9.
14. C. S. Buxton, 'Ruskin College, an Educational Experiment', *The Cornhill Magazine*, 25 Aug. 1908, pp. 192-200. Cf. Millar, *The Labour College Movement*, p. 9. In this article, Buxton cleaves to the idea of Ruskin enabling its students 'to raise, not rise out of their class' (p. 193).
15. Noah Ablett, 'The Relation of Ruskin College to the Labour Movement', *Plebs Magazine*, Vol. 1, No. 1, February 1909.
16. The name was changed to *The Plebs* in 1921, and it continued until 1969.
17. Daniel de Leon, *Two Pages from Roman History ('Plebs Leaders and Labor Leaders' and 'The Warning of the Gracchi')*, New York Labor News Co., 1903.
18. Jackson claims to have sought support for the CLC within the ILP in 1908 — an improbably early date. See Unpublished Autobiography, First Draft, p. 116.
19. See W. W. Craik, *Central Labour College 1909-29*, London, Lawrence and Wishart, 1964. See also Rowland Kenney, 'The Brains behind the Labour Revolt', *The English Review*, March 1912, pp. 683-96.
20. Unpublished Autobiography, First Draft, p. 116. There is a summary of the early days of Ruskin and of the Ruskin strike in Brian Simon, *Education and the Labour Movement 1870-1920*, London, Lawrence and Wishart, 1965, pp. 311-42. See also John A. McIlroy, 'Education for the Labour Movement: United Kingdom Experience Past and Present', *Labour Studies Journal*, Vol. 4, No. 3, Winter 1980, pp. 198-213; and especially the reminiscences in *The Plebs*, Vol. 27, No. 2, February 1935, pp. 1-35, by S. Rees, G. H. Mellhuish, and others.
21. The Home Office was worried, its Directorate of Intelligence

noting that 'class prejudice and ignorance of elementary economics has a firmer grip upon the working-class than ever before' (1919, p. 18) and that 'revolutionary classes were increased and well-supported, and lantern-lectures became a successful feature of Bolshevik propaganda. . . . The College is the fountain-head of Marxian teaching in this country and is responsible for the training of more dangerous revolutionaries than all the communist parties put together.' (1920 pp. 7, 40.) These reports are quoted in Challinor, *The Origins of British Bolshevism*, p. 261.

22.   But presumably the number of students was less, since each could enrol for several different courses. Still, the number of Colleges and Class Groups also grew impressively, from 27 in 1921, to 91 in 1923, 139 in 1924, and 173 in 1925. The numbers of classes and enrolments were as follows:

Date	No. of Classes	No. of Enrolments
1922–3	529	11,993
1923–4	698	16,909
1924–5	1,048	25,071
1925–6	1,237	30,329

Source: J. F. Horrabin, 'Independent Working-Class Education', *The Journal of Adult Education*, Vol. 1, No. 1, September 1926, pp. 80–6; p. 85, n. For fuller figures, see Anne Phillips and Tim Putnam, 'Education for Emancipation', *Capital and Class* 10, Spring 1980, pp. 18–42, p. 47.

23.   See J. P. M. Millar, *The Labour College Movement*, p. 123. This means that Labour College classes were much more male-dominated than either WEA or University Extra-Mural Classes. The Central Labour College in London had fourteen male students in residence in 1914, and two women students living out (ibid., p. 8). Of nearly eighty Central Labour College students listed in Craik's *Central Labour College*, not one is a woman. In 1935, there were fewer than 300 women to more than 7,000 men taking NCLC correspondence courses. (See *The Plebs*, Vol. 28, No. 3, March 1936, p. 68.)

24.   Eden and Cedar Paul, *Proletcult (Proletarian Culture)*, London, Leonard Parsons, 1921, pp. 60, 19. See also Jackson, *Solo Trumpet*, pp. 145, 149.

25.   1964 is the date of the absorption of the National Council of Labour Colleges into the TUC. See Millar, *The Labour College Movement*, pp. 145–74. An excellent brief general history of workers' education in Britain, from committed Plebs-Leaguers, is J. F. and Winifred Horrabin, *Working-Class Education*, London, Labour Publishing Co., 1924. See also the comparative study (rather academic) by the Californian Margaret T. Hodgen, *Workers' Education in England and the United States*, London, Kegan Paul, New York, Dutton, 1925.

Three: Jospeh Dietzgen and Proletarian Philosophy

1. See Dorothy Emmett, 'Joseph Dietzgen, the Philosopher of Proletarian Logic', *Journal of Adult Education*, Vol. 3, No. 1, October 1928, pp. 26–35; p. 26.
2. See Eugene Dietzgen, 'Joseph Dietzgen – A Sketch of his Life', translated from *Neue Zeit*, 1894–5, in Eugene Dietzgen and Joseph Dietzgen, Jr., eds., *Some of the Philosophical Essays on Socialism and Science, Religion, Ethics, Critique-of-Reason and the World at Large* by Joseph Dietzgen, trans. M. Beer and T. Rothstein, Chicago, Charles Kerr, 1906, p. 19.
3. See E. A. Korolcuk and N. B. Kruskol, 'Über die Propagierung der ökonomischen Lehre von Karl Marx in Russland in den sechziger Jahren des 19 Jahrhunderts', *Beiträge zur Geschichte der Arbeiterbewegung*, Vol. 15, No. 1, 1973, pp. 64–95, pp. 65–6.
4. 'Social-Democratic Philosophy' (1876), translated in *Philosophical Essays*, pp. 173–223, p. 180. For the original, see Joseph Dietzgen, *Sämtliche Schriften*, ed. Eugene Dietzgen, 3 vols., Wiesbaden, 1911, Vol. 1, pp. 159–98.
5. 'Scientific Socialism' (1876), translated in *Philosophical Essays*, pp. 79–89, pp. 81, 85; *Sämtliche Schriften*, Vol. 1, pp. 227–34.
6. 'The Limits of Cognition' (1877), trans. in *Philosophical Essays* pp. 224–35; p. 225; cf. *Sämtliche Schriften*, Vol. I, pp. 205–13.
7. 'The Nature of Human Brainwork', *The Positive Outcome of Philosophy* [*The Nature of Human Brain Work; Letters on Logic; The Positive Outcome of Philosophy*], trans. Ernest Unterman, eds. Eugene Dietzgen and Joseph Dietzgen, Jr., Chicago, Charles Kerr, 1906, pp. 43–160, p. 62. The German original – 'Das Wesen der menschlichen Kopfarbeit, dargestellt von einem Handarbeiter' is available in *Sämtliche Schriften*, Vol. 1, pp. xxxi–xxxiv and 1–87; see p. 11.
8. For a lucid and sympathetic account of Dietzgen's moral philosophy, arguing that Dietzgen anticipates Dewey, see Lloyd D. Easton, 'Empiricism and Ethics in Dietzgen', *Journal of the History of Ideas*, Vol. 19, No. 1, January 1958, pp. 77–90.
9. 'The Nature of Human Brain Work', p. 156 (*Sämtliche Schriften*, Vol. I, p. 76).
10. 'The Nature of Human Brain Work', pp. 43–4 (*Sämtliche Schriften*, Vol. I, p. xxxii).
11. 'Social-Democratic Philosophy', *Philosophical Essays*, p. 183; cf. p. 182: 'As the alchemistic errors generated modern chemistry, so have the errors of Philosophy generated a Universal Doctrine of Knowledge and Science' (*Sämtliche Schriften*, Vol. 1, p. 168).
12. *Philosophical Essays*, pp. 215–16. The English translation (1906) actually uses the phrase 'dialectic Materialists', whereas the German original simply has 'Materialisten' without qualification (*Sämtliche Schriften*, Vol. I, p. 193). This seems to have misled certain commentators into crediting Dietzgen with using the phrase 'dialectical materialism' in 1876, i.e. long before Plekhanov's

reference to 'dialektische Materialismus' in 1891. See for example, Adam Buick, 'Joseph Dietzgen', *Radical Philosophy* 10, Spring 1975, pp. 3–7; David McLellan, *Marxism after Marx, an Introduction*, London, MacMillan, 1979, p. 11, n. 10. (See above, p. 134, Notes to Introduction, n. 6.) There is, however (as David McLellan has pointed out to me), another passage in Dietzgen on which the attribution might be based. This occurs in 'Excursions of a Socialist into the Domain of Epistemology' (1886), and was faithfully translated in *Philosophical Essays* as follows: 'Engels called this materialism metaphysical, and the materialism of Social-Democracy, which has received a better schooling through the preceding German idealism, the dialectical' (*Philosophical Essays*, p. 311). (Cf. *Sämtliche Schriften*, Vol. 2, p. 216.) However, the phrase as used here is not fused into a kind of compound name, 'dialectical materialism', as it was to be later, and the credit for the first use of the phrase in this way probably belongs to Plekhanov after all, though the first use of 'dialectic materialist' in English may be due to Dietzgen's translator.

13. *Sämtliche Schriften*, Vol. 2, pp. 1–175, translated by Untermann in *The Positive Outcome*, pp. 177–323; pp. 193–4, 228, 220, 291, 244, 289, 301–2, 180–1.

14. He described it, for instance, as 'the photographic organ of the infinite motion and transformations called the "world"' ('Letters on Logic', p. 270; see also p. 244).

15. 'Gedankendinge sind Bilder, wirkliche Bilder, Bilder der Wirklichkeit.' See 'Das Akquisit der Philosophie', *Sämtliche Schriften*, Vol. 2, pp. 261–356, translated as 'The Positive Outcome of Philosophy' in *The Positive Outcome*, pp. 327–444, pp. 348, 404, 440; cf. *Sämtliche Schriften*, Vol. 2, p. 352.

16. 'The Positive Outcome of Philosophy', p. 346. Maybe this metaphor, these phrases, and this entire doctrine can be likened to Wittgenstein's early philosophy, especially his 'picture theory of the proposition'. Dietzgen, like Wittgenstein, was led by this theory to the conclusion that, as he put it, 'so called apodictical facts are nothing but tautologies' ('The Positive Outcome of Philosophy', p. 434).

17. 'The Positive Outcome of Philosophy', p. 444.

18. On Dietzgen, see further Henriette Roland-Holst, *Joseph Dietzgens Philosophie*, Munich, 1910; Ernest Unterman, *Die Logische Mängel des engeren Marxismus, Georg Plekhanov et alii gegen Josef Dietzgen*, Munich, 1910; Adolf Hopner, *Josef Dietzgens Philosophische Lehren*, Stuttgart, 1916; Vittorio Ancarani, 'La Teoria della Conoscenza nel primo Dietzgen', *Annali, Fondazione Giangiacomo Feltrinelli*, Milan, 1976, pp. 137–64.

19. Marx visited Ludwig Kugelmann's household in Hanover in 1867 and 1869, and according to the (possibly unreliable) recollection of Kugelmann's daughter, 'Party friends often came to see Marx during this period. One of them was Herr Dietzgen, a calm, distinguished man whom Marx and Jenny held in high esteem. . . .

They jokingly called him "das Dietzchen"'. See Franzisca Kugelmann, 'Small Traits of Marx's Great Character' (written 1928), in F. Engels *et. al., Reminiscences of Marx and Engels*, Moscow, FLPH, n.d., pp. 273–87, p. 282. The story that Marx and Jenny visited Dietzgen in Siegburg in 1869 (see Korolcuk and Kruskol, p. 74) appears to be unfounded.

20. See Eugene Dietzgen, 'Joseph Dietzgen — A sketch of his Life', *Philosophical Essays*, p. 15. This phrase, often quoted with pride by Dietzgenites, may have had a sting of mocking condescension in the tail. Certainly an exchange of letters between Marx and Engels in November 1868 was less complimentary: 'The man is not a born philosopher. . . . His terminology is of course still very confused. . . . On the whole, however, a remarkable instinct, to think so much that is correct with such deficient preliminary studies' (Engels). 'It is hard luck that it is precisely Hegel whom he did not study' (Marx). Marx and Engels, *Selected Correspondence*, 3rd edition, Moscow, 1975, pp. 203–4.

21. 'And this materialist dialectic which for years has been our best working tool and our sharpest weapon was, remarkably enough, discovered not only by us, but also independently of us and even of Hegel by a German worker, Joseph Dietzgen', Friedrich Engels, *Ludwig Feuerbach and the Outcome of Classical German Philosophy*, 1934, p. 54; MEW, 21, p. 293.

22. *The Postive Outcome*, trans. P. Dauge and A. Orlov, St. Petersburg, 1906; *Philosophical Essays*, St. Petersburg, 1906; *The Future of Social-Democracy*, Kiev, 1907; *The Nature of Human Brainwork*, trans. P. Dauge, Moscow, 1907. An article on Dietzgen by Plekhanov appeared in *Sovremmeny Mir*, No. 7, 1907.

23. 'In that worker-philosopher, who discovered dialectical materialism in his own way, there is much that is great! . . . To class him not only with Leclair but even with Mach is to lay stress on Dietzgen the muddlehead as distinct from Dietzgen the materialist', V. I. Lenin, *Materialism and Empirio-Criticism*, Ch. IV, Section 8; *Collected Works*, Vol. 14, pp. 247–8. Lenin returned to the defence of Dietzgen on several other occasions — for instance in an article in *Pravda* on 5 May 1913, commemorating the twenty-fifth anniversary of Dietzgen's death (*Collected Works*, Vol. 19, pp. 79–82), and in an article in an early issue of *Under the Banner of Marxism* (1922) entitled 'On the Significance of Militant Materialism', translated in *Labour Monthly*, Vol. 13, No. 1, January 1931, pp. 54–62, reprinted in *Collected Works*, Vol. 33, pp. 227–36.

24. Notably Ernest Untermann, author of what is probably the first article on Dietzgen in English ('A Pioneer of Proletarian Science', *International Socialist Review*, Vol. 6, No. 10, April 1906, pp. 605–9). Untermann claimed (p. 609) that 'a proletarian armed with the intellectual weapons of Darwin's natural selection theory, Marx's historical materialism, and Dietzgen's theory of understanding, can approach every phenomenon in society and nature

with scientific objectiveness and precision'. Letters to Upton Sinclair (now amongst the Sinclair MSS at Indiana University) show Untermann in 1930 still querulously evangelizing for Dietzgen.

25. Anton Pannekoek, 'The Position and Significance of J. Dietzgen's Philosophical Works' (1902), trans. Ernest Untermann, *The Positive Outcome of Philosophy*, pp. 7–73; p. 28, p. 37. See also Pannekoek's *Lenin als Philosoph* (1938) translated as *Lenin as Philosopher*, New York, 1948.

26. Eugene Dietzgen, 'An Illustration of the Proletarian Method of Research' in *Some of the Philosophical Essays*, pp. 35–77, pp. 70, 72, 74, 77.

27. W. W. Craik, *The Central Labour College*, 1909–29, London, Lawrence and Wishart, 1964, p. 121.

28. For mentions of courses in Rochdale, Oldham, and Halifax, for example, see *Plebs Magazine*, Vol. 7, No. I, February 1915, p. 17; No. 2, March 1915, p. 45.

29. According to Easton ('Empiricism and Ethics in Dietzgen', p. 79, n. 7) Craik was responsible for the translation of 'The Nature of Human Brain Work' in *The Positive Outcome*.

30. A synopsis of a course of lectures on the History of Philosophy given by Craik at the Central Labour College in or about 1915 can be found in the Casey Collection at Ruskin College, Oxford.

31. See *Plebs Magazine*, Vol. 7, No. 10, November 1915, p. 232; Vol. 7, No. 5, June 1915, p. 115; see also his article on 'The Outcome of Philosophy', pp. 100–5.

32. The agenda for a joint SLP-Plebs League 'Workers' Educational Conference' held in Glasgow in September 1917 (bound with *Plebs Magazine*, Vol. 9, 1917, in the Marx Memorial Library) includes the statement that 'the subjects we recommend students to take up are Economics and History, and for advanced students, Philosophy' and remarks that 'the working class has need to formulate a working-class philosophy: such philosophy to be founded upon dialectical reasoning and an interpretation of the universe by the actual facts of science'. J. F. and Winifred Horrabin (*Working-Class Education*, p. 79) nominated 'world history' as the main goal of working-class education, regarding 'Scientific Method and Science of Understanding' as 'more advanced education for the Minority'.

33. For further discussion of the conflict between the Labour College and the Central Labour College, see Anne Phillips and Tim Putnam, 'Education for Emancipation', esp. pp. 28–31.

34. The prospectus explained: 'How can the brain arrive at truth? This is the centuries-old problem of philosophy. . . . Kant and Marx transferred the subject-matter of philosophical speculation to the domain of objective science. As alchemy developed into chemistry, so passed philosophy into the sober science of human brainwork. The theoretical elaboration of this new science was the meritorious achievement of Joseph Dietzgen whose main

work, *The Positive Outcome of Philosophy,* serves as a textbook for the course of study'. (Prospectus of the Labour College, 1919, bound with *Plebs Magazine,* Vol. 11 in the Marx Memorial Library). See also J. R., 'The Test of Theory', *Plebs Magazine,* Vol. 10, No. 5, June 1918, pp. 125–8; 'What to read', *Plebs Magazine,* Vol. 10, No. 6, July 1918, p. 167.

35. Craik, *Central Labour College,* p. 120.

36. The conference is reported in *Plebs Magazine,* Vol. 12, No. 2, February 1920, pp. 17–21.

37. *Plebs Magazine,* Vol. 12, No. 4, April 1921, pp. 60–2. Alice Pratt (née Smith) attended the Central Labour College in 1913, returning to her native North West 'an able teacher of "Philosophic Logic"'. See Edmund and Ruth Frow, 'Educating Marxists: study of the Early Days of the Plebs League in the North West', *Marxism Today,* Vol. 12, No. 10, October 1968, pp. 304–10.

38. Judging by correspondence in the Casey collection at Ruskin College, Oxford, Craik was still hoping to complete the book in 1928. Its title was to be 'The Science of Understanding; or Proletarian-Democratic Logic', and it was announced as 'to be published in 1925' in Fred Casey, *Thinking,* Second Edition, Chicago, 1926, p. 186, and as 'to be published in 1927' in the Second English Edition, London, Labour Publishing Co., 1927, p. 199.

39. The Plebs League pamphlet, *What to Read: A guide for Worker-Students* (London, Plebs League, 1923) included a section by Craik which recommended a course in the History of Philosophy culminating in Dietzgen. But the rival subjects were proliferating — not only Economics, History, and Geography, but also Modern Problems, Psychology, Biology, Exact Science, English, and Esperanto.

40. See Christine Millar, 'Workers' Education by Post', *The Plebs,* Vol. 28, Nos. 2–4, February–April 1936, pp. 45–6, 66–8; 94–5.

41. 'It is a tragic blot on our work and we feel it keenly', as Fred Casey wrote in a very informative letter to Eugene Dietzgen of 17 Mar. 1926 (Casey Collection). Cf. Millar, *The Labour College Movement,* p. 44.

42. See Millar, *The Labour College Movement,* pp. 91–9.

43. Letter to Eugene Dietzgen, 16 Jan. 1926 (Casey Collection).

44. Casey, *Thinking, an Introduction to its History and Science,* London, Labour Publishing Co., 1922.

45. Casey, *Thinking,* Chicago, 1926, p. 113.

46. Letter from Casey to W. W. Craik, 4 July 1928 (Casey Collection).

47. Fred Casey, 'Joseph Dietzgen, 1828–1928', *The Plebs,* Vol. 20, No. 12, December 1928, pp. 269–70; Fred Casey, 'Dietzgen's Logic — A Plain Introduction to "The Positive Outcome of Philosophy", written for the Plain Man', published by the author, Bury, 1928; Henry Sara, 'Dietzgen, the Tanner who confuted the Pundits', *Sunday Worker,* 9 Dec. 1928, p. 4. Casey's papers include copies of a fraternal message from 'The Manchester section

of British students of Dietzgen', and a telegram from the Proletarian party of America in Chicago: 'Let us strive to promote greater understanding of understanding.'

48. Fred Casey, *Method in Thinking*, Manchester, 1933, p. 13. On abstraction: 'To construct the General, take the thoughts that men are living, plants are living, that protoplasm is living, and so on. Then split the thoughts of livingness from the other parts of the things, and add the separate thoughts of livingness together to form one general thought of livingness as a whole. . . . The knowledge of this process of understanding enables us to see that there can be no life apart from bodies that live' (pp. 127–8). On the problem of freedom: 'all that is needed to settle it is the knowledge that one thing can be at the same time two things' (p. 118). Casey referred to the 'continuance of the immortal work of Marx, Engels, and Dietzgen' as 'our mission'. (*Method in Thinking*, p. 190, cf. p. 7.)

49. See *Method in Thinking*, p. 8. Casey's final book — 'How people Think: How Brains form ideas' — was also turned down by the NCLC, and published by Casey privately in 1953.

50. Letter to the Editor of *Labour's Northern Voice*, 1952, refused publication (Casey Collection). Local studies might well reveal other, comparable enthusiastic local teachers of Dietzgenism — such as 'Comrade Tom' with his open-air lectures in Glasgow. See Comrade Tom (Anderson), *Comrade Joseph Dietzgen: Proletarian School Lessons*, Glasgow, 1935. Clearly there were Dietzgenian tutors at work in South Wales too, and *The Positive Outcome of Philosophy* was a widely used book. Cf. Hywel Francis, 'Workers' Libraries: The Origins of the South Wales Miners' Library'. *History Workshop 2*, Autumn 1976, pp. 183–205, esp. p. 197.

51. Letter to Stuart Macintyre, quoted in Macintyre's *A Proletarian Science*, p. 130.

52. Dorothy Emmett, 'Joseph Dietzgen, the Philosopher of Proletarian Logic', pp. 31–2. A further evidence of the way students interpreted Dietzgen is to be found in an article written in 1920 by a 'Labour College Student' on 'The Miners' Progress: Five Years in the South Wales Coal Fields'. The author, under the name 'Plebs', begins by trying to place the political progress of the last five years in a cosmic context, drawing attention to 'the realms of past human social development, which extend over such a long period, compared to an individual's life, or to the life of any one social system which is but a short period compared with general biological evolution', and remarks that, from this point of view, 'glancing at the changes in outlook and economic structure which have characterised the mining industry during recent years, one cannot but marvel and become exuberantly enthusiastic and optimistic'. See *Workers' Dreadnought*, Vol. 7, No. 4, Sat. 17 Apr. 1920, Supplement, pp. II–IV, p. II.

53. Shanley singled out *Capital*, Vol. 1, the *Eighteenth Brumaire*, the *Critique of Political Economy*, and *The Poverty of Philosophy*,

as well as Labriola's *The Materialist Conception of History*, and the Chicago edition of extracts from *Anti-Duhring*. Jock Shanley, interviewed 24 May 1977.

54. 'I was always in trouble, because the last thing a craftsman believes is that anyone can take his place. . . . I gave a lecture at a branch. They said, you'll never replace an upholsterer working with a mouthful of tacks. Now dialectics is not an answer. Dialectics tells you nothing. But it enables you to understand everything.' (Interview.)

55. But Shanley exaggerated when he said that Casey 'became the central theorist for the NCLC'. (Interview.)

56. Arthur Ransome, *Six Weeks in Russia in 1919*, p. viii, quoted in David Caute, *The Fellow-Travellers: A Postscript to the Enlightenment*, London, Weidenfeld and Nicholson, 1973, p. 21.

57. Lancelot Hogben, 'The Wisdom of Joseph Dietzgen: an Appreciation', *Plebs Magazine*, Vol. 11, No. 4, May 1919, pp. 53–4, pp. 53, 54. Further on Hogben, see Gary Werskey's *The Visible College: A Collective Biography of British Scientists and Socialists of the 1930s*, London, Allen Lane, 1978.

58. 'The Need for Science Textbooks', *Plebs Magazine*, Vol. 12, No. 10, October 1920, pp. 167–9, p. 169.

59. The subjects recommended in this document (bound with Vol. 12 of *Plebs Magazine* in the Bodleian Library) were physical sciences, geography, development of the tool, economics of labour, and the modern working-class movement.

60. *The Plebs*, Vol. 13, No. 7, July 1921, p. 197.

61. Pollitt, *Serving My Time*, p. 93.

62. The Pauls defended this omission in *The Plebs*, Vol. 13, No. 10, October 1921, p. 310.

63. *The Plebs*, Vol. 13, No. 10, October 1921, p. 290.

64. Eden and Cedar Paul, *Creative Revolution: A Study of Communist Ergatocracy*, London, Allen and Unwin, 1920, p. 191. The Pauls nominated Newton, Darwin, Marx, Bergson, and Freud as the chief theorists of 'Social progress' (p. 184).

65. Maurice H. Dobb, 'Communism or Reformism — Which?', *Communist Review*, Vol. 2, No. 4, February 1922, pp. 273–98; pp. 280, 281. Harry Waton is quoted from *Radical Review*, 1917.

66. Letter from John Lewis, *The Plebs*, Vol. 14, No. 2, February 1922, p. 52. Lewis was particularly offended by 'E and C P' (the Pauls), PLEB (Hogben?), Nordicus (Henry Lyster Jameson), and Postgate. See also the letter in support of Lewis in the next issue: 'Scrap the Plebs League: Inaugurate a Revolutionary Council of Action' (*The Plebs*, Vol. 14, No. 3, March 1922, p. 88). Ironically, it is probably the same John Lewis who later became a prominent Communist intellectual.

67. Letter from A. Fisher, *The Plebs*, Vol. 14, No. 10, October 1922, pp. 361–2, with reply by Craik; see also T. Ashcroft's defence of Dietzgenism: 'The Science of Reasoning' in *The Plebs*, Vol. 14, No. 11, November 1922, pp. 410–11. Fisher's position was echoed

in 1924, when a correspondent claimed that no worker could ever understand Dietzgen. (Letter from J. G. C., (Crowther?) *The Plebs*, Vol. 16, No. 2, February 1924, p. 79.)

68. *The Plebs*, Vol. 15, No. 11, November 1923, pp. 516–17.

69. Margaret Cole, 'Postgate, Raymond William', *Dictionary of Labour Biography*, eds. J. Bellamy and J. Saville, Vol. 2, London, Macmillan, 1974, pp. 304–10.

70. *The Plebs*, Vol. 15, No. 12, December 1923, p. 566.

71. *The Plebs*, Vol. 17, No. 4, April 1925, p. 162. The article names Riazanov as the instigator of the new policy.

72. Letter from 'A Tutor', *The Plebs*, Vol. 13, No. 8, August 1921, p. 250.

73. S. M. Connelly, *The Plebs*, Vol. 13, No. 9, September 1921, pp. 276–7.

74. Oliver Jones, *The Plebs*, Vol. 13, No. 9, September 1921, p. 277.

75. Robert Holder, *The Plebs*, Vol. 16, No. 1, January 1924, p. 40.

76. T. Gordon Nowell, *The Plebs*, Vol. 16, No. 1, January 1924, p. 40.

77. James Johnstone, 'The Method of Science', *The Plebs*, Vol. 16, Nos. 10–12, October–December 1924, pp. 390–4, 427–30, 469–72; Vol. 17, No. 2, February 1925, pp. 75–8. Johnstone had tried but failed to make an ally of Casey, complimenting him on his summary of the history of philosophy, but criticizing his 'logic' with amiable finality. This failed to woo Casey. (See letters from Johnstone in the Casey Collection.)

78. Later he became renowned as a scholar of Buddhism, and was professor of Far Eastern Studies of the University of Washington in Seattle.

79. Edward Conze, 'What is the Scientific Way of Thinking?', *The Plebs*, Vol. 26, Nos. 11, 12, November–December 1934, pp. 252–4, 278–81; Vol. 27, Nos. 1, 2, January–February 1935, pp. 8–11, 36–42, p. 252. These articles are colloquial in style, unlike Conze's earlier study, in German, of the same problems (Edward [Eberhard] Conze: *Der Satz vom Widerspruch: Zur Theorie des dialektischen Materialismus*, Hamburg, 1932).

80. 'His disciples often impress the observer by the laborious and ponderous way in which they express rather simple ideas' (Edward Conze, *The Scientific Method of Thinking: An Introduction to Dialectical Materialism*, London, Chapman and Hall, 1935, p. 51).

81. See Casey's letter to J. P. M. Millar, 10 Dec. 1935. (Casey Collection.)

82. Edward Conze, *An Introduction to Dialectical Materialism*, NCLC Publishing Society, 1936. The course was discontinued after a while on the grounds that 'some of the illustrations became decidedly out of date'. See Millar, *The Labour College Movement*, pp. 213–14.

83. 'The General Plan of our Studies', *The Plebs*, Vol. 12, No. 10, October 1920, pp. 164–7, p. 164.

84. 'The General Plan of our Studies Cont'd', *The Plebs*, Vol. 12, No. 11, November 1920, pp. 192–5, p. 194.

85. *The Plebs*, Vol. 12, No. 2, February 1920, p. 20.
86. T. A. Jackson, 'A comment on ergatocracy', *The Plebs*, Vol. 11, No. 8, September 1919, pp. 120-1, p. 121.
87. 'Ergatocracy — and Greek: in Conclusion', *The Plebs*, Vol. 12, No. 3, March 1920, pp. 42-4, p. 43.
88. Unpublished Autobiography, First Draft, p. 128, Third Draft, p. 123.

Four: British Communists and Dialectical Materialism 1920-1937

1. Nan Milton, *John MacLean*, London, Pluto Press, 1973, p. 227.
2. Unpublished Autobiography, Third Draft, p. 8.
3. Challinor, *The Origins of British Bolshevism*, Chapter 10.
4. William Gallacher, *The Rolling of the Thunder*, London, Lawrence and Wishart, 1947, pp. 8-12.
5. See V. I. Lenin, *'Left-Wing' Communism, An Infantile Disorder* (April 1920), *Collected Works*, Vol. 31, pp. 21-118, p. 62. See also the whole of the ninth chapter of this essay, and Lenin's speech at the Second Congress of the Third International, 6 August 1920, *Collected Works*, Vol. 31, pp. 257-63.
6. Jackson, *Solo Trumpet*, p. 162; Unpublished Autobiography, Second Draft, Part Two, p. 31.
7. Leslie Paul, *Angry Young Man*, London, Faber and Faber, 1951, p. 76.
8. This position was advocated by Eden and Cedar Paul, who sought to replace the catch-phrase 'dictatorship of the proletariat' with 'ergatocracy' — the Greek for 'Workers' control'. See their *Creative Revolution*, which developed ideas first aired in *The Plebs* in 1919.
9. Francis Meynell, *My Lives*, London, Bodley Head, 1971, pp. 127-8. Meynell continues: 'I doubt whether there could ever have been a political party organ that showed so little awareness of its party's ideology.'
10. *The Communist*, Vol. 1, No. 8, 23 Sept. 1920, p. 6; cf. No. 13, 28 Oct. 1920, p. 6: 'No Communist can afford to save sixpence at the expense of the *Plebs*.'
11. *The Communist*, No. 10, 7 Oct. 1920, p. 6.
12. *The Communist*, No. 20, 16 Dec. 1920, p. 5.
13. T. A. Jackson, *Solo Trumpet*, p. 166.
14. James Klugman, *History of the Communist Party of Great Britain*, Vol. 1, London, Lawrence and Wishart, 1968, p. 215.
15. See especially the feature by Stella Browne and Cedar Paul, *The Communist*, No. 84, 11 Mar. 1922, pp. 6-7.
16. *The Communist*, No. 68, 19 Nov. 1922, p. 10.
17. *The Communist*, No. 86, 25 Mar. 1922, p. 8.
18. See *The Communist*, No. 95, 27 May 1922, p. 4.
19. It was asserted that 'what Jackson said had reference to the Second International' — 'Shinwell Lies', *The Communist*, No. 91, 29 Apr. 1922, p. 4.

20. S. Francis wrote: 'There are other things in life besides the sex act. . . . If our comrades were to spend less of their energy on that, and more on the teaching of Marxian ethics, the CPGB would be a more efficient section of the Third International' – *The Communist*, No. 108, 26 Aug. 1922, p. 6.

21. At first entitled *The Communist Review*, this became *The Communist* in February 1927, reverting to the original title in January 1929.

22. See Klugmann, *History of the Communist Party of Great Britain*, p. 206, and Henry Pelling, *The British Communist Party* (2nd edition) London, A. and C. Black, 1975, pp. 21-2.

23. *Labour Monthly* was owned and controlled by Dutt personally, and he in turn put it at the disposal of the Party. See R. Page Arnot, *Forging the Weapon: The Struggle of the Labour Monthly 1921-1941*, London, Labour Monthly, 1941. The original idea of the *Monthly* was that it should be 'devoted primarily to reporting and explaining to British workers the developments of the Labour movement in other countries'. (*Labour Monthly*, Vol. 1, No. 1, July 1921, p. 3.)

24. However, the *Weekly* did carry a brief statement from the Plebs League, affirming that the League, whilst jealous of its independence, would welcome Party members into its ranks (*Workers' Weekly*, No. 18, 9 June 1923, p. 4). But see also the incongruous article by Cedar Paul, based on conversations with Krupskaya, about the failures of socialist education policies in the Soviet Union (*Workers' Weekly*, 17 Apr. 1923, p. 2).

25. Lenin's death (21 Jan. 1924) released a cult of Lenin, and its anniversary became a main event in the Communist calendar (see especially *Workers' Weekly*, 16 Jan. 1925).

26. T. A. Jackson, 'The Party Conference', *Communist Review*, Vol. IV, No. 12, April 1924, pp. 537-41.

27. Morton and Saville, 'Thomas Alfred Jackson', p. 103.

28. See especially 'Revolution by Hire Purchase', *Workers' Weekly*, 2 May 1924, p. 5.

29. William Paul, *Sunday Worker*, 9 Aug. 1925, p. 6.

30. *Sunday Worker*, 29 Aug. 1926; September and October 1927; 18 Mar. 1928.

31. *Sunday Worker*, 21 Oct., 4 Nov., 11 Nov., 9 Dec., 1928.

32. *Sunday Worker*, 13 Dec. 1925.

33. Unpublished Autobiography, Third Draft, p. 63.

34. *Sunday Worker*, 8 July 1928, p. 9.

35. *Sunday Worker*, 31 Mar. 1929, p. 8.

36. *Sunday Worker*, 7 Apr. 1929, p. 4.

37. *Sunday Worker*, 14 Apr. 1929, p. 4.

38. William Paul, 'Neither Honest nor History' (a review of the Plebs League's 'Workers' History of the Great Strike', by J. F. Horrabin, R. W. Postgate, and Ellen Wilkinson), *Sunday Worker*, 6 Feb. 1927. See also the indignant replies by Postgate and Horrabin in the next week's issue, and Cedar Paul's forthright attack on 'this

opportunist and un-Plebeian history' in *Workers' Life*, 11 Feb. 1927, p. 2.

39.   T. A. Jackson, 'Where is the NCLC: is it deserting to Marx's enemies?' (a review of 'Marxism and History' by John S. Clarke, published by the NCLC), *Sunday Worker*, 8 Jan. 1928. See replies by Millar and others, *Sunday Worker*, 22 Jan. 1928.

40.   T. A. Jackson, 'Lenin and Marxian Materialism', *The Communist*, Vol. 3, No. 2, February 1928, pp. 83–8, pp. 84–5.

41.   See in particular Bert Williams's attack on J. F. Horrabin's *Short History of the British Empire* (NCLC 1929), for being haunted by 'fear of hurting the susceptibilities of certain prominent trade union and labour leaders whose support for the NCLC is ardently desired'. Williams concluded that it would henceforth be necessary to 'go where education is conceived of as a weapon of revolutionary struggle' —*Sunday Worker*, 7 Apr. 1929.

42.   C.E.L.T., 'The Labour College Passes', *Sunday Worker*, 4 Aug. 1929.

43.   *Sunday Worker*, 10 Nov. 1929, p. 8; see also Palme Dutt's 'Notes of the Month' in *Labour Monthly*, Vol. 11, No. 11, November 1929.

44.   Unpublished Autobiography, Second Draft, Part Two, p. 103; First Draft, p. 195.

45.   T. A. Jackson, 'Why Militant Workers should study Marx', *Sunday Worker*, 1 Sept. 1929, p. 6.

46.   Unpublished Autobiography, Second Draft, Part Two, pp. 104, 113.

47.   Vivien Morton, interviewed 9 June 1978. The 'gag' is also recorded in the Unpublished Autobiography, First Draft, p. 215.

48.   A.L. Morton, interviewed 9 June 1978.

49.   CPGB circular, 'On C.P. Policy towards the Plebs League' (1924): Klugman, *History of the Communist Party of Great Britain*, p. 335.

50.   'Ideally the segregation into different sections . . . is bad, and these subjects should be treated dialectically, as they arise from the study of capitalism. In fact, such an arrangement has proved impossible. . . .' T.B[ell] Preface to CPGB, *Communist Party Training*, New Revised Edition, October 1927, p. 7.

51.   *Communist Review*, Vol. 7, No. 8, December 1926, pp. 377–82; see also Vol. 7, No. 9, January 1927, p. 427.

52.   A.G.P., 'Communist Schools and Education in Britain, a summary of recent activities', *The Communist*, Vol. 2, No. 8, September 1927, pp. 81–3, p. 82. The syllabus covered Political Economy, Industrial History, Political Theory, Imperialism, History of Socialism, Party Organization, History of the International Labour Movement, and Leninism.

53.   See A.G.P., *The Communist*, Vol. 2, No. 8, September 1927, p.81.

54.   Andrew Rothstein, 'On Lenin's Method', *The Communist*, Vol. 2, No. 10, November 1927, pp. 214–21. See also A.G.P., 'Ten Millions of Enlightened People', ibid., pp. 205–9.

55. See above, p. 142, Notes to Chapter Three, n. 12.
56. *The Communist*, Vol. 2, No. 10, November 1927, pp. 233–4; Vol. 2, No. 11, December 1927, pp. 283–5. Stalin's book was then available in a cheap pamphlet entitled 'Theory and Practice of Leninism'.
57. 'Lenin and Marxian Materialism', *The Communist*, Vol. 3, No. 2, February 1928, pp. 83–8.
58. Central Committee of the CPGB, 'Ourselves and the Labour Party', *The Communist*, Vol. 3, No. 2, February 1928, pp. 89–105.
59. *The Communist*, Vol. 3, No. 3, March 1928, pp. 141–53.
60. Harold Heslop, 'Raymond W. Postgate, A Memoir', *The Communist*, Vol. 3, No. 4, April 1928, pp. 228–31. Heslop claimed that his article had first been offered to *The Plebs*, which had turned it down. See also Heslop's letter in support of Jackson's doubts about the Labour College Movement, *Sunday Worker*, 8 July 1928, p. 9.
61. Henry Sara, 'Further Jottings on R. W. Postgate', *The Communist*, Vol. 3, No. 5, May 1928, pp. 290–6, p. 290.
62. Agitprop Department of the Communist International, 'A Criticism of the Party Training Manual', *The Communist*, Vol. 3, No. 8, August 1928, pp. 450–60, pp. 452, 456.
63. See D.R., 'The Present State of Party Education', *Communist Review*, Vol. 3, No. 1, January 1931, pp. 25–9, esp. p. 27.
64. A. L. Morton, interviewed 9 June 1978.
65. Anonymous, interviewed 24 June 1977.
66. 'Party Training Notes', *Communist Review*, Vol. 7, No. 9, January 1927, p. 427; see also D.R., 'The Present State of Party Education', p. 26.
67. Anonymous, interviewed 24 June 1977.
68. Vivien Morton recalled an evening in a London University Students' Group about 1933: 'We used to have to prepare pieces and I was a bit overwhelmed — I was so shy anyway — I prepared something about *State and Revolution* but I couldn't get a word out. They let me off I think.' (Vivien Morton, interviewed 9 June 1978.)
69. See for example the eleven 'lessons' (each occupying one pamphlet of fifty or sixty pages) of the 'Marxist Study Course' on *Political Economy*, London, Martin Lawrence, 1933; or the eighteen-page pamphlet, *What Every Worker Wants to Know: A Syllabus of Current Economic and Philosophical Problems*, London, Marx Memorial Library and Workers' School, 1934.
70. Unpublished Autobiography, First Draft, p. 198.
71. Olive Budden, 'The Materialist Conception of History', *Communist Review*, Vol. 2, No. 11, November 1930, pp. 30–9, p. 31.
72. S. Knight, 'The NCLC and Working Class Education', *Communist Review*, Vol. 3, No. 8, August 1931, pp. 323–7, p. 323.
73. Fred Casey, *Method in Thinking*, Manchester, published by voluntary tutors and others attached to the S.E. Lancashire Labour College, 1933, p. 179. Casey notes that 'a detailed exposition of this particular error considered as an example of dialectical

reasoning was published by South East Lancashire Labour College in November 1931'.

74. Knight, 'The NCLC and Independent Working-Class Education', pp. 325-6.
75. Letter to J. P. M. Millar, 16 Dec. 1937, Casey Collection.
76. D.R., 'Thinking', *Communist Review,* Vol. 3, No. 9, October 1931, pp. 373-6.
77. A. Fogarasi, 'Reactionary Idealism — the Philosophy of Social Fascism' (a review of Max Adler's *Lehrbuch der materialistischen Geschichstsauffassung*), trans. Jack Cohen, *Communist Review,* Vol. 4, Nos. 2, 3, and 5, February, March, and May 1932, pp. 92-8, 154-8, 251-6.
78. Jack Cohen, 'Critical Thoughts on our Agitation and Propaganda', *Communist Review,* Vol. 4, No. 6, June 1932, pp. 292-7, p. 296.
79. D.R., 'Thinking', p. 376.
80. Cohen, 'Critical Thoughts on our Agitation and Propaganda', p. 296.
81. H.R., 'Marxism Vulgarised', *Communist Review,* Vol. 4, No. 7, July 1932, pp. 343-8, p. 344.
82. For a general survey, see Leszek Kolakowski, *Main Currents of Marxism,* Oxford University Press, 1978, 3 Vols.; Vol. 2, pp. 305-80.
83. 'The Monist View of History', cited in Wetter, *Dialectical Materialism,* p. 107. Plekhanov's Darwinist evolutionism made him stalwartly Menshevik, since it rendered the Bolshevik project of hurrying from 'feudalism' to 'socialism' unthinkable.
84. See above, p. 134, Notes to Introduction, n. 6.
85. 'It is impossible to become an intelligent, *real* communist without studying — precisely studying — all that Plekhanov wrote on philosophy. . . .', V. I. Lenin, 'Once again on the Trade Unions' (January 1921), *Collected Works,* Vol. 32, p. 94.
86. See above, pp. 29-30.
87. S. Minin, 'Overboard with Philosophy', *Under the Banner of Marxism,* 1922. Quoted in David Joravsky, *Soviet Marxism and Natural Science, 1917-32,* London, Routledge, 1961, p. 96. See also Wetter, *Dialectical Materialism,* pp. 129-30.
88. Natalie Duddington, 'Philosophy in Russia', *Journal of Philosophical Studies,* Vol. 1, No. 1, January 1926, pp. 100-3. Cf. Kolakowski, *Main Currents of Marxism,* Vol. 3, pp. 56-76.
89. Quoted in Wetter, *Dialectical Materialism,* p. 138.
90. See Loren R. Graham, *The Soviet Academy of Sciences and the Communist Party,* Princeton University Press, 1967, p. 99.
91. See V. I. Lenin, Letter to A. M. Gorky, 25 Feb. 1908, *Collected Works,* Vol. 15, pp. 448-54. Joravsky, *Soviet Marxism and Natural Science,* Chapter 2, provides a subtle account of Lenin's doctrine. Althusser's essay 'Lenin and Philosophy' (1968) is an accurate but unimpressive incantation of some of its implications, though Althusser's claim that Lenin inaugurated a 'new practice' of philosophy, but not a new philosophy, is distressingly obscure. See *Lenin and Philosophy and Other Essays,* trans. Brewster,

London, New Left Books, 1971, pp. 27-68, esp. pp. 63-7.

92. V. I. Lenin, 'The Meaning of Militant Materialism', *Under the Banner of Marxism*, 1922, *Collected Works*, Vol. 33, pp. 227-36, pp. 233-4; translation from *Labour Monthly*, Vol. 13, No. 1, January 1931, pp. 54-62.

93. Karl Korsch, 'Marxism and Philosophy' (1923) in *Marxism and Philosophy*, trans. Fred Halliday, London, New Left Books, 1970, p. 31, n. 6; p. 50, n. 30; p. 61, n. 42.

94. Georg Lukacs, 'What is Orthodox Marxism?', written in 1919, was published in German along with other essays in 1923; English translation by Rodney Livingstone, *History and Class Consciousness*, London, Merlin, 1971.

95. See Perry Anderson, *Considerations on Western Marxism*. Anderson argues that these essays by Lukacs and Korsch determined the future preoccupation of Western Marxism with epistemological and methodological issues. This judgement, however, neglects the fact that Korsch and Lukacs were actually denying (on philosophical grounds) Lenin's philosophism, that is, the supreme importance which Lenin (on political grounds) accorded to philosophy. In 1930, Korsch was able to explain the position more clearly. Lenin, he wrote, had made a fetish of defending 'the *materialist* position, which no one has ever seriously thought of questioning'. Engels, a better philosopher, had realized however that modern materialism ' "does not in addition need a philosophy which stands above the other branches of knowledge". Lenin, however, insistently carps at "philosophical deviations". . . . His "materialist philosophy" becomes a kind of supreme judicial authority for evaluating the findings of individual sciences, past, present or future. This materialist "philosophical" domination covers all the sciences, whether of nature or society, as well as all other cultural developments. . . . Under the slogan of what is called "Marxism-Leninism", this dictatorship is applied in Russia today to the whole intellectual life not only of the ruling Party but of the working-class in general. There are now attempts to extend it from Russia . . .'. 'The Problem of Marxism and Philosophy', *Marxism and Philosophy*, pp. 120-1.

96. Laszlo Rudas, 'Orthodoxer Marxismus?', *Arbeiterliteratur* (Vienna), Nos. 9, 10, and 12, 1924. See also Bela Kun, 'Die Propaganda des Leninismus', *Kommunistische Internationale*, April 1924. I am grateful to Helena Sheehan for these references.

97. *Fifth Congress of the Communist International, Abridged Report*, CPGB, n.d., p. 17.

98. See Hedda Korsch, 'Memories of Karl Korsch', *New Left Review* 76, November-December 1972, pp. 34-45.

99. See Georg Lukacs, 'Lukacs on his Life and Work', *New Left Review* 60, March-April 1970, pp. 36-47.

100. A. M. Deborin, 'Lukacs und seine Kritik des Marxismus', *Under the Banner of Marxism*, 1924, and *Arbeiterliteratur*, No. 10. See Korsch, *Marxism and Philosophy*, p. 107, n. 19; Guy Planty-Bonjour, *The Categories of Dialectical Materialism*, pp. 1-2.

101. In 1924-5, Deborin published several works on Lenin and Dialectical Materialism: see René Ahlberg, *A. M. Deborin*, Berlin, 1959.

102. Bukharin was editor of *Pravda* from December 1917, and head of the Communist International 1925-9; his chief theoretical work, *Historical Materialism* (1921) was influential in Russia throughout the 1920s. Whether Bukharin really was a mechanist is a debatable point, well discussed in Stephen F. Cohen's formidable *Bukharin and the Bolshevik Revolution*, New York, Knopf, 1973, pp. 108-9. See also Roy Medvedev, 'Bukharin's Last Years', *New Left Review* 109, May-June 1978, pp. 49-73. The other leading 'mechanists' were Stepanov and Axelrod ('Ortodox').

103. See Wetter, *Dialectical Materialism*, p. 132.

104. Lenin's 'Notes on Hegel', composed in 1914-16, reverse the emphasis on materialism at the expense of dialectics in *Materialism and Empirio-Criticism*. See *Collected Works*, Vol. 38.

105. Graham, *The Soviet Academy of Sciences and the Communist Party*, pp. 114, 168.

106. See Natalie Duddington, 'Philosophy in Russia', *Journal of Philosophical Studies*, Vol. 5, No. 20, October 1930, pp. 598-601.

107. See Julius Hecker, *Moscow Dialogues, Discussions on Red Philosophy*, London, Chapman and Hall, 1933, p. 173.

108. In 1928, 60 per cent of the 14,805 academic workers had been educated before the revolution (four years later, the proportion was 20 per cent); and only 678 of them (less than 5 per cent) were Party members. See John Barber, 'The Establishment of Intellectual Orthodoxy in the USSR, 1928-34', *Past and Present* 83, May 1979, pp. 141-64, p. 146, p. 145, n. 17. In January 1929 not a single member of the Academy of Sciences was in the Party (see Loren R. Graham, *Science and Philosophy in the Soviet Union*, p. 11).

109. James C. McLelland, 'Proletarianising the Student Body: The Soviet Experience during the New Economic Policy', *Past and Present* 80, August 1978, pp. 122-46. The Institute of Red Professors, formed in 1921 specifically to produce 'Red' teachers, had, by 1929, produced 236 specialists, twenty-seven from worker or peasant families. See David Joravsky, *Soviet Marxism and Natural Science*, p. 251.

110. Quoted in Joravsky, *Soviet Marxism and Natural Science*, p. 252.

111. *Isvestiya*, 21 Dec. 1929, quoted in Barber, 'The Establishment of Intellectual Orthodoxy', p. 157, n. 77.

112. J. Stalin, 'Problems of Agrarian Policy in the USSR', in Stalin's *Problems of Leninism*, Moscow, 1947, pp. 301-21; the passage quoted is on p. 301. See Cohen, *Bukharin*, p. 336; Barber, 'The Establishment of Intellectual Orthodoxy', p. 146, n. 20; and Joravsky, *Soviet Marxism and Natural Science*, pp. 52-3.

113. See Wetter, *Dialectical Materialism*, p. 133.

114. Barber, 'The Establishment of Intellectual Orthodoxy', p. 153.

115. Joravsky, *Soviet Marxism and Natural Science*, p. 252.

116. Deborin defended himself in a book entitled *Dialectics and*

Natural Science (1930). See Wetter, *Dialectical Materialism*, pp. 160-1.

117. Barber, 'The Establishment of Intellectual Orthodoxy', p. 160.

118. J. V. Stalin, Speech to the Bureau of the Cell of The Institute of Red Professors, 9 Dec. 1930. See Wetter, *Dialectical Materialism*, p. 133. In an interview given in 1977, Mitin told Helena Sheehan that it was Stalin himself who suggested that Deborinism could be defined as a 'Menshevik' variety of idealism. I am grateful to Helena Sheehan for this information.

119. Central Committee of the CPSU(B), resolution of 25 Jan. 1931. The resolution included an instruction to *Under the Banner of Marxism*: 'the journal must wage a relentless struggle on two fronts.' See Wetter, *Dialectical Materialism*, p. 135.

120. Graham, *Science and Philosophy in the Soviet Union*, p. 478, n. 29.

121. Joravsky, *Soviet Marxism and Natural Science*, pp. 264-7.

122. Barber, 'The Establishment of Intellectual Orthodoxy', p. 154; Hecker, *Moscow Dialogues*, pp. 181-2.

123. Wetter, *Dialectical Materialism*, p. 112.

124. Engels, *Dialectics of Nature*, p. 62. The new philosophers stressed the second of these laws, on the authority of Lenin's *Philosophical Notebooks*, but insisted that 'interpenetration' should not be interpreted (as it had been by the Deborinites) to mean 'unity'; rather it meant 'unity and struggle'. Cf. Wetter, *Dialectical Materialism*, p. 161.

125. Marcuse, *Soviet Marxism*, p. 153; Wetter, *Dialectical Materialism*, pp. 242-6.

126. 'Antagonism and contradiction are far from being the same. The first will disappear, the second will remain in Socialism.' Rudas quotes this remark, and describes it as coming from Lenin's 'Remarks on Bukharin's Transition Period', in the pamphlet *Dialectical Materialism and Communism* (Labour Monthly Pamphlet No. 4, 1934, p. 28) but not in the articles on which it was based. The statement is not to be found, I think, in Lenin's *Collected Works*. The truth seems to be that Lenin often referred to antagonisms and contradictions, which he regarded as entirely different from each other, and that whilst he never confused them, he never explicitly distinguished between them either, still less between antagonistic and non-antagonistic contradictions. Rudas's further claim, that the distinction is made in Engels's *Anti-Dühring*, also seems to be unwarranted.

127. There is a distressingly inadequate attempt at such an argument in Rudas, 'Dialectical Materialism and Communism — a Postscript', *Labour Monthly*, Vol. 16, No. 9, September 1934, pp. 563-72, pp. 568-9, reprinted as Part Four of *Dialectical Materialism and Communism*, Fourth Edition, Labour Monthly Pamphlets, 1935, pp. 34-43.

128. On the new interpretation of this slogan see Joravsky, *Soviet Marxism and Natural Science*, p. 256.

129. The complete work was first published by the Marx-Engels-

Lenin Institute, Moscow, in 1932. See above, p. 133, Notes to Introduction, n. 1.

130. Quoted in Wetter, *Dialectical Materialism*, p. 177.

131. Quoted in Wetter, *Dialectical Materialism*, p. 136.

132. In November 1930. the Party had 86 trainers, 192 members in District Schools, and 72 workers' study circles, attended by a total of 597 members and 197 non-members. (D.R., 'The Present State of Party Education', p. 25.) The Labour Colleges could claim nearly thirty times that number (19, 273). (See Putnam and Phillips, 'Education for Emancipation', p. 27.) See also Steve Boddington, 'Marxism and Education', *Labour Monthly*, Vol. 17, No. 9, September 1935, pp. 560–1.

133. Cohen, *Bukharin and the Bolshevik Revolution*, pp. 216, 301.

134. D. S. Mirsky, 'The Philosophical Discussion in the CPSU in 1930–31', *Labour Monthly*, Vol. 13, No. 10, October 1931, pp. 649–56, pp. 649, 652, 654.

135. *The German Ideology* was not available in English until 1964: see above, p. 133, Notes to Introduction, n. 1. Clemens Dutt gave an English version of Lenin's sixteen points in 'Dialectical Materialism and Natural Science', *Labour Monthly*, Vol. 15, No. 2, February 1933, pp. 84–95, p. 87; another was given in *The Communist* (New York), Vol. 14, No. 5, May 1935, p. 428. A complete English edition of the *Notebooks* appeared as *Collected Works*, Vol. 38 in 1961 (the sixteen points are on pp. 221–2). See also N. Krupskaya, 'How Lenin Studied Marx', *Labour Monthly*, Vol. 15, No. 3, March 1933, pp. 170–81.

136. Clemens Dutt, 'Dialectical Materialism and Natural Science', pp. 89, 95.

137. See above, pp. 64–5.

138. L. Rudas, 'Dialectical Materialism and Communism', *Labour Monthly*, Vol. 15, Nos. 9 and 10, September and October 1933, pp. 568–74, 633–44, pp. 572, 574.

139. 'Dialectical Materialism and Communism', pp. 570, 569, 573, 644, 572.

140. *Dialectical Materialism and Communism* was revised in 1935 after going through three editions (13,000 copies) in its first year.

141. V. Adoratsky, *Dialectical Materialism – The Theoretical Foundations of Marxism-Leninism*, London, Martin Lawrence, 1935, pp. 37, 43, 30, 63.

142. *A Textbook of Marxist Philosophy*, prepared under the direction of M. Shirokov, trans. A. C. Moseley, ed. John Lewis, London, Gollancz (Left Book Club 'Additional Book'), 1937.

143. Pelling, *The British Communist Party*, pp. 87–8.

144. John Lewis, *The Left Book Club, An Historical Record*, London, Gollancz, 1970. Not that these numbers necessarily represent a high degree of knowledge or commitment: George Orwell's character George Bowling says: 'Mrs Wheeler thought it had something to do with books which had been left in railway carriages and were being sold off cheap.' (George Orwell, *Coming up for Air*

(1939), Harmondsworth, Penguin Books, 1962, p. 141; see also pp. 143-8.)

145. Lawrence Daly, interviewed 30 Sept. 1977.

146. Edward Upward, *In the Thirties*, Vol. 1 of *The Spiral Ascent*, (1962), London, Quartet, 1978, p. 66.

147. E.R., 'A Wage-Worker's Reflections on the NCLC', *The Plebs*, Vol. 24, No. 8, August 1932, pp. 189-90.

148. Anonymous, interviewed 24 June 1977.

149. Jock Shanley, interviewed 24 May 1977.

150. Dudley Edwards, interviewed 5 July 1977.

151. Rudas, 'Dialectical Materialism and Communism', pp. 569, 570.

Five: Dialectical Materialism and the Scientists

1. See above, pp. 39-43.

2. 'We sometimes wonder whether "dialectic", as used by many Marxists, means any more than "that blessed word Mesopotamia"'. Eden and Cedar Paul, 'Lenin on Materialism' (a review of Lenin's *Materialism and Empirio-Criticism*), *The Plebs*, Vol. 20, No. 5, May-June 1928, pp. 116-17.

3. 'The out of date portion of Marxism, then, is probably the dialectic, important though Marx and even Lenin considered it to be' (Raymond Postgate, *Karl Marx*, London, Hamish Hamilton, 1933, p. 82).

4. J. T. Murphy was editor of the *Communist Review*, but in May 1932 he was dismissed from the post and expelled from the Party, ostensibly for his 'anti-working class views'. (W. T. Joss, 'The Expulsion of J. T. Murphy', *Communist Review*, Vol. 4, No. 6, June 1932, p. 304.) According to A. L. Morton, however (letter to author, 7 Nov. 1982), 'he was *formally* expelled only after he had expelled himself. . . . Later, Murphy made successful efforts to present himself as having been expelled because of opposition to our sectarian policy. But the fact is that he was one of the people most involved in drafting and pushing the Class-against-Class policy and was noted for his rigid adherence to whatever line the Comintern was advocating.'

5. On the history of the Socialist League (founded 1932), which grew out of the disintegration of the ILP, see Ben Pimlott, 'The Socialist League: Intellectuals and the Labour Left in the 1930s', *Journal of Contemporary History*, Vol. 6, No. 3, 1971, pp. 12-38.

6. J. S. Haldane, *Mechanism, Life and Personality: An Examination of the Mechanistic Theory of Life and Mind*, London, John Murray, 1913.

7. Lancelot Hogben, *The Nature of Living Matter*, London, Kegan Paul, Trench, Trubner, 1930, p. 301.

8. Joseph Needham, 'The Inadequacy of Scientific Deism' in *The Great Amphibium*, London, SCM Press, 1931, p. 57. Needham's source of information on Russian philosophy was Natalie

Duddington's misleading article on 'Philosophy in Russia', see above, pp. 66-7, p. 156, Notes to Chapter Four, n. 106.

9. V. I. Lenin, *The State and Revolution* (1917), *Collected Works*, pp. 383-492, pp. 474, 426-7.

10. 'The immediate tasks of the Soviet Government' (March–April 1918), *Collected Works*, Vol. 27, pp. 258-9. Cf. Carmen Claudin-Urondo, *Lenin and the Cultural Revolution* (1975), trans. Pearce, Hassocks, Harvester Press, 1977, pp. 91-2. On Trotsky, see ibid., p. 112.

11. J. Stalin, 'The Foundations of Leninism', Part Nine; *Works*, Vol. 6, p. 194.

12. Julian Huxley, *A Scientist Among the Soviets*, London, Chatto and Windus, 1932, pp. 100, 49. When he visited Russia in 1931, Huxley was looked after by Bukharin, and was able to form the extraordinary opinion that the official 'Marxist philosophy' was 'mechanistic' and committed to the view that 'the method of science is the only method' and that its designation as 'Dialectical Materialism' was merely an unfortunate accident (p. 52).

13. Hyman Levy, *Social Thinking*, London, Cobbett Press, 1945, p. 6.

14. H. Levy, 'Science and Labour', *Nature*, Vol. 114, No. 2876, 13 Dec. 1924, pp. 849-51.

15. Werskey, *The Visible College*, p. 125.

16. Quoted in Werskey, *The Visible College*, p. 71.

17. On Bernal's relations to the Party, and his reasons for working outside it, see Werskey, *The Visible College*, pp. 74, 166-7.

18. Under the pseudonym 'X-Ray', he wrote on 'The Great Poison-Gas Plot' (*The Communist*, Vol. 1, nos. 3-5, April–June 1927, pp. 113-20, 1973-80, and 225-32) and on 'The Unmasking of the D.S.I.R.' (Vol. 3, nos. 5-6, May–June 1928, pp. 281-6, 339-45). Cf. Werskey, *The Visible College*, p. 350.

19. J. D. Bernal, *The World, the Flesh and the Devil: an Enquiry into the Future of the Three Enemies of the Rational Soul*, London, Kegan Paul, Trench, Trubner, 1929, pp. 53, 95, 93-4.

20. Werskey, *The Visible College*, p. 318, pp. 166-7.

21. J. B. S. Haldane, 'The Inequality of Man', in *The Inequality of Man and other Essays* (1932), Harmondsworth, Penguin Books, 1937, pp. 22-35, pp. 35, 33.

22. Ronald Clark, *J. B. S.: The Life and Work of J. B. S. Haldane*, London, Hodder and Stoughton, 1968, p. 89.

23. J. B. S. Haldane, 'Science in Western Civilisation' (1928), *The Inequality of Man*, pp. 119-39, pp. 134, 135, 136, 137.

24. See J. G. Crowther, *Fifty Years with Science*, London, Barrie and Jenkins, 1970, pp. 21, 35, 41, 52.

25. *Sunday Worker*, 20 Oct. 1929, p. 8; 27 Oct., p. 4; 10 Nov., p. 4. Crowther forgets about his run-in with the *Sunday Worker* in his autobiography, *Fifty Years with Science*.

26. V. I. Lenin, *What is to be Done* (1902), as quoted by Freda Utley; cf. *Collected Works*, Vol. 5, pp. 416-17.

27. Freda Utley, 'Economism Today: The "Iskra Period" and Ourselves', *The Communist Review*, Vol. 2, No. 5, May 1930, pp. 196-207, 199-201.

28. See W. Tapsell, 'Economism: A Reply to F. Utley', *Communist Review*, Vol. 2, No. 7, July 1930, pp. 302-6; Allen Hutt, 'Fundamental Questions for our Party' (No. 9, September 1930, pp. 393-400); Freda Utley, 'Raising the Theoretical Level of Our Party' (No. 10, October 1930, pp. 432-41); W. Tapsell, 'The opportunism of Comrade Utley' (No. 12, December 1930, pp. 82-7).

29. 'The theoretician of "Left" Sectarianism and Spontaneity: the Political Bureau's Reply to Freda Utley', *Communist Review*, Vol. 3, No. 1, January 1931, pp. 11-19. Freda Utley subsequently lived in Moscow, and her experiences there are touchingly recorded in her despairing autobiography, *Lost Illusion*, London, George Allen and Unwin, 1949.

30. Pelling, *The British Communist Party*, p. 15; Klugmann, *History of the Communist Party of Great Britain*, Vol. 1, pp. 197-8, 331; Idris Cox, 'Carrying out the CC Resolution', *Communist Review*, Vol. 4, No. 8, August 1932, pp. 383-8.

31. R. Palme Dutt, 'Intellectuals and Communism', *Communist Review*, Vol. 4, No. 9, September 1932, pp. 421-30, pp. 422, 428, 426.

32. Max Black, 'Göttingen', in Carmel Haden Guest, *David Guest: a Scientist Fights for Freedom*, London, Lawrence and Wishart, 1939, pp. 58-73.

33. One of them was Maurice Cornforth, upon whose recollections this account of Guest at Cambridge is based. See *David Guest*, p. 97.

34. M. Y. Lang, 'The Growth of the Student Movement'; *David Guest*, pp. 85-103.

35. David Guest, *A Textbook of Dialectical Materialism*, London, Lawrence and Wishart, 1939.

36. *David Guest*, p. 175.

37. Vivien Morton, interviewed 9 June 1978.

38. The taste for such plain English was shared by them all, and was systematically theorized in Ogden and Richards's neo-Benthamite theory of meaning (*The Meaning of Meaning*, 1923) and in Ogden's promotion of 'Panoptic English' or 'Basic English' — a simplified language with a vocabulary of 850 words designed for the purposes of 'General Science' — from the 'Orthographical Institute' in Cambridge and in the journal *Psyche*. William Empson translated two volumes of Haldane's essays into 'Basic' (*The Outlook of Science* and *Science and Well Being*, London, Kegan Paul, Trench, Trubner, 1935), and some of Crowther's writing was given similar treatment (see Crowther, *Fifty Years with Science*, p. 45).

39. N. Bukharin *et al.*, *Science at the Crossroads*, London, Kniga, 1931. For this account of the Congress, I am greatly indebted to Werskey, *The Visible College*, pp. 138-49. See also Crowther, *Fifty Years with Science*, pp. 76-80.

40. M. Rubinstein, 'Electrification as the basis of technical reconstruction in the Soviet Union', *Science at the Crossroads*, pp. 115–45, pp. 116–17.

41. Zavadovsky went on to assert that the practical imperatives of the 'Socialist Five Year Plan' were bound to lead, in the Soviet Union, to a proper appreciation of 'the role and importance of the rest of man's social measures. . . . in the development of the phenotype and the possible emergence of new inherited variations'. (B. Zavadovsky, 'The "Physical" and the "Biological" in the Process of Organic Evolution", *Science at the Crossroads*, pp. 67–80, 73, 75, 79.)

42. N. I. Bukharin, 'Theory and Practice from the Standpoint of Dialectical Materialism', *Science at the Crossroads*, pp. 11–33.

43. B. Hessen, 'The Social and Economic Roots of Newton's "Principia"', *Science at the Crossroads*, pp. 149–212.

44. Hyman Levy, 'The Mathematician in the Struggle', in Guest, *David Guest*, pp. 151–2.

45. J. D. Bernal, *The Social Function of Science*, London, Routledge, 1939, p. 406; Hyman Levy, *Science in Perspective: an essay introductory to Twenty-Four Talks*, London, BBC, 1931, p. 47. See Werskey, *The Visible College*, pp. 146–7.

46. J. G. Crowther, *British Scientists of the Nineteenth Century* (1935), Harmondsworth, Penguin Books, 1940, p. 9; *Fifty Years with Science*, p. 79.

47. Joseph Needham, *A History of Embryology*, Cambridge University Press, 1934, p. xvi. See Werskey, *The Visible College*, p. 147.

48. Lancelot Hogben, *Mathematics for the Million: A Popular Self-Educator* and *Science for the Citizen*, both with illustrations by J. F. Horrabin, the first and second in a series of 'Primers for the Age of Plenty', London, George Allen and Unwin, 1936, dedicated to C. K. Ogden.

49. J. D. Bernal, *Science in History*, London, Watts, 1954.

50. Cohen, *Bukharin and the Bolshevik Revolution*, pp. 351–2.

51. Lancelot Hogben, 'Contemporary Philosophy in Soviet Russia', *Psyche*, No. 46, October 1931, pp. 2–18.

52. Dutt hung his denunciation of Hogben on a review of *The Nature of Living Matter* ('The Hesitant Materialist', *Labour Monthly*, Vol. 14, No. 10, October 1932); Hogben returned with 'Materialism and the Concept of Behaviour' in *Labour Monthly*, Vol. 15, No. 1, January 1933; and Dutt had the last word the following month.

53. Clemens Dutt, 'Dialectical Materialism and Natural Science', pp. 88, 95.

54. It depended, he said, on the idealistic 'identification of history with the reasoning process as a corollary of the belief that ultimate reality is mental . . .'. Lancelot Hogben, *Lancelot Hogben's Dangerous Thoughts*, London, George Allen and Unwin, 1939, pp. 269–70.

55. Hyman Levy, 'A Scientific Worker Looks at Dialectical Materialism' (lecture delivered May 1933), in Hyman Levy *et al.*, *Aspects*

of Dialectical Materialism, London, Watts, 1934, pp. 1–30; pp. 21, 13, 17–18, 30. This lecture was an application of ideas Levy had presented at considerable length in his *The Universe of Science,* London, Watts, 1932. See also J. M. Hay, 'Professor Levy and Dialectical Materialism', *The Plebs,* Vol. 25, No. 6, June 1933, pp. 137–8.

56. Hyman Levy, *Thinking,* London, Newnes, 1936; *A Philosophy for a Modern Man,* London, Gollancz, 1938; *Social Thinking,* London, Cobbett Press, 1945.

57. Clemens Dutt gave a patronizing review of *A Philosophy for a Modern Man* in *Labour Monthly,* Vol. 20, No. 4, April 1938, pp. 254–60; Levy wrote a pained reply (*Labour Monthly,* Vol. 20, No. 5, May 1938, pp. 318–23). The quotation is from Dutt's rejoinder (*Labour Monthly,* Vol. 20, No. 6, June 1938, p. 392) which attempts to associate Levy's parochialism with the Plebs League.

58. See Hyman Levy, *Jews and the National Question,* London, Hillway, 1958. See also Werskey, *The Visible College,* p. 310. There is some mystery about the process of Levy's disappointment. A. L. Morton, who was a member of the same delegation, recalls that during the visit 'like the rest of us he had criticisms to make but these were not about the Jewish question' (letter to author, 7 November 1982). However, Soviet mistreatment of Jews in the past is unflinchingly detailed in the delegation report in *World News,* Vol. 4, No. 2, 12 Jan. 1957, pp. 20–2.

59. Lawrence Daly, interviewed 30 Sept. 1977.

60. J. D. Bernal, 'Dialectical Materialism', in Levy *et al., Aspects of Dialectical Materialism,* pp. 89–122, pp. 122, 89, 109.

61. N. I. Bukharin *et al., Marxism and Modern Thought,* trans. Fox, London, Routledge, 1935. Cf. Crowther, *Fifty Years with Science,* pp. 143–4, and see above, p. 160, Notes to Chapter Five, n. 12.

62. J. G. Crowther, *Soviet Science,* London, Kegan Paul, Trench, Trubner, 1936, pp. 2–11.

63. Bernal's explanations, however, were as vague as ever: Dialectical Materialism, he said 'points the way in which it may be useful to look for new solutions.... From my own experience I have found Marxism invaluable for arriving at new conceptions.' 'Dialectical Materialism and Modern Science', *Science and Society,* Vol. 2, No. 1, Winter 1937, pp. 58–66, p. 64.

64. J. B. S. Haldane, *The Marxist Philosophy,* 9th Haldane Memorial Lecture Birkbeck College, London, 1938, p. 3.

65. J. B. S. Haldane, *The Marxist Philosophy and the Sciences,* London, George Allen and Unwin, 1938, p. 13.

66. *The Marxist Philosophy,* p. 6.

67. *The Marxist Philosophy and the Sciences,* p. 15.

68. *Dialectical Materialism and Natural Science* (Labour Monthly Pamphlet, 1942), p. 13.

69. *The Marxist Philosophy,* p. 3; *The Marxist Philosophy and the Sciences,* p. 23.

70. *The Marxist Philosophy*, p. 8. This trenchant statement is hard to reconcile, however, with Haldane's interpretation of Einstein: *The Marxist Philosophy and the Sciences*, p. 61.
71. *Dialectical Materialism and Natural Science, passim; The Marxist Philosophy*, pp. 9–11; *The Marxist Philosophy and the Sciences*, p. 23.
72. *The Marxist Philosophy*, pp. 14–15.
73. See above, p. 86.
74. *The Marxist Philosophy and the Sciences*, p. 16.
75. J. B. S. Haldane, 'A Dialectical Account of Evolution' *Science and Society*, Vol. 1, No. 4, Summer 1937, pp. 473–86.
76. A. P. Lerner, 'Is Professor Haldane's Account of Evolution Dialectical?' *Science and Society*, Vol. 12, No. 2, Spring 1938, pp. 232–9.
77. 'I claim that a good deal of my recently published research has been inspired by my gradually increasing knowledge of dialectical materialism. . . . Some years earlier, I had discussed the equilibrium (or near equilibrium) between mutation and selection in mathematical terms. The intellectual effort of doing so exhausted me, and it was not until (thanks to Engels) I could state the situation verbally, that I could see how this approximate equilibrium gave the key to many surprising facts. . . . I do not claim that these results could not have been obtained without a study of Engels. I merely state that they were not reached without such a study. . . .' J. B. S. Haldane, 'Professor Haldane replies', *Science and Society*, Vol. 2, No. 2, Spring 1938, pp. 239–242. Haldane also wrote: 'I had it [gastritis] for fifteen years until I read Lenin and other writers, who showed me what was wrong with our society and how to cure it. Since then I have needed no magnesia. . . . The *Daily Worker* may effect a permanent cure.' J. B. S. Haldane, *Science and Everyday Life*, London, Lawrence and Wishart, 1939, pp. 228–9.
78. Clark, *J.B.S.*, pp. 164–6.
79. Clark, *J.B.S.*, pp. 178–9; Werskey, *The Visible College*, pp. 301–3, 313.
80. *The Marxist Philosophy*, p. 5.
81. Joseph Needham, 'A Discussion of Religion: Thoughts of a Young Scientist on the Testament of an Old One', *Science and Society*, Vol. 1, No. 4, Summer 1937, pp. 487–95.
82. In 1932, commenting on his non-identity with his father, J. B. S. Haldane added that 'our opinions differ mainly on questions of emphasis and terminology rather than of fact' (*The Inequality of Man*, p. viii); in 1938 he remarked that his father's 'views on biology were close enough to Dialectical Materialism to cause a Moscow radio speaker to recommend one of his books to British readers' (*The Marxist Philosophy*, p. 20). On his similarity to his uncle, see the remarks in the introduction and peroration to the same lecture.

Six: Dialectical Materialism and the Philosophers

1. Haldane, *The Marxist Philosophy*, p. 20.
2. Bertrand Russell, *The Practice and Theory of Bolshevism*, London, George Allen and Unwin, 1920, pp. 119–21.
3. Bertrand Russell, 'Philosophy and Common Sense', *The New Statesman and Nation*, 12 Feb. 1938, pp. 252–4.
4. L. Susan Stebbing, 'The Creed of a Dialectical Materialist', *The Modern Quarterly*, Vol. 1, No. 2, March 1938, pp. 121–8. Laski's review appeared in the Left Book Club's periodical, *Left News*, in January 1938.
5. See Sidney Hook, 'The Philosophy of Dialectical Materialism', *Journal of Philosophy* 25, March 1928, Nos. 5 and 6, pp. 113–24, 141–55, p. 145.
6. Ibid., pp. 118–21.
7. Cf. E[dward] C[onze], 'Is Socialism Inevitable?', *The Plebs*, Vol. 26, No. 6, June 1934, p. 138.
8. Cf. E. F. Carritt, 'Dialectical Materialism', in Levy *et al.*, *Aspects of Dialectical Materialism*, pp. 129–30.
9. See above, pp. 16–17.
10. See Jonathan Rée, 'Philosophy as an Academic Discipline: the changing place of philosophy in an arts education', *Studies in Higher Education*, Vol. 3, No. 1, March 1978, pp. 5–23; 'The Rise of American Philosophy', *Modern Language Notes*, Vol. 93, Fall 1978, pp. 972–81.
11. L. Susan Stebbing, 'The Creed of a Dialectical Materialist', p. 126.
12. For instance, H. W. B. Joseph, in 1913, lectured on the fallacies of the Ricardian 'Labour Theory of Value', which he thought to be the basis of Marxist economics (*Karl Marx's Theory of Value*, London, Oxford University Press, 1923); A. D. Lindsay, Master of Balliol and enthusiast for the WEA, wrote an intelligent philosophical defence in 1925 (*Karl Marx's 'Capital'*, London, Oxford University Press, 1925).
13. 'The Philosophy of Dialectical Materialism', pp. 114, 117, 144, 118, 147, 146. Hook's own philosophical orientation had been spelt out in *The Metaphysics of Pragmatism*, Chicago, Open Court, 1927, whose deliberately paradoxical title signalled Hook's intention to combine the 'technical philosophy' of the twentieth century with the stately metaphysics of the past.
14. Sidney Hook, *Towards the Understanding of Karl Marx, A Revolutionary Interpretation*, London, Gollancz, 1933, pp. 15, 6, 9.
15. 'Philosophical Burlesque: On some Stalinist Antics in Philosophy', *Modern Monthly*, Vol. IX, No. 3, May 1935, pp. 163–72, p. 164. Hook's first attack on Rudas appeared in his 'Communism without Dogmas' in B. Russell, John Dewey, Morris Cohen, Sidney Hook, and Sharwood Eddy, *The Meaning of Marx, A Symposium*, New York, Farrar, 1934; see also his 'The Fallacy of Social-Fascism' and 'Workers' Democracy' in *Modern Monthly*, Vol. VIII, Nos. 2,

6, and 9, April, July, and October 1934, and 'Dialectic and Nature', *Marxist Quarterly*, April–June 1937.

16. L. Rudas, 'The Meaning of Sidney Hook', *The Communist* (New York), Vol. XIV, No. 4, April 1935, pp. 326–49, *Labour Monthly*, Vol. 17, Nos. 3, 4, and 6, March, April, and June 1935, pp. 177–84, 249–56, 312–20.

17. Sidney Hook, *From Hegel to Marx* (1936), New Edition, University of Michigan Press, 1962, p. 14. According to Helena Sheehan (private communication), it is probable that Riazanov did not die till 1938.

18. Sidney Hook, *Marx and the Marxists: The Ambiguous Legacy*, Princeton, Norstrand, 1955, pp. 80–1.

19. Sidney Hook, *From Hegel to Marx*, New Introduction, 1962, p. 1.

20. John MacMurray, *The Philosophy of Communism*, London, Faber and Faber, 1933, p. 80. Cf. his 'Dialectical Materialism as a Philosophy', in Levy *et al.*, *Aspects of Dialectical Materialism*, pp. 31–53, and 'Christianity and Communism: Towards a Synthesis' in John Lewis *et al.*, eds., *Christianity and the Social Revolution*, London, Gollancz, 1935, pp. 505–26.

21. Julius F. Hecker, *Moscow Dialogues: Discussions on Red Philosophy*, with a foreword by John MacMurray, London, Chapman and Hall, 1933, pp. x, 164.

22. Julius F. Hecker, 'Christianity and Communism in the Light of the Russian Revolution', in John Lewis *et al.*, eds., *Christianity and the Social Revolution*, pp. 297–328, p. 328.

23. John Lewis, Karl Polanyi, Donald Kitchin, Joseph Needham, Charles Raven, and John MacMurray, eds., *Christianity and the Social Revolution*, London, Gollancz, 1935.

24. John Lewis, 'Communism the Heir to the Christian Tradition', in Lewis *et al.*, eds., *Christianity and the Social Revolution*, pp. 473–504, pp. 501, 503–4.

25. Reissued as a pamphlet, *Socialism and the Churches: A Plea for a United Front*, London, Gollancz, 1937.

26. John Lewis, ed., *A Textbook of Marxist Philosophy*, p. 29.

27. E. F. Carritt, 'A Discussion of Dialectical Materialism', *Labour Monthly*, Vol. 15, Nos. 5 and 6, May–June 1933, pp. 324–9, 383–91; 391, 324, 391. Cf. Sidney Hook, 'Philosophical Burlesque', p. 170.

28. E. F. Carritt, *Fifty Years a Don* (privately printed), Oxford, 1960, p. 28.

29. See Society for Cultural Relations, *Tenth Annual Report* 1933–4. The symposium was the culmination of a series of lectures all collected in Hyman Levy *et al.*, *Aspects of Dialectical Materialism*.

30. J. D. Bernal, 'Dialectical Materialism', in Levy *et al.*, *Aspects of Dialectical Materialism*, pp. 89–122, pp. 93, 118–19.

31. The attribution of 'Trotskyism' to Hook was false but frequent, and surprising to Hook (letter to author, 13 Dec. 1980).

32. J. D. Bernal, 'Notes in reply to Mr Carritt's paper', *Aspects of Dialectical Materialism*, pp. 147–54. Bernal gave a further

pugnacious attack on a philosopher in his notice of Conze's *Textbook, The Plebs*, Vol. 28, No. 2, February 1936, pp. 92–3.

33. E[dward] C[onze], 'Is socialism inevitable?', *The Plebs*, June 1934, p. 138.

34. *Aspects of Dialectical Materialism*, p. v.

35. Ralph Fox, 'The Relation of Literature to Dialectical Materialism', *Aspects of Dialectical Materialism*, pp. 54–72. On the appalling abuse to which such 'wet, wishy-washy, Liberal, Oxonian writing' as Carritt's was subjected by Communists, see Stephen Spender, *World Within World*, London, Hamish Hamilton, 1951, pp. 253–4.

36. Hook, 'Philosophical Burlesque', p. 167.

37. 'Dialectical Materialism and Communism', pp. 569–70.

38. J.G., 'An Approach to Marxist Philosophy', *Labour Monthly*, Vol. 15, No. 10, October 1933, pp. 653–4.

39. L. Rudas, 'Dialectical Materialism and Communism — a postscript', *Labour Monthly*, Vol. 16, No. 9, September 1934, pp. 563–72, pp. 564, 567. Rudas's attempted definition of antagonism (p. 568) is, as far as I can see, nonsense.

40. Edward Conze, 'A Reply to Rudas', *Labour Monthly*, Vol. 15, No. 11, November 1934, pp. 692–4.

41. 'I must renounce the pleasure of entering into a discussion with Mr. Conze. . . . His review . . . was nothing but an attempt to counteract the revolutionary effect my pamphlet may have on the proletarian reader.' 'Conze answered', *Labour Monthly*, Vol. 16, No. 11, November 1934, pp. 694–5.

42. Quoting Marx's identification of the 'practical materialist' with the 'communist' in *The German Ideology*, Rudas commented: 'you cannot be a practical, that is, a dialectical materialist without being a communist, that is the adherent of a "definite revolutionary party"', the Communist Party', 'The Meaning of Sidney Hook', *Labour Monthly*, Vol. 17, pp. 317, 314.

43. See, for instance, Wetter, *Dialectical Materialism*, pp. 177–81.

44. J. Stalin, *History of the CPSU(B)* (1938), Chapter Four, Part Two: 'Dialectical and Historical Materialism'; English translation, Moscow, 1939.

45. The only innovation in Stalin's presentation was the omission — which was for some years emulated by soviet philosophers — of any principle corresponding to Engels's 'Law of the Negation of the Negation'.

46. 'The only time there was a systematic study of philosophy, was when we came to the chapter of the *History of the CPSU(B)*' — Anonymous, interviewed 24 June 1977.

Seven: Farce and Tragedy

1. See above, pp. 54–55.

2. T. A. Jackson, 'Self-criticism', *Communist Review*, Vol. 1, No. 2, February 1929, pp. 132–6, pp. 134, 135, 136, 132, 133, 136.

3. Closed letter, 27 Feb. 1929. See L. J. MacFarlane, *The British Communist Party*, pp. 309–19; Morton and Saville, 'Thomas Alfred Jackson', p. 103.
4. From 1933 to 1943 he was usually the delegate of Crawley Co-operative Society to the NCLC Annual Conferences. See the Unpublished Autobiography, Third Draft, p. 123.
5. Unpublished Autobiography, First Draft, p. 131.
6. Vivien Morton, interviewed 9 June 1978; Lawrence Daly, 30 Sept. 1977; Anonymous, 24 June 1977; Dudley Edwards, 5 July 1977; Jock Shanley, 24 May 1977.
7. Unpublished Autobiography, Third Draft, p. 72.
8. Jackson welcomed the Chicago reprint of Casey's *Thinking* in *Sunday Worker*, 2 Oct. 1927, p. 9.
9. Unpublished Autobiography, First Draft, p. 191; Third Draft, p. 74.
10. Unpublished Autobiography, Third Draft, p. 73.
11. This account of the composition of *Dialectics* is drawn from the Unpublished Autobiography, Second Draft, Part Two, p. 112; Third Draft, pp. 74–5. The reference to Comintern is due to Morton and Saville, 'Thomas Alfred Jackson', p. 105.
12. *Charles Dickens, the Progress of a Radical* (1937); *Trials of British Freedom* (1940); *Socialism: What? Why? and How?* (1945); *Ireland Her Own* (1946); *Old Friends to Keep* (1950); *Solo Trumpet* (1953).
13. Unpublished Autobiography, Second Draft, Part Two, pp. 114, 121; Third Draft, pp. 76, 83.
14. *Dialectics: The Logic of Marxism, and its critics — an essay in exploration*, London, Lawrence and Wishart, 1936, p. 236, pp. 209–10.
15. *Dialectics*, p. 211. In the same spirit, Jackson rejected the fashion amongst the 'less well-informed members of the intelligentsia' who took the Einsteinian revolution to have 'destroyed the foundation for Materialism and Marxism'. Einstein's demonstrations were really 'simply what the Dialectical Materialist has always contended' (p. 273).
16. *Dialectics*, pp. 605, 20, 26, 103–7.
17. See above, p. 133, Notes to Introduction, n. 1.
18. *Dialectics*, pp. 524, 190. Cf. 626: 'Its conception of the inter-relation of Theory and Practice, is the vital essence of Marxism ...'.
19. *Dialectics*, p. 206, cf. pp. 118, 287; p. 35, pp. 189–90; pp. 398–400.
20. *Dialectics*, pp. 549–51. Jackson was attacking especially Max Eastman and Raymond Postgate, 'the Castor and Pollux of Freudian Marxism' (p. 148), referring to the former's *Marx, Lenin and the Science of Revolution* (London, 1926) and the latter's *Karl Marx* (1933). The following year, the Left Book Club issued Reuben Osborn's *Freud and Marx, a Dialectical Study*, with an introduction by John Strachey (London, Gollancz, 1937), which argued (p. 244) for the shocking proposition that

'the best evidence of the validity of dialectical materialism can be found in psycho-analysis itself'. J. D. Bernal duly notified *Labour Monthly* readers of the outrage, claiming that Freudianism was 'just one more form of subjective philosophy and must be understood and rejected as such' and that 'politically, it is a profoundly dangerous influence, paralysing action and leading to fascism'. ('Psycho-analysis and Marxism', *Labour Monthly*, Vol. 19, No. 7, July 1937, pp. 433–7, pp. 434, 437.) See also Francis H. Bartlett, *Sigmund Freud, A Marxian Essay*, London, Gollancz, 1938, and Christopher Caudwell, 'Freud, A Study in Bourgeois Psychology', in *Studies in a Dying Culture*, London, John Lane, 1938.

21. Unpublished Autobiography, Third Draft, p. 78.
22. *Labour Monthly*, Vol. 18, No. 6, July 1936, p. 443.
23. This anonymous attack was translated in *Modern Quarterly*, Vol. 1, No. 3, August 1938, pp. 297–304.
24. Unpublished Autobiography, Second Draft, Part Two, p. 123.
25. Unpublished Autobiography, Third Draft, p. 72.
26. Unpublished Autobiography, Second Draft, Part Two, p. 117. A simultaneous edition had been produced in America (New York, International Publishers, 1936); a later one in India (Benares, Oriental Publishing House, September 1945).
27. Unpublished Autobiography, Second Draft, Part Two, p. 116. In the Third Draft, p. 78, Jackson says: 'an unvoiced tradition had grown up that in order to be authoritative a Marxist work simply had to be imported, and should be, for preference, translated, at one time from the German, later from the Russian.' See also First Draft, p. 198.
28. Unpublished Autobiography, First Draft, pp. 199–200; Second Draft, Part Two, p. 110, Third Draft, p. 79.
29. Lawrence Daly, interviewed 30 Sept. 1977.
30. Unpublished Autobiography, Third Draft, p. 123. Jackson added that 'naturally, I have at times been in a minority on questions of practical application. . . '. I imagine this myth . . . arose from nothing more recondite than my constant endeavour to find fresh ways of stating the Communist case'.
31. Unpublished Autobiography, First Draft, p. 215.
32. Unpublished Autobiography, Second Draft, Part Two, p. 117. Jackson claims to have written this to Dona Torr following the success of his pamphlet on the Jubilee of George V.
33. Unpublished Autobiography, Second Draft, pp. 115–16.
34. Unpublished Autobiography, First Draft, p. 195, p. 203, p. 131.
35. 'Contribution to the Critique of Hegel's Philosophy of Right: Introduction', MEW, Vol. 1, p. 391; *Collected Works*, Vol. 3, p. 187.

Index